The Story of the Bible

The Bible's story is a unique account of *salvation,* the means whereby a loving and just God transforms the lives of men and women and brings them into his believing community, the Church. Although it begins with a vivid portrait of God as the world's creator, the Bible does not claim to be a complete account of everything which He did in the ancient world, not even of every event which occurred in the life of the Hebrew people. It *is* history, but it is more than history. As it tells the history of God's people, the Bible reveals the great truths of God's salvation.

HarperEssentials

BIBLE GUIDE
CARD GAMES
FAMILY AND PARTY GAMES
FIRST AID
STRESS SURVIVAL GUIDE
THE ULTIMATE SURVIVAL GUIDE
UNDERSTANDING DREAMS
WINE GUIDE
YOGA
ZODIAC SIGNS

HARPERESSENTIALS

Bible Guide

(Previously published as *The Bible Book by Book*)

RAYMOND BROWN

HarperTorch
An Imprint of HarperCollinsPublishers

First published as *The Bible Book by Book* in 1990 by Marshall
Pickering, an Imprint of HarperCollins Publishers

HARPERTORCH
An Imprint of HarperCollins*Publishers*
10 East 53rd Street
New York, New York 10022-5299

Copyright © 1990, 1993 by Raymond Brown
ISBN: 0-06-073442-6

First HarperTorch paperback printing: February 2005

HarperCollins ®, HarperTorch™, and ❦ ™ are trademarks of
HarperCollins Publishers Inc.

Printed in the United States of America

Visit HarperTorch on the World Wide Web at www.harpercollins.com

10 9 8 7 6 5 4 3 2 1

Contents

BOOKS OF THE BIBLE

The Story of the Bible

❦

The Bible's story is a unique account of *salvation,* the means whereby a loving and just God transforms the lives of men and women and brings them into his believing community, the Church. Although it begins with a vivid portrait of God as the world's creator, the Bible does not claim to be a complete account of everything which he did in the ancient world, nor even of every event which occurred in the life of the Hebrew people. It *is* history, but it is more than history. As it tells the history of God's people, the Bible reveals the great truths of God's salvation.

THE PATRIARCHS

God needed a particular nation to be a special instrument to present his truth, his name and nature, to the world, and he chose the Hebrew people, or "the Israelites," as they are also called.

The Bible's first book provides a graphic presentation of the devastating effects of sin and God's answer to human need. *Genesis* means *beginnings,* and it describes the origin of the world, and of sin in the world, before going on to the call of Abraham to be God's servant, and "father" of the Is-raelite race. It follows this with an account of leading events in the lives of Abraham's immediate successors and fellow patriarchs—Isaac and Jacob.

THE EXODUS

Severe famine conditions throughout the ancient near-east led the old man Jacob and his family to Egypt, where there were good supplies of food, thanks to the statesmanship of Jacob's long-lost son, Joseph, now governor over all Egypt.

The family settled in Egypt, but in the decades after Joseph's death their numbers rapidly increased. In an attempt to suppress them, the Egyptians made them slaves, and treated them roughly, even ordering the execution of their male babies. One such infant was hidden by his parents for three months, and was then providentially delivered from death and brought up in Pharaoh's court. His name was Moses, and he was the deliverer chosen by God to lead the Israelites out of Egyptian bondage and back to the land God had prepared for them—Canaan, roughly the present state of Israel.

THE PROMISED LAND

The Israelites' miraculous escape from Egypt was followed by their journey across the desert toward the "promised land." Early in that journey God revealed himself to the people through Moses, and made a "covenant" (agreement) with them.

The making of such treaties was a familiar feature in the life of the surrounding nations. A smaller country might at times feel compelled to make such an agreement with a larger, more powerful nation. The terms of the treaty would demand allegiance from the smaller (vassal) nation and in turn the larger (suzerain) would promise full support and protection. The treaty always included a promise that the weaker nation would not make similar alliances with other nations; the loyalty was to be complete and exclusive.

God's covenant with his people followed the same pattern. They were to obey his laws and not worship other "gods." The covenant's terms are clearly set out in EXODUS (Exod. 20:1–17) and DEUTERONOMY (Deut. 5:6–21) and are brilliantly summarized in the Ten Commandments.

Instead of being grateful for God's miraculous salvation from Egyptian tyranny, many of the Israelite pilgrims often grumbled and complained during their desert journey, sometimes wishing they had never left Egypt. When they got to the borders of Canaan, they were particularly stubborn and rebellious, refusing to believe that God was able to make them victorious over the existing inhabitants of the land. God therefore told them that their generation would not enter the land. When, several decades later, that entire unbelieving generation had died, their children resumed the journey and, under Joshua's leadership, entered the land of Canaan.

They entered a land whose people worshipped many idols. The Canaanite religion was a fertility cult, a particularly immoral form of worship, involving such practices as "sacred" prostitution. God had told the Israelites that they must have no other gods, but they often disobeyed that part of the covenant-agreement.

Initially, the leadership of the land was the responsibility of "judges," or tribal leaders, but eventually the people asked for a king, and Saul was appointed by the prophet Samuel. Saul, like some other biblical characters, failed to achieve his rich potential. David was chosen as Saul's successor and the rule then passed to David's son, Solomon.

THE DIVIDED KINGDOM

After Solomon's death, there was a serious division among the people, and the nation split into two. Those who endeavored to maintain the line of David and Solomon formed the Southern Kingdom, Judah; those who broke away from that allegiance are known as the Northern Kingdom, Israel.

Relationships between the two nations were often

strained, and the northerners frequently adopted idolatrous practices. Prophets like Elijah, Elisha, Amos and Hosea sought to bring their disloyal contemporaries back to the nation's agreed spiritual values, but without lasting success. Eventually, to discipline them, the Lord allowed the Assyrian nation to be "the rod of my anger" (Isa. 10:5) and in 721/2 BC their capital city, Samaria, fell to the Assyrian invading armies. That event virtually marked the end of the story of the northern kingdom of Israel. Those Israelites who survived in the north frequently married people belonging to other nations, who naturally had an allegiance to other gods. Over the centuries this group became known as "Samaritans" and were seriously alienated from Jewish people. They later had their own temple on Mount Gerizim and were regarded by pious Jews as a heretical sect.

THE EXILE

Following the collapse of the northern kingdom, things were not easy for Judah. Some arrogant southerners imagined that they had been kept safe because they were specially privileged people and that, whatever their conduct, the temple guaranteed their security. Although the nation often had good kings who were loyal to God and had high moral values, people became lax in their worship and behavior. Outstanding prophets such as Isaiah, Micah and Jeremiah repeatedly warned them that if they did not abandon their idolatry and turn wholeheartedly to God, they too would be judged. This message was largely unheeded and the threatened judgment came with the invasion of the Babylonian armies in the sixth century BC. Solomon's magnificent temple was destroyed, their homes and farms ravaged, a scene which is movingly described in LAMENTATIONS. Judah's leading citizens—those likely to incite a revolt against Babylonian domination—were taken away into captivity.

The story of the Hebrew people from Saul through to the

Babylonian captivity is told in the books of SAMUEL and KINGS, and also, from a different perspective, in the books of CHRONICLES.

THE RETURN

Despite these grim circumstances, both Jeremiah and Ezekiel had a message of hope for the exiles. God, the sovereign Lord of the universe, was in control of what happened to them and still loved them, even though they had disappointed him. In order to judge them, the Babylonian king had been used as God's "servant" (Jer. 25:9), but when the chastisement was over, God then used a Persian prince, Cyrus, to overcome the Babylonians, and become God's "shepherd" to lead his people back to Judah (Isa. 44:28). So after approximately seventy years of refining correction in Babylon the Jewish people returned to their own land in circumstances described in EZRA and NEHEMIAH. The broken walls of Jerusalem were rebuilt as, eventually, was the Temple. The prophets Haggai, Zechariah and Malachi had a message for the returned exiles after they had settled back in Judah.

BETWEEN THE TESTAMENTS

A 400-year ("inter-testamental") period separates the Old and New Testaments. During this time the Hebrew people were left without any uniquely inspired prophetic leader and they eagerly looked forward to the coming of their Messiah, God's appointed deliverer. As a nation, Israel was in a geographically difficult and vulnerable position, sometimes set, as if in the jaws of a nutcracker, between rival powers, as, for example, when Persia and Egypt struggled for supremacy.

Eventually control of these nations was usurped by the Greeks through the famous conquests of Alexander the Great. He and his successors endeavored to spread Greek culture and values throughout the empire and this produced immense problems for the Jews. It was impossible for genuine, spiritually-minded Jews to adopt these Greek (Hellenistic) ways of life, for Greek ideas and God's laws simply could not mix.

Struggles for power continued between the successive Greek/Macedonian rulers of Egypt—the Ptolemies—and the Seleucids who ruled Syria and Babylonia. But throughout it all, Israel continued to be a dominated people, sometimes reacting fiercely against attempts to corrupt their religious life with alien influences, as in the famous "Maccabean revolt" in 168 BC, led by the Jewish hero Judas ben Mattathias (whose Greek name was Maccabaeos), when many orthodox Jews died for their faith.

The Maccabees eventually obtained their religious and political freedom, and Israel was ruled by a number of its high-priests (the Hasmoneans) who extended the Israelite territory to include Samaria and Galilee and managed to keep on reasonably friendly terms with the next world power to dominate the international scene, the Romans.

During this inter-testamental period the Old Testament was translated into Greek; it was said to be the work of seventy-two translators, hence its name "Septuagint." In the two to three hundred years prior to the birth of Christ a number of additional religious writings began to circulate among the Jewish people; these are known as the "Apocrypha"; which means "the hidden [things]." These books covered events such as the Maccabean revolt and portrayed Jewish courage and fortitude in times of severe persecution.

THE COMING OF CHRIST

In 63 BC Pompey, the Roman empire's commander in the East, conquered the Israelites' territory and, once again, the Jewish people were under foreign control. During the rule of the emperor Augustus God sent his only Son, Jesus, into the world to be its unique deliverer. It was the perfect time for the long-awaited Jewish Messiah to appear. The Romans had built excellent roads along which Christian preachers were to travel for several centuries, sharing the good news ("gospel") of Christ's message. Greek had become the common language of almost every known country. Those thousands of Jews who, under recurrent persecutions, had been "dispersed" throughout the known world, had shared their high ideals with their Gentile neighbors and some of these "God-fearers," as they were called, were consequently seeking a better way of life. How right Paul was to say that Christ came at exactly the right moment in world history (Gal. 4:4).

Jesus was born at Bethlehem in Judea, son of Mary, a young Galilean virgin who was engaged to be married to a devout carpenter named Joseph. Within hours of the baby's birth his life was in danger because of the jealous threats of a local king, Herod. Joseph and Mary escaped with the child to Egypt, where they remained until Herod's death, when it was safe to come back.

On their return, the family settled at Nazareth, a very ordinary town in the north (John 1:46). We know little about Christ's boyhood other than that, at the age of twelve, he accepted spiritual responsibility by becoming a "son of the law" like every other Jewish boy. At that time he was certainly aware of his unique relationship with God, his Father (Luke 2:48–49).

THE MINISTRY OF JESUS

Conscious of his unique destiny, Jesus was baptized in the Jordan river by his cousin, John the Baptist, a courageous preacher of repentance. Although he was sinless, he did this as a deliberate act of identification with our sinful humanity, and as a righteous act before men (Matt. 3:13–15). At his baptism a voice from heaven confirmed his unique nature, mission and destiny as God's Messiah-Son and Suffering Servant (Matt. 3:17; Ps. 2:7; Isa. 42:1).

After his baptism, Jesus was led to spend almost six weeks in the wilderness. During that time of quiet prayer and preparation, he was fiercely tempted by the devil, but his mind was well-stored with strong and supportive words of Scripture and he emerged victoriously from the conflict.

He selected twelve very different men to be his associates or "disciples" (the word means "learners"), and they stayed with him until his arrest by Roman soldiers three years later. During those years they and thousands of others had heard his magnetic preaching (richly preserved in the four "Gospels") and witnessed his unique power to change and transform human lives, physically, morally and spiritually.

He was briefly imprisoned at the instigation of Jewish religious opponents who objected to many aspects of his teaching and particularly his claim to be God's only Son. He was crucified between two criminals on that first Good Friday. The New Testament message is that when he died he carried in his body to that cross the sins of all mankind so that those who repent and seek his pardon, might be immediately and eternally forgiven. At the end of that unforgettable day, the most significant day in world history, his dead body was buried in a garden tomb, but, as irrefutable proof of God's vindicating power, Jesus was raised from the dead. Over the next few weeks he was seen repeatedly by different individuals: a couple out walking, several groups, and on one occasion 500 people at one meeting (1 Cor. 15:3–6).

THE BIRTH OF THE CHURCH

During his ministry, Jesus had frequently told his disciples that though he would eventually have to leave them, the Holy Spirit would take his place among them, actually making his home in their hearts and living with them as an indwelling new friend. Before leaving this world, Jesus told his followers to wait for this promised new gift of the Spirit's permanent presence. After Christ's ascension into heaven, the Holy Spirit came, no longer, as in Old Testament times, on rare and specially selected individuals for "one-off" tasks, but on *all* who trusted Jesus. The Church was born.

Peter, a disciple transformed by the Holy Spirit, preached

to huge crowds who were visiting Jerusalem for the Festival of Pentecost, and several thousands from different nations became committed Christians. The Church grew so quickly that the religious authorities in Jerusalem began to be worried, and one extremely well-educated, fanatical Jew, Saul of Tarsus, embarked on an intense persecution campaign, during which many Christians were arrested and imprisoned, and one was executed. At a key stage in Saul's campaign, he was himself converted to personal faith in Christ, becoming Paul, the outstanding missionary and pastor, as well as author of a number of the letters in our New Testament.

The Church's story over the next few decades is that of a steadily growing community. The initial chapters of early Church history are told in the ACTS OF THE APOSTLES, the sequel which doctor Luke wrote to his famous "Gospel." The book of Acts, together with the many letters and tracts written by church leaders like Paul, Peter, James, John and others, present us with a vivid and detailed picture of Church life in the mid and late first century. This literature, together with the Gospels, make up the twenty-seven books of the New Testament. Added to the thirty-nine books of the Old Testament, it completes the "canon" (literally "rod," "rule" or agreed list) of authentic Scripture.

The Structure of the Bible

❧❦❧

It is often maintained, and rightly so, that the Bible is more than a book—it is a library. If we go into a public library, one of the first features we will notice is that different types of literature are placed on different shelves, so that if we want to read about English social life under Henry VII we do not have to rummage through endless rows of intriguing paperbacks by Agatha Christie! The library shelves are clearly marked—History, Geography, Religion, Economics, Drama, Poetry, Music, Songs, Biography, and so on. Actually, the Bible contains books which, in one form or another, deal with all the subjects we have just mentioned. God knew that men and women are vastly different in their interests and outlook; in the art of communicating a message, one type of approach may leave one person totally unmoved while another is immediately persuaded and responsive. God used all sorts of people, with a wide variety of gifts, to convey his message to mankind. It might be helpful, therefore, if we look briefly at the Bible's library so that we can see the various books which are to be found in its pages.

The main divisions of the OLD TESTAMENT are history, poetry and prophecy:

HISTORY

Although this collection carefully records the story of God's people, it does far more than relate a series of major historical events. It contains an account of the Covenant or Law given to the Israelites by God, and it comments on how they kept to that agreement in the succeeding centuries.

- Early history (prior to their possession of the land): Genesis—Exodus—Leviticus—Numbers—Deuteronomy
- Later history (from settlement in the land to the exile) Early Settlement: Joshua—Judges—Ruth
- From the beginning of the monarchy to the Babylonian captivity: 1 and 2 Samuel—1 and 2 Kings—1 and 2 Chronicles
- The release from Babylon and the return to the land: Ezra—Nehemiah—Esther

POETRY

This includes the songs of Israel's worship and the sayings of Israel's "wise men," those who, under God, shaped and recalled their people's great truths about life and how it ought to be lived and enjoyed—the so-called "Wisdom literature": Job—Psalms—Proverbs—Ecclesiastes—Song of Solomon.

PROPHECY

This large group of books contains the preaching of the great Hebrew prophets. Their message was written down by their devoted followers (usually in a minority) and naturally contains a great deal of historical material as well. For the approximate dates of each of the prophets see the chapters on the Old Testament books.

- Major Prophets: Isaiah—Jeremiah (with Lamentations)—Ezekiel
- Minor Prophets (the term "minor" relates only to their size; it has nothing to do with their importance): Daniel (though this book is almost in a class on its own; the Jewish canon did not include it with the prophetical books. It contains a combination of history and what is more strictly known as "apocalyptic" ["unveiling"].)—Hosea—Joel—Amos—Obadiah—Jonah—Micah—Nahum—Habakkuk—Zephaniah—Haggai— Zechariah—Malachi.

The main divisions of the NEW TESTAMENT are history, letters and prophecy:

HISTORY

- The life of Jesus on earth: Matthew—Mark—Luke—John.
- The work of the early Church: The Acts of the Apostles.

LETTERS

- Letters by Paul: Romans—1 and 2 Corinthians—Galatians.

Three prison epistles: Ephesians—Philippians—Colossians. 1 and 2 Thessalonians—1 and 2 Timothy—Titus—Philemon (which was also written from prison).

- Letters by other Christian leaders: Hebrews—James—1 and 2 Peter—1, 2 and 3 John—Jude.

PROPHECY

The Book of Revelation.

The Study of the Bible

❄❄❄

We have seen that the Bible is a unique library, written over many centuries by an impressive panel of about forty authors who had been carefully chosen by God. They were drawn from a wide variety of different social backgrounds and daily occupations. These writers included kings, priests, prophets, poets, shepherds, government officials, civil servants, itinerant preachers, at least one physician, a tax collector, an exiled prisoner and several local church leaders. Each book of the Bible deserves to be read thoroughly and unhurriedly. They do not all have the same aim and purpose, and each book will certainly repay the attentive study which every serious reader may give to it.

The aim of this book is to introduce the Bible book by book and to do it in such a way that, by carefully studying the biblical text, the distinctive message of every book may not only be understood but applied to everyday life and conduct. Each of the following chapters takes the reader through one book of the Bible and provides an outline of its content and leading ideas. Every one of the Bible's sixty-six books ought to be read like any other book, that is, from beginning to end. But all too often they are only read in short extracts or selected passages. That obviously has its uses but it can rob us of an essential overview of the main message of each book. How, then, can we set about serious Bible study which can be not only profitable but thoroughly enjoyable as well?

First, we ought to read it *regularly*. When Luke was describing the early Christian people at Berea, he tells us that "they examined the Scriptures *every day* to see if what Paul said was true" (Acts 17:11, NIV). At one time every committed Christian recognized the necessity of some definite time in every day for Bible reading and prayer. A decade or two ago, a daily "Quiet Time" was widely regarded as a spiritual necessity and many thousands of believers can still testify to its supreme importance and lasting value. We now live at a time when "discipline" is hardly a popular concept, and some Christians are so eager to avoid "legalism" that even biblically based traditions are dismissed with a slightly superior air. In any time of spiritual awakening, one always has to guard against what is known as the "antinomian" danger— the teaching asserted by those who so emphasize the doctrine of grace that they minimize or even despise what the Scripture has to say about law. These are times, therefore, when it is important to say, once again, that the blessings and benefits of regular, disciplined Bible reading and Bible study are incalculable for every Christian.

Secondly, we must read it *gratefully*. God has given the Bible to us and it has come down to us across the centuries at immense cost. We have already seen that he used a variety of different writers and this unique book took a long time to compile. The Old Testament writers span a period of over 2,000 years, while the New Testament events (and the task of recording those events) cover the best part of a century.

Moreover, over the centuries many thousands of gifted linguists have translated the Bible from its original Hebrew (the Old Testament) and Greek (the New Testament) texts into the language of the people in various parts of the world. That painstaking, laborious yet exciting work of translation, the careful search for the right word, for the best means of conveying in a different language some idea or word-

picture, is an exacting responsibility. Thousands of dedicated people have given their best years to it, people we will
never meet on this earth but whose specialist ministry has
been used to transform our lives. Additionally, we have seen
that some heroic people have risked and, in many cases,
given their lives that we might read this book. In some periods of world history the vernacular Bible has been a forbidden book but the ministry of its translation and distribution
was gladly undertaken by people willing to shed their blood
that its message might be read and understood. They believed that it was not given only for literate priests with a
knowledge of Latin but for the ordinary man or woman in
every town and village. We ought never to take this marvelous book for granted. Every time we turn its pages we ought
to think with gratitude of the price which has been willingly
paid to make it our own.

Thirdly, we must read it *dependently*. We must apply our
minds to it, and read it with sensitivity and imagination, but
we need something far more than our sharpest intellect,
good and essential as that is. The Bible is God's gift to us
and its initial writing was the unique work of God's Holy
Spirit. One writer tells us that the work of these different authors did not have "its origin in the will of man" but each
one "spoke from God as they were carried along by the Holy
Spirit" (2 Pet. 1:2, NIV). We must always remember that the
same Holy Spirit who inspired the original authors is eager
to inspire us as its dependent readers. The Spirit who gave
the book is its best interpreter. Whenever we open the Bible,
we ought to ask for the Spirit's promised help to understand
and apply its message.

Fourthly, we should read it *obediently*. We need a responsive will as well as an alert mind. The message of God's
word has to be worked out in everyday life. We are never
meant to become precocious Bible "book-worms," with our
minds stuffed full of biblical facts which are interesting but
scarcely related and applied to our daily conduct. If there is
a command from God in the book we are reading, then we

must *do* it and not leave it simply as a revealed truth on the pages of our Bible. If there is a promise in the chapter before us, then we are meant to *accept* it and seek to apply its benefits to our lives. If God has pointed out through that passage of Scripture something in our lives which is not pleasing to him, then we must *forsake* it.

Finally, we ought to read it *carefully*. When Luke says that the Berean people gave themselves wholeheartedly to the task of examining the Scriptures every day, he employs a word which was often used in legal circles during the first century to describe the careful and meticulous interrogation of an offender, or the careful sifting of evidence. Bible study is not an exercise which can be done properly when it is frantically pushed into a few spare minutes in an overcrowded day. We can only examine the Bible with the thoroughness of the Bereans if we give time to it. The Bible cannot possibly yield its treasures to the man or woman who is in too much of a hurry to read it properly.

We are all capable of devoting plenty of time in most weeks to some regular but frequently profitless activities. A lot of our time is wasted. It's very easy to devote more time to the newspaper, for example, or to a particular television program than we would dream of giving to the Bible, and those activities are not always profitable, as we all know; they can even be damaging. But every single moment we give to this best of all books will be more than repaid. Exploring this vast mine of truth will make us better people. Obeying its commands and accepting its promises will issue in deeper peace, increased confidence, richer faith, greater power and, best of all, renewed love for others as well as for him who has given us this priceless treasure.

Genesis

n the Hebrew, the first word of this book means *beginning*. There are many ways of studying the message of *Genesis,* but our method is to see it as the beginning of God's relationship with man and God's revelation to man. Consider the book's tremendous teaching on the doctrine of God, and note its relevance to our own times.

1. CHAPTERS 1–5
THE HOLINESS OF GOD

Much discussion about Genesis has centered on the creation story, but the book is also concerned with people. Note the concentration of interest on God's holiness and man's reaction to it. Three men are given prominence in this section of the book:

- ADAM—man hides himself (3:8–10)
- CAIN—man excuses himself (4:9–12). Sin not only breaks our relationship with God (chapter 3), but our relationship with men (chapter 4).
- ENOCH—man submits himself (5:22, 24)

In chapter 3 man is a *rebel;* in chapter 4 he is a *fugitive,* in chapter 5 he is a *friend,* he walks with God.

2. CHAPTERS 6–11
THE JUDGMENT OF GOD

God is not only *holy,* he is *just.*

The two great events which dominate this section are the
Flood and Babel. In both stories God's purpose is to judge
man's sin and to restrain its serious effects in the world.
Man's thoughts are evil (6:5; 11:6). There is no vindictiveness in God's judgment: he is deeply grieved about man's
stubborn rebellion (6:6).

NOAH is the central character here:

- he rejoices God's heart (6:8)
- he obeys God's word (6:22; 7:5)
- he acknowledges God's goodness (8:20)
- he experiences God's favor (9).

Man is a strange mixture. He can build an altar (8:20) but
he also wants to build a tower (11:5); one symbolizes his fellowship with God, the other portrays his fight against God.

Note how God has the last word. Man may say, "Let us
build . . . a tower" (11:4), but God says, "Come, let us go
down and confuse their language" (11:7).

3. CHAPTERS 12–20
THE POWER OF GOD

The key figure here is ABRAHAM. Chapter 12 begins with a
demand ("Leave your country") and a promise ("I will bless
you"). When God asks us to do something he always provides the strength to obey.

Note God's unlimited power in Abraham's life:

- power to overrule his sins (12:17–20)
- power to overcome his difficulties (13:7–18)
- power to vanquish his enemies (14:15–24)
- power to satisfy his longings ("What can you give me
  since I remain childless?" 15:2).

Chapters 15–18 record the story of God's message to Abraham and Sarah, and also record their impatience (16). God does not always impart his gifts immediately. He knows the best time for his benefits. Abraham does not believe it possible at first (17:17); neither does Sarah (18:12). They have to learn that nothing is too hard for the God of all power (18:14).

Holy Scripture is wonderfully balanced in its comment on man. True, Abraham is portrayed in these chapters as someone who lacks faith at times, and demonstrates serious impatience, but he is also a man concerned about his fellows (18:22), and pleads with God for sinners like himself.

Chapter 19 records another act of God's judgment on a sinful community—not now by water, but by fire. How slow we are to learn! Abraham makes the same mistake in chapter 20 as in chapter 12. Note his desire for prayer: 15:2; 18:22–33; 20:17.

4. CHAPTERS 21–26
THE MERCY OF GOD

Abraham is still on the scene, of course, but interest is now focused on ISAAC, the promised son. The theme here is God's undeserved mercy. He is not only merciful in providing them with a son and thus realizing their dreams, but he is merciful to Hagar and her son (21:9–20). He is merciful, too, in providing the lamb (22:11–14) at a time when Abraham's faith and reliance was put to the test; in providing a bride for Isaac (24:12, "show kindness"); and in giving them children (25:21).

But notice how easily the child can repeat the father's sins (26:7; compare 12:13; 20:5).

The Isaac story is a story of the generous mercy of God. God:

- spares Isaac's life (22)
- provides Isaac's partner (24)
- answers Isaac's prayers (25:21).

5. Chapters 27–36
THE PATIENCE OF GOD

Now we come to JACOB, not an attractive character in many ways, but a clear demonstration in this "book of beginnings" that God is able to transform a man's nature and use him as an instrument of his purposes.

Parental example is a repeated theme in this section: Isaac commits the same sin as Abraham (26:7); note it is Rebekah who leads her son astray (27:6–13).

Observe the power of the spoken word in Hebrew thought: once the blessing is given it cannot be revoked (27:37).

Sin costs a heavy price. Rebekah's action brings grief to their home (27:41) and to her heart (27:46); Jacob becomes as self-centered as his mother (28:20, "If . . . then . . ."), thinking only about his gains.

The overall picture is of God's patience. His people are self-seeking and unkind to their fellows. The chapters record tales of greed (31:1–33), lies (31:34, 35), strife (31:51, 52), fear (32:4–33, especially 32:7), deceit (34:13–15), murder (34:24–31), robbery (34:2; compare 35:4), idolatry (35:2). They are not happy chapters, but throughout it all God communes and pleads with his servant (28:13; 31:11; 32:24; 35:7, 9–15), and is patient with Jacob and his family.

6. Chapters 37–50
THE SOVEREIGNTY OF GOD

Finally we come to JOSEPH. It's thrilling to see how he triumphs over his unhappy family background. All the scheming of the previous chapters drops away. Here we have a story of:

- holiness (39:9; 41:38; 50:15–21)
- heroism (39:20; 40:15)
- hope (50:24)

God is sovereign and his providential care is illustrated throughout the Joseph story (39:21, 23; 45:5–7). Joseph sums it all up magnificently: "You intended to harm me, but God intended it for good" (50:20).

Exodus

xodus, like *Genesis*, is a Greek title; it means *departure* or *going out*, and the book's theme is the victorious act of God in delivering his people from Egyptian slavery and oppression. The book can be divided into three parts:

1. CHAPTERS 1–6
GOD'S MESSENGER

MOSES is the key figure in this book, and the opening chapters trace the story of his birth, call and response. There are three clearly defined stages in the story:

a. GOD'S MESSENGER IN DANGER (1–2) His life is twice in great danger:

- as a baby (1:16, 22; 2:1–10) and
- as an adult (2:15).

But Moses' name—the Hebrew word means *drawn out* (of the water)—is an abiding testimony to the providential care of God. In his goodness, God constantly preserves his people.

b. GOD'S MESSENGER IN DOUBT (3–4) The account of God's call to Moses demonstrates God's sovereign choice and man's frightened response (3:10–11). Moses feels unequal to the task and gives a series of excuses (3:11, 13; 4:1, 10, 13, "Send, I pray, some other person," RSV).

c. GOD'S MESSENGER IN DIFFICULTY (5–6) These chapters record some of the problems that arise when Moses and Aaron go to see Pharaoh. Their people are angry with them because Pharaoh increases their burden (5:19–21), and although Moses gives them the reassuring word of God (6: 6–9) they will not believe. If the Hebrews will not accept God's truth, how can the Egyptians be expected to believe (6:10–12)?

2. CHAPTERS 7–18
GOD'S DELIVERANCE

These chapters deal with the great act of redemption:

- PLAGUES (7–11)
- PASSOVER (12–13)
- PROTECTION (14)
- PRAISE (15:1–21) The song is a magnificent hymn of thanksgiving to the Lord who saves (15:2), guides (15:13), owns (15:16) and rules (15:18) his people.
- PROVISION (15:22–18:27) God provides pure water (15:22–25; 17:1–6), necessary shelter (15:27), daily bread (16:4, 15), overwhelming victory (17:8–16), and human companionship (18).

JETHRO is kind and encouraging (18:8–12) and realizes that Moses cannot possibly manage on his own (18:13–18). He makes the excellent suggestion that others might assist Moses in ruling the people (18:19–27).

3. CHAPTERS 19–40
GOD'S COVENANT

This third main section of the book divides into three parts. The covenant theme (19:3–6) is developed as follows:

a. IT EXPOUNDS THE PRIORITIES OF GOD'S PEOPLE (19–20)
God reminds them of:

- his deliverance (19:4; 20:2)
- his demands (19:5, "obey" and "keep")
- his desire (19:5b, 6, "you will be")

The priorities are carefully listed in the Ten Commandments. The first four are directed to man's relationship with God (20:3–11); the last six to man's relationship with man (20:12–16). A very important aspect of the covenant is that it concerns our attitude toward God *and* man.

b. IT ENFORCES THE RIGHTEOUSNESS OF GOD'S PEOPLE (21–23) Observe the detailed provision for men in their need. Community problems are dealt with here: laws concerning the release of slaves (21:2–11); murder (21:12–14); strife (21:18, 19); carelessness regarding dangerous cattle (21:28–32); theft (22:1–4); straying cattle (22:5); fire (22:6); theft or loss of property left in the care of a friend (22:7, 8)—to name only a few. They reflect God's loving involvement in the very down-to-earth, practical, everyday difficulties of community life. The term "law" sounds harsh, but a careful study of these legal provisions demonstrates the *kindness* of God, for example, he is concerned about the physical protection of a pregnant woman (21:22), about the bedclothes of a man in debt (22:26, 27), about caring for cattle even when it belongs to your enemy (23:4, 5), about feeding the poor (23:10, 11). He even plans to remove the Canaanite people gradually rather than at one dramatic moment, so that the country is not left to become desolate wasteland (23:29–31).

c. IT EXPLAINS THE WORSHIP OF GOD'S PEOPLE (24–40) This concluding section deals mainly with God's spiritual provisions for the Hebrews during their desert wanderings.

Moses goes to the mount (24:15) and is given detailed instructions about the tabernacle and priestly robes.

There is one very sad passage (32) which reflects something of the impatience (32:1), idolatry (32:2–6), and immorality (32:25) of the Hebrews. There are deep spiritual lessons here. We begin to fall away from God when we are impatient with him because he is not acting as and when we want. The next stage is to turn to "other gods," and finally, having left him, we forget his standards for our lives.

Moses stands out in contrast. See:

- Moses' contrition (32:31)
- Moses' communion (33:11)
- Moses' commission (34:9, 10)

No wonder his face shines (34:29)!

The generous giving of God's people may be an expression of their genuine repentance (36:5, "The people bring much more than enough . . . ," RSV). Is that kind of liberality typical of us?

EXODUS

illegible faint text at top of page

Leviticus

xodus contains preliminary legislation regarding Hebrew worship. Leviticus considers this important theme in greater detail. It describes the Jewish people's sacrificial system, and presents "types" or "figures" of Christ's greater, eternal and sufficient sacrifice. The title is derived from "Levi," the name of Jacob's third son, whose descendants were the levitical priests, dedicated to caring for the tabernacle and, later, the Temple.

1. CHAPTERS 1–7
OFFERINGS

Leviticus begins on the demanding note of *entire surrender*. The command is to "burn the whole . . ." (1:9). Five offerings are described in detail:

a. BURNT OFFERING (1) At some sacrifices part of the sacrifice was given to the priests (2:3), but the burnt offering was offered to God in its entirety.

b. MEAL OFFERING (2) (The RSV calls this the Cereal Offering; NIV has Grain Offering.) It has something to do with the dedication of our work and service to God.

c. PEACE OFFERING (3) This offering concerns our relationship with others. It is consummated by a covenant

meal with one's friends (7:13–15), and expresses gratitude to God (7:12), or marks the moment when a vow is
fulfilled (7:16).

d. SIN OFFERING (4) This conveys the assurance that sins
of ignorance have been forgiven. The Hebrews did not
view sin lightly; there was no sacrifice for deliberate sinning ("defiantly," Num. 15:30, NIV). The Sin Offering
covers unintended acts of wrong before God.

e. TRESPASS OFFERING (5) This mediates pardon for sins toward man, for example, when anyone refused to be a witness in a controversy, and so did not speak in the cause of
justice (5:1), or was accused of embezzlement, deceit or
fraud (6:2–3). In these cases of financial misconduct, full
restitution has to be made, plus an extra fifth (6:5); there is
no easy way out. For the Hebrews, faith was very practical.

Further details about these five offerings are given in
6:8–7:38.

2. CHAPTERS 8–10
PRIESTS

Attention now turns from the sacrifices to the men who offered them. The priests are appointed in the presence of the
congregation (8:4, 35) so that everyone knows the priestly
group and recognizes the holy nature of their office (see
2 Chron. 26:18). They are then clothed and anointed (8:5–13).

At the anointing, blood (signifying cleansing) is symbolically placed upon the right ear, right thumb and right big toe
of each priest (8:23–24). There is a message here for every
Christian, for every Christian is a priest in God's kingdom
(1 Pet. 2:9; Rev. 1:6, Isa. 61:6). The cleansing made possible by Christ's death ought to affect:

a. WHAT WE HEAR The priest was a teacher (10:11; Deut.
24:8; Mail. 2:7) and so he gave himself to the hearing of
good things from God and not grim things from men.

b. HOW WE WORK Do we realize that the service of our hands can be a sacrifice to God? Remember Colossians 3:17, 23–24.

c. WHERE WE WALK Once forgiven we need to pray that our steps may be kept in his way (see Ps. 1:1; 37:23–24). Note that the priests had to look after their own fellowship with God if they were to minister to others (9:7, "for yourself and the people"). A priest first filled his hand with gifts for God (9:17) and then he could lift up his hand in blessing on the people (9:22).

The story in chapter 10 is a warning to any who would dare to serve God presumptuously. NADAB and ABIHU were stupidly self-assertive (10:1). Some have wondered whether the injunction about strong drink (10:8–9) suggests that these two careless men were drunk when they sinned; it could be. One thing is definite; priests were expected to be morally different in order that they might be effective teachers ("distinguish between . . . the unclean and the clean . . . and you must teach," 10:10–11).

3. CHAPTERS 11–40
RULES

The series of regulations which follow contain detailed instructions regarding a multitude of different issues. Ceremonial, moral and social questions are discussed side by side for they are inseparably related in Jewish thought.

a. FOOD AND HEALTH (11–15) Diet laws (11) are followed by rules regarding birth (12), and skin diseases (13–15). In the Hebrew community the priest was a public health officer (compare Lev. 14:2, 33–57; Luke 17:14).

b. SACRIFICE AND SACRILEGE (16–17) The theologically important and spiritually significant Day of Atonement ritual is described (16) with its use of the scapegoat to symbolize the removal of sin (16:8–10, 21–22; compare John 1:29; 1 Pet. 2:24).

The next chapter warns about unlawful sacrifices (17:3–4). These provisions were intended to avert the danger of sacrificing to other gods (17:7).

c. IMPURITY AND GENEROSITY (18–20) Rules prohibiting sexual misconduct (e.g., 18:20) are found alongside compassionate provisions for the needy (19:9, 13, 14, 33, etc.).

d. PRIESTS AND FEASTS (21–24) These chapters outline regulations about the priesthood and details regarding the Sabbath and the feasts of Passover, Pentecost, Atonement and Tabernacles.

e. PROPERTY AND POVERTY (25) Regulations about the Sabbath and Jubilee are given; these have agricultural and humanitarian benefits as well as spiritual value. The poor are of special concern to God (25:25, 35, 39).

f. PLEDGES AND PROMISES (26–27) The words: "If . . . I will . . ." are key terms here (e.g., 26:3–4); likewise: "But if you will not . . . then I will . . ." (26:14–16). There are serious warnings in these closing chapters. Are we willing to be reformed by him (26:23–24)?

WHY READ LEVITICUS?

- It describes God's holiness (11:44–45; 19:2; 20:26; 21:8)
- It demonstrates God's kindness (e.g., 25:25)
- It declares God's faithfulness (11:45; 26:2–12)

Numbers

ince the numbering of the people accounts for only a small fraction of the book, the title seems strange. However, it is difficult to suggest another title, when the subject matter is so varied in interest, theme and presentation. Some chapters give detailed legislation regarding Hebrew religious and social life, but other passages are straightforward narrative, telling the frequently grim story of disobedience and rebellion as the Hebrew pilgrims journey from Egypt to the Promised Land. But it is possible to outline the book under three key ideas.

1. CHAPTERS 1–10
INSTRUCTION

These early chapters record a series of laws and instructions about:

a. TRIBAL LOCATION (1–2)
b. LEVITICAL ORGANIZATION (3–4) Remember that the tribe of Levi was specially appointed for religious service.
c. COMMUNITY PURIFICATION (5) Here are regulations concerning hygiene (5:1–4); stolen goods (5:5–10; compare Lev. 6:1–7); and broken relationships (5:11–31).
d. NAZIRITE DEDICATION (6) This act of dedication was

for a set period (6:18). There were three requirements: no strong drink; hair must not be cut; and there must be no contact with a dead body. The strong drink prohibition is possibly meant to emphasize the pilgrim nature of the godly life (no vineyards, etc., which belong only to a settled community). The uncut hair was an outward indication of the inward spiritual vow. A dead body was viewed as unclean, so this regulation stressed the need for purity. The Nazirite vow is thus a declaration of the need for pilgrims, witnesses and saints; the eternal ambition, outward testimony and holiness of God's people are the dominant themes of Numbers.

The Benediction in 6:24–26 is one of the most comprehensive prayer pronouncements in the whole Bible.

e. PRIESTLY LEGISLATION (7–9:14) This provides us with details about the offerings of the princes (leaders) of tribes (7), and regulations regarding the care of the lampstand (8:1–4); the purifying of the Levites for service (8:5–26); and the celebration of the Passover, when the people remember God's goodness in the past (9:1–14).

f. TRAVEL INFORMATION (9:15–10:36) Crowd management in the days before loudspeaker hailers and shortwave radio:

- the guiding cloud (9:15–23)—the people experience God's goodness as he leads them in the present
- the silver trumpets (10:1–10)—the priests communicate with the people by blowing different blasts on the trumpets
- marching orders (10:11–28)—this is no unruly rabble; each group of people know when they have to move and whom they have to obey.

2. CHAPTERS 11–25
INSURRECTION

This is a depressing story; it tells of disloyalty and disaffection, discontent and discouragement. It is a serious warning to all God's people. Once we depart from God's will and seek only our own pleasure, we can be sure of unhappiness and frustration. The Israelites complained about:

- the food which was provided for them (11)
- the leader who was appointed over them (12)
- the land that was offered to them (13)

In all of life's experiences there are giants (13:33), as well as grapes (13:23–24). Once again God's appointed leaders come in for trouble (14:2–6), and at this point God tells the multitude that only their children will inherit the land (14:23, 29).

Some rules are given about offerings and Sabbath (15) and we then read of further rebellion (16) led by KORAH, DATHAN and ABIRAM (compare Jude 11; 2 Pet 2:10). God's appointed leadership was authenticated by a miraculous sign (17). The New Testament has a good deal to say about those who just cannot submit to authority (see also Heb. 13:7, 17; 1 Cor. 12:28, "*God* has appointed").

There is a serious word here for our own time. Any kind of submission to authority is despised today, even when the authority has the best interests of people at heart. But this is hardly a Christian attitude: some kind of leadership is essential in any well-organized society, the Church included. No group or community can hope to work effectively without recognized and respected leaders. But to guard against rigidly authoritarian or dictatorial church leadership, the New Testament emphasizes the necessity of *mutual submission* (Rom. 12:10; Gal. 5:13; Eph. 5:21; Phil. 2:3–4).

Priestly dues (18) and *purificatory demands* (19) occupy the main place in the next chapters, and we are then faced with yet another rebellious encounter (20), this time about the lack of water. Moses, normally a meek (that is, teachable) man (12:3), does not do exactly as God commanded him (compare 20:8 and 11). He may have struck the rock twice as an act of impatience with the people or disobedience to God. Obviously we are not intended to know the precise nature of the sin other than that it reflected some kind of *unbelief* (20:12).

The *discontent* of the people, and the *disobedience* of Moses is now followed by their *discouragement* "on the way" (21:4), causing them to fall into the serious sin of speaking "against God" (21:5). This results in the plague of serpents (21:6). Their deliverance when they have repented of their sin is wonderfully symbolic of our deliverance (John 3:14–15).

The main point of the intriguing BALAAM-BALAK narrative (22–24) is the *sovereignty of God*. A foreign prophet hired by an enemy king is consistently frustrated in his attempt to curse God's people. This incident shows how at this very early period the Israelites are aware that God is not only concerned with their little nation, but that he rules the world, even when it does not recognize his reign. Tragically, although Balak does not confound the Israelites by cursing, he corrupts them by immorality (25:1–3).

3. CHAPTERS 26–36
INTENTION

The concluding chapters of the book deal with *God's plans* for his people's future; it records what he intends to do once their children settle in the Promised Land. It deals with matters like tribal census (26); legal inheritance and the rights of daughters (27); offerings, feasts, vows and spoils (28–31). Reubenites and Gadites ask if they can have the land east of the Jordan (32). Finally:

- the journey is described (33)
- the land is divided (34)
- the refuge cities are demanded (35)
- the inheritance (of daughters) is discussed (36)

POSTSCRIPT

Numbers is an unusual book in many ways, but it has some
very pointed things to say to our own generation. It clearly:

- illustrates the seriousness of sin (20:12; 25:3; 32:23)
- expounds the sovereignty of God (23:19–20; 23:8,
  21)
- exemplifies the surrender of men (6:2–12; 14:24;
  32:11–12)

Deuteronomy

euteronomy takes up the story of the children of Israel to explain how Moses reminded the people of the covenant they had made with God before entering the Promised Land: the title means "second law." It is one of the most important books in the Bible, and is quoted in seventeen out of the twenty-seven books in the New Testament. The main themes of the book are so closely related that it is not easy to suggest clear divisions, and any attempt at analysis is bound to be slightly artificial. However, the following outline may help to focus our attention on the leading ideas.

1. CHAPTERS 1–11
LOOK BACK IN GRATITUDE

The first section of the book surveys God's dealings with his people from their stay at Horeb (1:6) to Beth Peor (3:29) and recalls some of the vital things God said to them in the course of their journey. It is easy to forget the Lord's mercies and Deuteronomy constantly demands the "backward look" of thanksgiving. "Remember" is a key word in the book.

The portraiture of God is fascinating. He is:

a. THE ARDENT LOVER (7:6–8; 10:15) God's love for us demands the response of our love (6:5; 7:9; 11:13). Be-

cause of this deep love which the Israelites were to have
for God, the call of Deuteronomy is to abandon other
gods. The book says a great deal about the perils of idolatry; the worship of images is disloyalty, due to loss of
love for God himself (compare 4:25; 6:14; 7:25; 11:16.
The same idea is behind the ban on mixed marriages: the
people will lose their love for Yahweh, 7:3–6).

b. THE UNFAILING DELIVERER (9:3) The Israelites have an
acute sense of history, and deliberately recall God's goodness to them in former days (8:2). But his deliverance in
the past is meant to encourage their reliance in the present. Hence a key phrase in Deuteronomy is "Do not be
afraid" (1:21, 29; 3:2, 22; 7:18).

c. THE PATIENT TEACHER "Consider the discipline [instruc-
tion, RSV margin] of the Lord" (11:2). Yahweh manifested
his love and power in times past in order that they might
learn of his ways (4:32–35; 6:20–23; 8:2) and share their
knowledge with others. It was also in order that they might
attend to his word. "Obedience" is another key concept in
this book (5:27, 31–32; 6:1–3, 17–18, 25; 7:11; 8:1, 6, 11,
20; 9:24; 11:8). God is thoroughly consistent and reliable
(4:31):

- the people fail to keep God's word—but God is always faithful
- the nation forgets God's goodness—but God never
  forgets his promises
- the people forsake God—but God will not abandon
  them

2. CHAPTERS 12–16
LOOK UP IN OBEDIENCE

We have already seen that "obey" is a key word. This section begins, "These are the decrees and laws" and a number
of instructions follow, all of which demand the obedient response of the people. The covenant loyalty of which the peo-

ple are reminded is toward God *and* man (God's people). Chapters 12–16 deal mainly with the right attitude to God while the following section is concerned with man's responsibilities in the light of the covenant. Once the people enter the land they must remember God's teaching about:

a. OFFERINGS (12; 16:21–22) No offerings are to be made to idols (12:2–3).

b. PROPHETS (13) This includes anyone who tries to lead others.

c. FOOD (14) Both that which is *prohibited by God* (diet laws, 14:1–21) and that which is *presented to God* (tithes, 14:22–29).

d. FESTIVALS (15–16) Instructions are given about the well known Year of Release (15), Passover (16:1–8), Weeks, that is, Pentecost (16:9–12), Tabernacles (16:13–15), Pilgrimages (16:16–17).

Chapter 16:18–20 demonstrates how closely woven are these important spiritual ideas. Sacrifices in the Temple (16:16) are no more important than justice before the rulers (16:18)—both are interrelated themes. A right approach to God should ensure a just attitude to man. The following section discusses these matters in greater detail.

3. CHAPTERS 17–25
LOOK AROUND IN COMPASSION

The Hebrew people must not only turn obediently toward God but compassionately toward their fellow men. Rules are now laid down which are intended to guide the people in their community life. Instruction is given about:

- judges (17:1–13)—the danger of bribery, for example
- kings (17:14–20)
- priests (18:1–8)
- spiritual leaders (18:9–22)

- offenders (19)—including a man accused of manslaughter (cities of refuge are provided), and false witnesses
- warriors (20)—regulations are given which affect both the soldiers (e.g., 20:8) and the land they conquer (e.g., 20:19–20, during a prolonged siege they must not cut down fruit trees in order to build bulwarks)
- families (21–22)—including provisions for unsolved murder; a worthless son; care of children (22:8); broken and unhappy relationships (22:13–21); even for a bird's family (22:6–7)
- worshippers (23)—and the need for purity in the camp as well as at the Temple (23:10–14)

Chapters 24–25 deal with a variety of matters like divorce, pledges, hire of servants, gleanings and care of the poor.

4. CHAPTERS 26–34
LOOK FORWARD IN CONFIDENCE

This closing section of Deuteronomy faces the future and anticipates the time when the community of God's people is no longer nomadic but enjoys a settled agricultural life.

a. Chapter 26:1–4 record a *first-fruits offering* and the words of the response (26:5–11) reveal something of the Hebrews' rich historical sense. Their idea was that when God had given them the land in an overwhelming victory, surely they should offer the fruit of that soil to him. Are we as responsive and sacrificial with the lives he has given to us?

b. Chapter 26:12–15 record another confession which is made as the tithes are offered. These gifts directly benefit the priests and the poor in Israel.

c. In these final chapters there are *prohibitions* (curses, warnings, etc., 27–28) and *promises* (29–31).

d. Chapter 32 records the *Song of Moses,* a lofty hymn of thanksgiving in which the leader of God's people rejoices in all God's providential care and direction.

e. Chapter 33 turns from rejoicing before God to blessings upon men; it relates the tribal promises.

f. Chapter 34 tells the story of Moses' death. The final challenge of Deuteronomy is to loyal worship and obedient service.

Is God *deliberately hiding* his face from us in judgment (32:19–20) or *clearly revealing* his face to us in fellowship (34:10)?

Joshua

he book takes its title from its leading character, Moses' successor, the man who led the Israelites into Canaan. It tells the story of invasion and settlement in the Promised Land.

1. CHAPTERS 1–12
CONQUERING THE LAND

In the opening chapter, which sets the scene, JOSHUA is assured of:

- the divine presence (1:5: "As I was with Moses, so . . .")
- the divine promise (1:5: "I will never leave you . . .")
- the divine plan (1:6: "You will lead these people to inherit the land I swore to their forefathers to give them.")
- the divine power (1:7: "Be strong and very courageous . . . that you may be successful wherever you go.")

The following chapters are dominated by three personalities:

a. A FOREIGNER WHO SERVES GOD (2) The RAHAB chapter is a majestic salvation story. The historian responsible for this narrative is at pains to stress belief in God's *un-*

hindered purpose (2:9: "I know that the Lord has given this land to you."); God's *unfailing might* (2:10); and God's *unlimited reign* (2:11; 3:11). It is a missionary story showing how one who was not formerly a "believer" enters *by faith* (as she believes the word of the spies) into a saving experience of God's grace.

b. A LEADER WHO OBEYS GOD (3–6) JOSHUA is the central character here. The ark (3:3) is a symbol of God's presence and the people are instructed to follow it (3:4) as they step on to strange territory. They cross Jordan at a difficult time (3:15) in a miraculous way (3:16) and as a spiritual lesson (4:1–3). The stone memorial is to be a permanent reminder of God's delivering power (4:20–24).

As a sign of the people's devotion, the rite of circumcision is renewed and the Passover is remembered (5). The victorious Captain meets the obedient leader at Jericho, and reminds Joshua of the immense spiritual resources which are at his right hand (5:13–6:2). Always remember this when you are up against difficulties and obstacles. If you have a vision of the Conqueror you will not be afraid (compare Rom. 8:37; 1 Cor. 15:57), for he is always at your side. No wonder Jericho was taken.

- Joshua worships (5:14)
- Joshua relies (5:14: "What message does my Lord have for his servant?")
- Joshua obeys (5:15; 6:2–26)

c. A BELIEVER WHO ROBS GOD (7) Rahab and Joshua stand out as rich examples of complete obedience, but a warning narrative follows: the sad story of ACHAN. God has said that the treasures are to be "devoted" to him, but Achan completely disobeys the word of God. If the land is to be occupied without internal strife among the Hebrews, some definite ruling has to be issued about property and theft. By ignoring this, Achan brings disaster not only upon his own life but on the lives of others. There is a warning for us here. Our selfish disregard of God's word

and our stubborn determination to please ourselves often
result in anguish for others. We cannot live isolated lives;
inevitably our conduct affects others. Our poor standards
are soon communicated to other people. But remember
that if you have sinned, you may be gloriously forgiven.
An eighth century prophet made passing reference to this
sad incident in a message of pardon and hope (Hos. 2:15).

Once the people recognize the need of utter reliance and
complete obedience, Ai is captured (8). Note how Achan's
sin is not only disobedience but *impatience.* God knows that
the people need money and clothing and at Ai they are free
to take what they want (8:2, compare 8:27).

The story told in chapter 9 is a further illustration of the
importance of the *word* in Hebrew thought. The men of
Gibeon, who only live three days' journey away, make it
look as if they live in a country far away from the Canaanite
border, so Joshua and his men gladly agree to leave them in
peace (9:15). But even when they discover they have been
fooled, the Israelite leaders will not break the promise they
have given (9:16–19), and the Gibeonites are made servants
of the Hebrew community (9:21–27).

Chapters 10–12 record further victories and achievements; even the giants they so much feared are removed
(11:21–22). Joshua is noted for his unhesitating and unre-
served obedience (11:12, 15: "he left nothing undone . . .").

2. CHAPTERS 13–21
DIVIDING THE LAND

The entire land has not been subdued (13:2) but is allocated
to different tribes, and this general theme occupies chapters
13–19.

In chapter 20 clear legislation is given about the *cities of
refuge.* These instructions illustrate truths we have noted
earlier about God's *mercy,* just as the Achan story emphasizes his *severity* (compare Rom. 11:22). The refuge cities

provide for those who kill anyone "unintentionally" (20:3), ensuring full protection until the case has been brought before the judges.

The territories allocated to the Levites are given in chapter 21. Society offenders and spiritual officials are equally God's concern.

3. CHAPTERS 22–24
UNIFYING THE LAND

These closing chapters indicate how the people were united. Chapter 22 relates a story about the danger of disunity. The tribes on the east side of the Jordan built an altar (22:10) and this caused trouble among the remaining tribes as they had all been instructed to have a *central* sanctuary (22:16–20). The offending tribes explained they did not want this altar for sacrificial purposes (22:22–23), but as a memorial or witness to the fact that they, as the others, were equally included in the provisions of God's favor. They naturally feared that distance might cause the others to disown them at some future time (22:24–25). The altar was therefore left as a testimony ("witness") to their place in the divine purposes for the entire nation (22:34).

Chapter 23 records the words of Joshua to the people. He is eager to share with them what God has told him (23:6; compare 1:6–9). "Cleave" (23:8, RSV) and "love" (23:11); it can hardly be bettered.

The final chapter tells of the covenant made by Joshua and the people (24:25). It has three aspects:

- God and the past (24:2–13)
- God and the present (24:14–28)—"Now . . . this day"
- God and the future (24:29–33)

Three burials are mentioned: Joshua, Joseph and Eleazar. They *served* the Lord faithfully and made it easier for others to serve him too.

Judges

his very sad book covers a period in Hebrew history of obvious embarrassment to the gifted author of this collection of tribal stories. The key to the book is the repeated statement in 17:6 and 21:25. Tribal leaders like Gideon, Jephthah, Samson and others lead the people, but the nation easily falls into corrupt and idolatrous practices. The book can be divided into three sections:

1. CHAPTERS 1–2
THEIR CONDITION

The grim story of King Adoni-Bezek in this opening section (1:5–7) introduces readers to one of the key themes of the book: *the inevitability of judgment.* Sin against others ultimately comes back upon ourselves.

There is a clear cyclic pattern:

a. PARTIAL OBEDIENCE (1:21, 27, 29, 30, 31; compare Num. 33:55; Josh. 23:13; Judg. 2:1–3)
b. CORRUPT WORSHIP (2:11–13)
c. INEVITABLE JUDGMENT (2:14–15)
d. UNDESERVED MERCY (2:16)
e. REPEATED APOSTASY (2:17)
f. FURTHER JUDGMENT, etc.

This pattern is repeated throughout the book.

2. CHAPTERS 3–16
THEIR CONQUESTS

A number of stories now follow, covering the exploits of thirteen "judges" or deliverers. Of these tribal leaders, Dr. Graham Scroggie has observed: "We cannot conclude that all these Judgeships were consecutive; indeed it is almost certain that some of them were contemporaneous."

In this section we are told of the adventures of Othniel (3:7–11); Ehud (3:12–30); Shamgar (3:31); Deborah and Barak (4:1–5:31); Gideon (6:1–8:35); Abimelech (9:1–57); Tola (10:1); Jair (10:3–5); Jephthah (11:1–12:7); Ibzan (12:8–10); Elon (12:11); Abdon (12:13–15) and Samson (13:1–16:31). Certain aspects of their personal experience are of continuing spiritual importance:

a. DIVINE APPOINTMENT Chapter 3:10 gives a brief summary of a judge's life and work. Spiritually equipped (3:10; 6:34; 11:29; 13:25), their duties appear to be both legal ("judge") and military ("and went to war").

b. CONSEQUENT HEROISM Like Jael (4:18–21), Ehud is quite fearless and kills the Moabite king within yards of the Moabite bodyguard (3:15–23).

c. TRANSFORMED PERSONALITY Gideon is frightened (6:27) but becomes fearless in the power of the Spirit (6:34).

d. SUBTLE TEMPTATIONS How sad that Gideon should spoil an otherwise admirable record by greed (8:24–27; compare Exod. 28:6–35: the ephod was to be for the High Priest only). Possibly there is spiritual pride here as well as materialistic avarice. Even religious things can become a snare. Do not forget 1 Tim. 6:10; 2 Tim. 3:2. Covetousness is a common peril.

e. INTENSE RIVALRY Chapter 9:1–21 illustrates the sad fact of internal strife and tension. Two sons of Gideon (or

Jerub-Baal, see 8:35) fight for leadership; the story which follows is a sad commentary on the weakening effect of discord and bitterness within families and communities.

f. CARELESS RESOLUTIONS The Jephthah narrative (11:30) ought to be a standing warning about thoughtless remarks and uncostly vows. It was easy for Jephthah to make such a promise. He never thought for a moment that his only child would rush out to meet him; doubtless he had a servant in mind. It was quite customary for a singer to greet the victors on their return (compare 1 Sam. 18:6) but Jephthah didn't think his daughter would be among the singers and musicians (11:34).

g. UNNECESSARY FAILURE Jephthah's story is distressing but the tale of Samson is even more pathetic. It was all so unnecessary. He had unique gifts and immense opportunities, but was dominated by selfishness. Chapters 13–16 record his various exploits. He has three sad love affairs (14:1, 7, 20; 16:1, 4); all three women are Philistines, and the towns Timnah and Gaza, and the Valley of Sorek are all in Philistine territory (compare Exod. 34:12–17; Deut. 7:3–6; Josh. 23:12; 2 Cor. 6:14). Samson's name meant "sunlight"! What irony. In the end he is blinded and spends his days in the darkness of a lonely prison-house (16:21). But his sacrificial death leads to ultimate victory.

3. CHAPTERS 17–21
THEIR CORRUPTION

It would seem that the compiler's aim here is to direct our attention from the leaders to the ordinary people in Israel at this time, and to show how defiled everything and everyone has become because of the selfish attitude of rulers and subjects alike (21:25). There is an utter disregard of God's will, their own walk and other people's welfare. The sad consequences of the people's stubborn rebellion are shown to be:

a. RELIGIOUS DECLENSION (17–18) A man without true devotion to the Law (17:1–6; see Exod. 20:1–6; Lev. 19:4) appoints a Levite as his household priest because he thinks this will assure him of prosperity (17:12–13) but the priest becomes equally self-seeking (18:19). As a Levite he should have opposed the suggestion of image-worship (18:20, 31) but deep religious convictions seem to have disappeared.

b. MORAL DEGRADATION (19) Here is an awful tale of lust and violence. The initially hospitable nature of the old Ephraimite stands out in marked contrast to the sordid behavior of his neighbors in Gibeah. Notice how quickly one sordid sin leads on to another. This grim incident results in:

c. TRIBAL DISSENSION (20–21) Determined to be avenged, the Israelites fight against the offending tribe of Benjamin (19:16; 20:12). When the Benjamites will not hand over the men responsible for the atrocity (20:13), there is a prolonged and debilitating struggle leading to further intertribal warfare (21:8–10).

WARNING

The book of Judges is a story of anguish and distress and yet it could have been so different. It illustrates with intense seriousness the folly of ungodly, selfish and willful behavior, and the consequent humiliation and despair. No Christian can read the book without realizing how important it is to maintain a close communion with the God who loves his people and demands and deserves their total allegiance.

Ruth

his little tract is of immense theological as well as historical importance. It was possibly circulated at a time when the Hebrew people were in danger of becoming very exclusive, and even fiercely restrictive in their attitude to non-Jews. Like Jonah, the book records the compassionate provision of God for Gentiles. It is of obvious additional importance in that the central figure is the great-grandmother of David.

The four chapters can be divided into four great scenes in this magnificent *drama of salvation*. The story unfolds the wonder of God's generous love for the homeless, the hungry and the lonely as we see how Ruth, who was without a proper home, without adequate food and without a reliable companion, found a home in Bethlehem (literally, "the house of bread") where she was cared for by her kinsman-redeemer (*Go'el*), a man named Boaz (literally, "strength"). The story speaks to all of us, for we are all spiritually lonely, hungry and homeless until we are found by our Redeemer.

1. CHAPTER I
A HOLY DECISION

The scene is in far-off Moab. Naomi plans to leave the country and return to Judah now that the famine is over, but it is an agonizing moment. She is a widow and has also lost both her married sons; she has only her two daughters-in-law, Orphah (possibly meaning "stiff-necked" and Ruth (possibly meaning "friend." The later rabbis attached spiritual significance to these names). There comes the moment of parting. Orphah returns to the place where she believes she will find security among her own people and their idols (1:14–15), but Ruth makes a decision which:

a. EXPRESSES HER LOYALTY (1:16) It is a decision of love: she refuses to be separated from one who has done so much for her over the years.

b. DEMANDS HER FAITH The journey is certainly a venture into the unknown, and her new-found faith is being put to the test. When she says, "Your God . . ." Ruth does not say *Elohim* (as foreigners often did, see 1 Kings 19:2; 20:10), but *Yahweh,* the name of Israel's God.

c. ILLUSTRATES HER HOPE Ruth speaks boldly about the ultimate future (1:17: "Where you die I will die . . ."). In the ancient near-Eastern world every nation believed that it had its own allocated place in Sheol (compare Ezek. 32:21–30). Ruth's decision, therefore, is an irrevocable commitment with definite eternal implications.

d. ANTICIPATES HER REWARD (1:22: "arriving in Bethlehem as the barley harvest was beginning.") Ruth has no idea of the path which lies before her; she is walking into an unknown country. But the God who calls is the Lord who cares and her loyalty to Naomi as well as to Naomi's God is graciously rewarded. These two needy women arrive in Bethlehem just at the time when the barley harvest is being reaped.

2. CHAPTER 2
A HEAVENLY PROVISION

Chapter 2 enlarges on the theme of "provision" announced in 1:22. Ruth is apparently unaware of the Hebrew practice of appointing a Go'el (kinsman-redeemer). This law states that a brother or male relative is obliged to make every possible provision for the family of his deceased kinsman—either by redeeming the widow's property or marrying her (Lev. 25:25). The Go'el was particularly responsible for the helpless members of a family.

In the story of Ruth, the wonderful thing is that without any knowledge of this law Ruth goes into a field where reapers are at work, and starts gleaning in the very part of the field owned by Boaz, a kinsman of her father-in-law. If we are obedient to God, we too are directed by him, even though we are not always aware of the importance and significance of our movements.

Ruth finds every sympathy in Boaz' part of the field. Notice that she is a hard worker (2:7: "without resting even for a moment," RSV). Although the Lord provides for us, he expects us to do our part too! The Lord's provision is:

- immediate—as soon as Ruth enters the field, she is given an opportunity to glean. God also meets our needs in his immense generosity (Phil. 4:19)
- undeserved (2:10)—Ruth accepts this loving provision with a deep sense of humility
- generous (2:9, 14–16)—there is plenty in God's storehouse. Remember Luke 15:17.
- promised—Ruth's freedom to glean in Boaz' field goes back to a law of God (Deut. 24:19–21). But the gleanings were often quite meager (compare Isa. 17:5–6) and Boaz goes well beyond the Law.

3. CHAPTER 3
A HUMBLE SUPPLICATION

In the evening Ruth follows the advice of Naomi and goes down to the threshing-floor where Boaz is sleeping—the grain is carefully guarded at night-time. Notice the attractive characteristics of this "new convert":

- she is completely obedient (3:5–6; compare John 2:5)
- utterly meek (3:7–8)
- graciously submissive (3:9: "I am Ruth, your maid-servant," RSV, that is, a female slave)
- absolutely dependent (3:9: "Spread the corner of your garment over me, since you are a kinsman-redeemer"). The word translated "garment" is the same as "wings" in the prayer of Boaz (2:12) and one imagines the parallel is quite intentional. The practical expression of the spiritual fact that Ruth is under God's "wings" will be that she is also in the care of Boaz
- morally pure (3:11)—both Ruth and Boaz are eager to avoid any appearance of evil (3:14; compare 1 Thess. 5:22). The sequel is that she is:
- abundantly rewarded (3:15)—if we have these qualities we will be cared for ourselves and be able to help others too (3:17)

4. CHAPTER 4
A HAPPY CONSUMMATION

The beautiful story reaches this very happy ending. The closing chapter provides a fascinating insight into the legal procedures involved in the Go'el provisions.

It is more than likely that the final sentence of the book indicates its primary purpose. It *may* have been originally circulated to counteract the fierce exclusivism of the post-exilic period. Chapter 4:7 suggests that the story was written down well after the events took place; obviously it was not written until after David's reign (4:22). The writer's aim could have been to remind the Hebrew people that the Lord God loved this Moabite convert and therefore the provisions of the Deuteronomic law (see Deut. 23:3) should not deter their missionary enthusiasm since after all even David had Moabite ancestry.

1 Samuel

 and 2 Samuel are concerned with the establishment of a united monarchy in Israel; their main theme is *kingship*. When 1 Samuel opens attention is focused on the last two of the judges (who were probably little more than exalted tribal leaders): ELI who served as judge/priest, and SAMUEL who served as judge/prophet. The book can be divided into three unequal parts, in which SAMUEL, SAUL and DAVID are the successive leading characters.

1. CHAPTERS 1–8
REQUESTING

The people want a godly leader. The priesthood is selfish and the nation lacks strong moral leadership and adequate military resources (4:1–10; compare 8:1–5).

The first section of the book has a "true to life" mixture of joy and tragedy; the story of Samuel's birth and HANNAH's delight dominates chapters 1–3, while the tragedy of Ichabod's birth and Eli's grief makes sad reading in chapter 4.

The families of ELKANAH and Eli present us with stark contrasts—godliness (1:1–3, 21; 2:1–11) and greed (2:12–17). There are fascinating similarities between Hannah's prayer of thanksgiving (2:1–10) and Mary's song (the Magnificat, Luke 1:46–55); even the language is the same let alone the ideas: for example, rejoicing, salvation, holiness, hatred of pride, help for the poor, defeat of adversaries, the mighty broken, the hungry fed, etc. Was Hannah's song in Mary's mind on the great day when she visited Elizabeth? There is so much value in *knowing* the word of God by heart.

THE ARK is the main theme in chapters 4–7. We see:

- the ark's capture (4)
- the ark's victory (5)
- the ark's return (6)
- the ark's rest (7)

In chapter 8 attention begins to turn from the ark to a *throne* (8:5). What was wrong was not the people's natural desire for a leader, but their willful rejection of the kingly rule of God (8:7). The omniscient Lord could see their future unhappiness (8:11–18). What we think is *naturally right* is not always *spiritually best* for us. God granted their desire but their self-centered request had tragic results (compare Ps. 106:15).

2. CHAPTERS 9–15
REGRETTING

The early period of Saul's reign seems rich with promise. He is attractive (9:2); strong (9:2); considerate (9:5, 7); meek (9:21); controlled (10:26–27); just (11:6); and courageous (11:7–11). But power corrupts, and Saul changes.

Samuel tells the people that God is deeply grieved by their request (12:17–19), but adds that if they obey God's voice all will be well (12:14, 20–22). The tragic thing is that their appointed leader, who ought to have been a good example, is *constantly disobedient* and *spiritually rebellious* (13:8–9, 13–14; 15:3, 9, 11, 13–15, 22–23). The reign which opened with such evident joy is *closed by God* in sorrow (15:26, 28, 35; 16:1) for though Saul stays on the Israelite throne, God no longer recognizes him as the monarch of the people.

Interest now moves away from this arrogant rebel in the palace to an insignificant shepherd-boy caring for his father's flock on the hills of Bethlehem (compare 1 Cor. 1:27–29; Psa. 78:70). God regrets that Saul was anointed and the people regret that they are still under his poor leadership.

3. CHAPTERS 16–31
REJECTING

God's new king is chosen (16:5–12), anointed (16:13) and equipped (16:13). God leaves Saul with his utter selfishness as his only assured possession; this final section of 1 Samuel records Saul's fierce rejection of David and his various attempts to destroy the fugitive king. The story of how this once devoted servant of God attempts to frustrate God's purposes makes pathetic reading and is a stark illustration of the failure that is bound to follow any such attempt to fight God.

Saul's son, JONATHAN, has no desire to be king. He knows that it is God's purpose that his friend David should be ruler (23:14–18).

This closing section might be summarized as follows:

a. DAVID IS ANOINTED (16) God knows his *heart* is right (16:7; Psa. 147:10–11).
b. DAVID IS TESTED (17) The encounter with Goliath proves David's utter reliance upon God (17:37, 47) rather than on human aids (17:38–39).
c. DAVID IS HATED (18) Saul soon becomes jealous (18:8, 29).
d. DAVID IS HUNTED (19) The tale of Saul's sad pursuit of David goes on almost until the close of the book.
e. DAVID IS SUPPORTED (20–22) David is not alone. He is encouraged by *a devoted friend,* Jonathan (20) and *a faithful priest* (21–22), whose kindness to the refugee king (21:3, 6) costs him his life (22:16–19).
f. DAVID IS FRUSTRATED (23–26) The theme of ingratitude runs throughout these four chapters. David saves Keilah

(23:1, 5), yet he is warned that their citizens will certainly hand him over to Saul (23:12); he spares Saul (24), but the king is merely emotional about it (24:16) and there is no real gratitude to David for his mercy (25). Yet again Saul is spared (26), but there is no genuine reconciliation (26:25).

g. DAVID IS PROTECTED (27–31) David makes a major decision: he will seek refuge at the Philistine court (27:1). However, he craftily uses his new protected state to fight battles against the enemies of Israel rather than against his own countrymen (27:8–12). From this unusual base he is able to keep away from Saul and at the same time serve his own nation!

The difficulty comes when David is asked to join the Philistine armies in a direct battle against the Hebrews but even in this God's sovereign, protecting hand is at work (29:3–11). So David turns to fight the Amalekites (30:1–20) and is victorious. Meanwhile, in the Philistine encounter with Israel the Hebrews are defeated and both Saul and Jonathan are killed (31:1–6).

The story of intense heroism with which the book closes indicates both the cruelty (31:8–10), bravery (31:11–13) and loyalty (see 1 Samuel 11:1–11) of those hard times.

POSTSCRIPT

Saul was ruined by greed and jealousy. Not long before he died he made this tragic confession: "I have played the fool, and have erred exceedingly" (1 Sam. 26:21). The story of his wasted life is one of several found in Scripture. The Bible is an honest book. It tells the story as it was and not how we would like it to have been.

2 Samuel

Samuel records the main events in the reign of David. A brilliant collection of historical and biographical narratives, it contains a vast number of important lessons for Christian people.

1. CHAPTERS 1–12
RECOGNITION

In our study of 1 Samuel we noted that although Saul had been rejected by God (1 Sam. 15:23, 26; 16:1) he remained on the throne. After Saul's death on the battlefield of Gilboa (1 Sam. 31:3–6) DAVID is free to assume the regal responsibilities earlier assigned to him by God (1 Sam. 16:1, 12–13) and the men of Judah publicly acknowledge David as their king (2 Sam. 2:4). In this first section of the book we see how, despite some initial opposition, David comes to be recognized as king by all the tribes of Israel. There are five main themes:

a. OPPOSITION (1–5) ABNER, Saul's able captain, believes ISH-BOSETH, Saul's son, to be the rightful heir to the throne, and he encourages the people to recognize him as king (2:8–10). JOAB, David's captain, and a cruel and dangerous man, is soon at cross-purposes with Abner (2:18–32), even though Abner later comes over to David's side. Joab cannot rest until he has put Abner out of the way (3:27) and David realizes that his reign is likely to be troubled by the intrigue and cruelty of his leading army official (3:27–39).

Some people are not at their best solely because they are dominated by unworthy and unhelpful friends. This was certainly so of David's relationship with Joab. Ish-Boseth is killed (4:5–7) and David is made sole king over all Israel (5:3).

b. AMBITION (6–7) After the atrocious bloodshed of these early chapters it is a delight to turn to David's two spiritual ambitions: *to bring the ark* back to Jerusalem (6:2), and *to build the Temple* (7:1–3). In both cases he meets with those who cool his ardor: MICHAL (6:16–24) and NATHAN (7:3–17)—though these two are entirely different. Michal is proud and resentful (6:20) while Nathan is meek and obedient (7:4–5, 17). These two chapters reveal the earnest sincerity of David's spirituality.

c. EXTENSION (8) David's heart was right and his prayer (7:29) for God's blessing upon his reign is certainly answered. Chapter 8 records the details of his increasing conquests and the extension of his vast kingdom (compare 1 Sam. 2:30).

d. COMPASSION (9–10) Two different events are set here side by side, and both portray something of David's generosity (9:1; 10:1–2). The word translated "kindness" is the Hebrew *hesed,* which means loving-kindness, mercy, covenant-love. It is the word that is found in Psalm 23.6: ". . . and *love* will follow me." David has experienced God's mercy (kindness) in his own life so he naturally wants to express that same attitude to others. These two chapters present us with a sharp contrast: kindness enjoyed (9:13) and kindness spurned (10:3–5).

e. TRANSGRESSION (11–12) One sin quickly gives birth to another. If the new king of Ammon had accepted and welcomed David's envoys and their kindness (10:2) then there would have been no war between them, and, presumably, Joab would not have gone fighting against them (11:1) and the awful incident recorded in 11:2–27 might never have happened. Joab emerges from the narrative with even more power over David (11:14, 18, 21).

Nathan's utter loyalty to the revealed word of God is further demonstrated in 12:1–15.

2. CHAPTERS 13–18
REBELLION

From distress in the family, the narrative turns to further unhappiness in the nation. Sin not only reproduces itself, it widens its influence:

a. ABSALOM'S ANGER (13) The immense upheaval in the life of the nation created by Absalom's rebellion starts with an evil suggestion made by David's nephew, JONADAB. The words, "Now Amnon had a friend . . ." (13:3) are a warning about relationships. Amnon listens to his friend. Absalom is responsible for Amnon's death (13:28–29) and flees.

b. ABSALOM'S RETURN (14) How ungrateful a man Absalom is! Joab is largely responsible for his return to Israel (14:2, 18–20, 22–23), and yet he sets Joab's fields on fire (14:30).

c. ABSALOM'S PLOT (15) He turns the hearts of the people from the king to himself, but there are loyal people in Jerusalem even in these dark days (15:15, 19–21, 32–37).

d. ABSALOM'S COLLEAGUE (16) AHITOPHEL is widely respected as an adviser, but he has gone over to Absalom's side (16:15).

e. ABSALOM'S ENEMY (17) HUSHAI is David's spy and he suggests a plan that gives David time to get away (17:8–15).

f. ABSALOM'S DEATH (18) His long hair, which has been his pride (14:26), possibly leads to his death (18:9).

3. Chapters 19–24
RESTORATION

In the final section, which deals with David's return, we are presented with five scenes:

a. A RETURNED EXILE (19) SHIMEI, MEPHIBOSHETH and BARZILLAI (19:18–30) are interesting miniature biographical studies. How will you meet *the* King on his return— with deep regret (Shimei), with vague excuses (Mephibosheth) or with unashamed joy (Barzillai)?
b. A VICIOUS SOLDIER (20) Joab obviously feared that AMASA was taking his place and so killed him (17:25; 19:13; 20:4, 8–13).
c. A DEVOTED MOTHER (21) RIZPAH's invincible love for her sons (21:10) shows that there could still be loyalty and heroism even in days of appalling cruelty and injustice.
d. A GRATEFUL WORSHIPPER (22:1–23:7) David's song of thanksgiving is about security, mercy, power and guidance.
   A parenthesis (23:8–39) lists the warriors.
e. A FAITHFUL PROPHET (24) GAD (1 Sam. 22:5) who recorded some events in David's reign (1 Chron. 29:29). Are we as faithful in proclaiming God's work even when we suspect it might not be well received?

1 Kings

he stories related in 1 Kings illustrate the *disruptive* effect of man's sin. The narrative begins with the kingdom led by one king (DAVID, then SOLOMON) and goes on to show how the careless policy of Solomon's successor (REHOBOAM) leads to the bitter division of the kingdom into Israel (North) and Judah (South).

This book is also a fascinating study in the importance of *prophetism* during the period. Many unnamed and lesser-known prophets are introduced into the story and they indicate the vital part played by these men in the religious life of the Hebrew people (see 1:22; 12:22–24; 13:1–10, 11–33; 14:4–5; 16:1–4, 7; 17:1–19:21; 20:13, 22, 28, 35; 21:17–28). This book is thus not only about godless *kings* but about loyal *prophets*.

1. CHAPTERS 1–11
THE UNITED KINGDOM

These chapters tell the story of the united people of God before the sad disruption under Rehoboam (Judah) and JEROBOAM (Israel).

a. UNDER DAVID (1:1–2:11) ADONIJAH, ABSALOM's brother (1:5–7), supported by JOAB tries to get the throne but is unsuccessful. David's last words are intensely disappointing—note the bitterness against SHIMEI (for example, 2:8–9), though Shimei would not have died but for his disobedience (2:36–46).

b. UNDER SOLOMON (2:12–11:43). The historian's main concerns are:

- SOLOMON'S WISDOM (3)—compare 3:5 with James 1:5; Proverbs 2:6; 3:13
- SOLOMON'S COURT (4)
- SOLOMON'S TEMPLE (5–8) using wood from Tyre (5:6–10) and labor from Israel (5:13–17; compare 2 Chron. 2:2, 17–18). The historian is at pains to stress Solomon's *selfishness* as well as his *wisdom* (see 6:38– 7:1: "He had spent seven years building it [the Temple]. It took Solomon thirteen years, however, to complete the construction of his palace."). The Temple prayer (8) is very moving; it comes to terms with *the universal fact of man's sin* (8:30, 33–34, 46) and the *universal appeal of God's mercy* (8:41–43)—it is a great missionary prayer (Isa. 2:2; 56:7–8)
- SOLOMON'S KINGDOM (9–10) Despite the obvious hardship involved in Solomon's heavy taxation and forced labor gangs (4:6; 5:13–14; 12:4) the historian here lists Solomon's extensive wealth as a spiritual principle—because he has honored he prospers (3:11–13; Matt. 6:33). But note that as he prospered so he came to rely on money rather than God, and turned to idols (9:6; compare 11:4).
- SOLOMON'S SIN (11) The same writer who earlier rejoiced that Solomon loved the Lord (3:3) now says, "Solomon loved many foreign women" (11:1). These mixed marriages were his downfall (compare Deut. 17:17; 2 Cor. 6:14).

2. CHAPTERS 12–22
THE DIVIDED KINGDOM

a. DEGENERATION (12–16) The kingdom is divided because of Rehoboam's stubborn refusal to heed obviously
good advice (12:6–8); Jeroboam leads the revolutionaries
(12:16–19). In the history recorded in these remaining
chapters there are four successive kings over Judah (two
bad and two good) and eight successive kings over Israel
(all bad!). It is a sad story of *idolatry* (12:28; 14:22–24),
immorality (14:24), *pretense* (14:25–28), *compromise*
(15:17–19), *bloodshed* (15:25–29: 16:8–10), and *suicide*
(16.7–18): conditions in the northern kingdom grew
steadily worse (16:25–33).

b. PROTESTATION (17–22) This closing section gives details of the prophetic reaction to all this sinning. ELIJAH is
the leading character in this section, though, as we have
observed, he is but one of many fearless spokesmen in
these sad days of declension and disobedience. Note:

- Elijah's loyalty (17:1)—as a servant and subject
- Elijah's heroism (17:1)—he has the courage to con-
  front Ahab with this serious warning
- Elijah's obedience (17:3, 5: "he did what the Lord
  had told him")
- Elijah's faith (17:13)
- Elijah's prayerfulness (17:17–24: "Elijah . . . laid him
  on his bed")—Elijah put the child between himself
  and his rest. Do we pray with that kind of sacrificial
  intensity (compare 18:42–44, Jas. 5:17: "He prayed
  earnestly")?
- Elijah's reliance (18:31–39)
- Elijah's patience (18:43–44) And do not forget:
- Elijah's tendency to depression (19:4–5)—he was a
  man just like us (Jas. 5:17)

The closing chapters deal with the continuing interplay
between cruel kings and fearless prophets. They concern:

a. AHAB'S VICTORY (20) over the Syrian king BEN-HADAD.

b. AHAB'S GREED (21) Ahab flagrantly disregarded the Law of Moses:

- in his longing for the vineyard (21:4)—Exodus 20:17: "You shall not covet."
- in his unjust accusation of Naboth (21:8–10)—Exodus 20:16: "You shall not give false testimony against your neighbor."
- in his plot to kill Naboth (21:13)—Exodus 20:13: "You shall not murder."
- in his seizure of the vineyard (21:15–16)—Exodus 20:15: "You shall not steal."

The word of the Lord to this royal thief was, "Have you not murdered a man and seized his property?" (21:19).

c. AHAB'S DEATH (22)

d. AHAB'S CONTINUING EVIL INFLUENCE (22:51–53).

Elijah and Ahab are intentionally set side by side in these stories so that we can clearly discern the enriching or corrupting influence of their lives. What kind of example are we leaving behind (see Heb. 11:4; 13:7; Rev. 14:13)?

2 Kings

e have just seen that in 1 Kings there is as much about prophets as about monarchs. The book closes with a lengthy narrative in which ELIJAH is the leading character. 2 Kings opens with a passage of similar length in which the story is dominated by Elijah's less familiar but equally important successor, ELISHA.

In the Hebrew Bible the section called *The Prophets* is divided into "former" and "latter" prophets, and the books of Joshua, Judges, Samuel and Kings are placed in the *Latter Prophets*. This is because the history is told from a *prophetic standpoint*. The books are certainly not written in support of the idea of the monarchy. The kings are often shown as men whose hearts and minds are set against the divine will. 2 Kings illustrates this regal resistance. It opens with the story of a prophet's approbation (Elijah's ascension into heaven) and it closes with the nation's condemnation (their enforced journey into Babylonian captivity).

The book contains a vast amount of detail but can be divided into five sections:

1. CHAPTERS 1–8
REVELATION

These vividly told stories reveal God's power (3:16–18; 7:6–7) and grace (4:42–44; 5:8–10). Elisha is a central figure. He is portrayed as a man of:

- WISDOM (2:9)—he could have asked for anything, but he longs to continue Elijah's heroic ministry
- FAITH (2:9)—"a double portion." Remember John Newton's words: "Thou art coming to a king, large petitions with thee bring." And he has too much faith in God to believe that Elijah has been dashed to earth (2:16).
- CERTAINTY (3:18)—"He will also hand Moab over to you."
- INSIGHT—there are many illustrations of this. Part of the equipment God gave Elisha for his difficult mission, is an awareness of the supernatural. He can *see* things which are about to happen or are happening elsewhere (6:8–23, 32–7:2, 16–20; 8:1, 10–13).

Notice in the Elisha narratives several illustrations of the Lord's power to heal a corrupt or troubled situation *not by rooting out* the corruption in the first place *but by adding* something good and wholesome to it (2:19–22: salt is added; 4:38–41: meal is added; 6:1–7: the stick is added). It *may* be that these miracle narratives were meant to enshrine an important spiritual principle for later generations, for example, much good could have been accomplished in both Israel and Judah if more holy people had taken the lead. Preeminently though, they demonstrate the effective power of God's word (2:21; 3:16; 4:43; 5:10; 7:1, 16).

2. CHAPTERS 9–10
REVOLUTION

The next two chapters tell the story of the JEHU revolution—an attempt to purge the land of AHAB'S corrupt influence. It is a grim record of bloodshed. Jehu was used to remove an intensely evil religious system (10:30), but he is a sad figure in many ways, a pathetic example of a man who has a passion for a necessary cause, but never learns to conquer himself (10:31) and live righteously before God.

3. CHAPTERS 11–17
REBELLION

These chapters tell the story of the two kingdoms down to the fall of Samaria, the Israelite capital. It is a sad tale of chaos and disorder, culminating in the Assyrian conquest of the northern kingdom (17:5–41). The historian is at pains to tell us how the offending Samaritans came into being (17:24–41). Two things are important in this section:

    a. THE FAITHFULNESS OF GOD Even though there is widespread religious and moral corruption, God still has his witnesses. We see occasional examples of loyalty and spiritual integrity: for example, the courageous priest JE-HOIADA in the cruel reign of QUEEN ATHALIAH (11:4–20)—note Jehoiada's good influence over the young king (11:21; 12:2). Do we view our spiritual responsibilities toward children with the seriousness they deserve? *Many* a child in this land of ours is yet waiting to meet a truly godly man or woman whose transformed character proclaims God's power and grace.
    b. THE JUDGMENT OF GOD Man's sin is punished; chapter 15 is an outstanding illustration of this spiritual principle (for example, 15:9–10, 17–19, 23–25, 27–31).

4. CHAPTERS 18–23
REFORMATION

These six chapters tell the story of two revivals—under HEZEKIAH (18–20) and under JOSIAH (22–23)—separated by the wicked reign of MANASSEH (21), a time of religious corruption and evil hitherto unknown in Judah.

A summary of Hezekiah's achievements and spiritual principles is found in 18:4–7: "He removed . . . trusted . . . held fast . . . kept the commands . . . And the Lord was with him." Hezekiah is famous for his *reliance* in time of foreign invasion (Isaiah is his adviser) and Josiah for *his reformation* in time of internal corruption.

Note that the word of God played a central part in both reformations (18:6; 22:8–13). Josiah, as others, encountered problems caused by an unbelieving ancestry, for example, Manasseh's sins (23:10, 12; compare 2 Chron. 33:6); Solomon's sins (23:13; see 1 Kings 11:7); Jeroboam's sins (23:15). What are *we* leaving behind us—good or evil?

5. CHAPTERS 24–25
RETRIBUTION

The sad corruption of these years demands an experience for Judah of *refining judgment* similar to Israel's, so the purifying exile follows (23:26–27; compare Heb. 12:9–11; 1 Pet. 4:17).

1 Chronicles

All history is a record of *interpreted fact* and any detailed historical narrative tells you almost as much about the historian as about the events he is describing. Variations in newspaper accounts of the same event, for example, reveal the political bias of the paper, and the paper's views of its readers.

1 and 2 Chronicles not only give a detailed account of Hebrew history, but set out to win our allegiance for a particularly important viewpoint. They are essentially *religious history (though all Jewish history is that); the Temple* is the central idea and the central figure is not now the prophet but the priest. It is extremely interesting and valuable to have the story of God's people told from entirely different points of view: that of the historians responsible for Samuel and Kings, and that of the Chronicler responsible for 1 and 2 Chronicles. An example of the contrasting viewpoints can be seen in the story of ABIJAH's reign (called ABIJAM in Kings). The prophetic account (1 Kings 15:1–8) tells only of Abijam's wickedness and wars, while the Chronicler gives details of the conflicts and, more importantly, includes an address Abijah gave to his northern kingdom opponents (2 Chron. 13:5–12). The address indicates the Chronicler's main interests—the united monarchy under David and his appointed successors, rightful priests, proper sacrifices and temple furnishings.

1 and 2 Chronicles were written after Samuel and Kings, narrating the story right up to the post-exilic period. 1 Chronicles begins with Adam and 2 Chronicles ends with the decree of Cyrus (King of Persia)—no mean stretch of history. The books are the work of a gifted and devout editor who used a variety of different sources: 1 Chronicles 29:29; 2 Chronicles 9:29; 12:15; 13:22; 20:34; 24:27; 26:22; 27:7; 32:32; 33:19.

1 Chronicles divides into two unequal parts.

1. CHAPTERS 1–9
THEIR HERITAGE

This is a series of genealogical tables. Note that there is no interest whatever in the northern tribes. The breakaway under Jeroboam is reckoned to be a serious spiritual, as well as national, disaster and the returned exiles (among whom *Chronicles* was circulated) are not interested in the story of disloyal Israel; only Judah is in their thoughts. Even the tables contain spiritual hints: they are more than a mere list of names. For example, the JABEZ story (4:9), told here for the first time, is possibly included to encourage the belief that the pain (see NIV footnote: the Hebrew word *Jabez* and the Hebrew for "pain" sound similar) felt by the dispirited returning exiles can be changed to blessing by the God who answers our prayers, enlarges our borders, dispels our loneliness (4:10: "let your hand be with me") and conquers our enemies (4:10: "Keep me from harm"). All these things are of the greatest possible importance to the post-exilic community in Judah, as are the principles that God:

- rewards those who trust him (5:18–22)
- chastises those who forsake him (5:24–26)

Even in these lists the Chronicler gets a word in about God's work deserving the best (9:13).

2. CHAPTERS 10–29
THEIR HERO

The remaining twenty chapters focus interest on David, the
national hero, and illustrate the importance of the idea of the
Davidic monarchy.

a. THRONE (10–12) There are three sub-sections here:

- the man who vacates the throne (10)—Saul. His rejection by God is due entirely to his disobedience to
  the divine word (10:13–14)
- the man who ascends the throne (11:1–9)—David.
  The prosperity of the new king is noted as a divine
  principle. Just as Saul became weaker because he had
  rejected God, so David becomes more and more powerful because he honors God (11:9)
- the men who surround the throne (11:10–12:7)—
  some of their exploits prior to the coronation are
  noted in detail

b. ARK (13–17) David does not want to repeat Saul's sin
(13:3; compare 10:13–14), but the Ark should have been
carried on the shoulders of priests (Exod. 12–14; 1 Chron.
15:12–15). Partial obedience often has serious consequences.

David's adoration (16) is followed by his ambition (17);
he longs to be practical about his thanksgiving and suggests the building of a more permanent home for the Ark.
c. BATTLEFIELD (18–21) The extension of David's kingdom is noted: if someone puts God first, things will be
added (Matt. 6:33; 1 Sam. 3:30). Here the Chronicler is
interested in:

- God's protection (18:6, 13)
- David's dedication
- the people's satisfaction—He omits David's sin of
  adultery (2 Sam. 11), though for those who know the
  story, there is a significant phrase: "but David re-

mained in Jerusalem" (20:1). But he does not ignore David's sin of *pride*—numbering the people (21). Yet the new Temple site is to be at the scene of David's penitence (21:16–22:5). Worthy things can be built on the ruins of our former sins.

d. TEMPLE (22–29) David hands over the responsibility to Solomon (22:6), who is made king (23:1). There are detailed lists of levites (23), priests (24), stewards (26), choristers and musicians (25), soldiers, treasurers and advisers (27:1–24, 25–35). Looking after people's spiritual welfare demands teamwork.

The closing chapters (28–29) record David's address to the national leaders: notice his plea that Solomon will not procrastinate: "Be strong and courageous, and do the work" (28:20). We sometimes fail in this. Do we have glorious intentions which seldom turn to actions (compare 2 Sam. 15:15; Matt. 21:30; John 2:5; Rom. 2:13; Jas. 1:22–23, 25)?

2 Chronicles

The second part of this composite work traces the story of the kings of Judah from the time of Solomon to the exile. There are two main themes, both inter-related: Temple and Throne. The compiler of *Chronicles* is out to win our allegiance to his viewpoint: put God first and ultimately everything will work out to his glory, your blessing, and the good of others; to ignore him is as foolish as fighting against your own firm ally.

1. CHAPTERS 1–9
SOLOMON'S TEMPLE

In these chapters all interests are subservient to the Temple. This is because 2 Chronicles is intended to guide the returned exiles and encourage their belief that the rebuilt Temple must always be central in their thinking for it symbolizes the essential priority of the things of God. Compare Solomon's determination (2:1) with David's plea (1 Chron. 28:10). How sad that this book which tells of the splendor and beauty of the Temple furnishings (3–4), ends with the story of its profanation and destruction (36:18–19).

Note how closely the Temple and Throne go together in the Chronicler's thinking (7:16–22). His preoccupation with the Solomonic Temple tends to make the Chronicler disregard the *sins* of Solomon, even as he did some of the sins of David; there is no mention, for example, of Solomon's *mixed marriages* and *idolatry,* the prophetic account in 1 Kings 11 is a bit more down-to-earth. But the Chronicler speaks out against ungodly relationships which lead to corrupt worship. These are vexed issues in the post-exilic period and Nehemiah uses Solomon to show that mixed marriages are perilous (Neh. 13:26).

2. CHAPTERS 10–36
DAVID'S THRONE

Note that it is *David's* throne which is the main subject in these chapters. The Davidic monarchy is of supreme importance to the Chronicler (7:17–18; 10:16, 19; 13:8; 21:7; 23:3). The northern kingdom (Israel) is regarded as a rebel organization and the Chronicler does not interest himself at all in their history except on the comparatively rare occasions when the two kingdoms either unite against a common foe or fight each other. He is at pains to emphasize that no alliance with the northern kingdom was ever wise: it always led to trouble (18:1–3; 19:2; 20:35–37; 21:4–6, 12–15; 22:4–5; 25–7; 30:6–9).

These chapters tell of the mixed regal successors of David, from Solomon's unwise and proud son Rehoboam, to the equally stupid and arrogant Zedekiah (36:11–12). The kings at each end of this long line of twenty monarchs lack the grace of humility; they just cannot accept the wise advice of others (10:8; 36:12). The senseless conduct of both monarchs leads to widespread grief. A willingness to *walk humbly* before God is an important theme in Chronicles (12:12; 30:8; 32:26; 33:12, 23).

This section cannot easily be analyzed by chapters; the kings tend to alternate, on average a good king being followed by an evil king, and so on. But this is only a rough guide. The material may be summarized, however, as follows:

a. INCREASING CORRUPTION: under the bad kings people deteriorated until they were even worse than the heathen (33:9).

b. OCCASIONAL CONSECRATION: some rulers were good, e.g., Jehoshaphat (17:3), Hezekiah (29:2) and Josiah (34:2).

c. ULTIMATE CORRECTION: the theme of the closing chapter. Note the recurrent "did evil" followed by an account of the way God punished each stubborn monarch (36:5–6, 9–10, 11–12).

There are six key ideas which deserve careful study:

a. The necessity of *absolute reliance upon God* (13:18; 14:11; 16:7–9; 20:12–17; 25:8; 32:7–8).

b. The importance of *obedience to the revealed word of God,* listening to his prophetic word, the Law of Moses, the advice of priests, etc. (14:4; 20:20; 23:18; 25:4; 30:16, 22; 34:14–31).

c. The demand to *forsake all forms of idolatry* (14:3, 5; 15:8, 16; 17:6; 23:17; 24:18; 31:1; 33:15; 34:3–4).

d. The *danger of power,* leading to self-reliance (12:1; 25:17–24; 26:11–18; 32:24–25).

e. The blessing which comes from *"seeking" God* in prayer and the serious consequences of failing to seek him (14:7; 15:4, 12; 16:12; 17:4; 18:31; 20:3–4; 26:5; 30:18–19; 31:21).

f. The *perils of partial allegiance,* for example, JEHOSHAPHAT (18:1; 19:1–4); AMAZIAH (25:2, 14–16); JOTHAM (27:2: "but . . . he did not enter the temple of the Lord"). These men did not follow God *wholly.* There was some kind of reservation about their commitment to him. Is it like that with us?

Ezra

zra-Nehemiah are from the same literary school as *Chronicles* (see 2 Chron. 36:22–23 and Ezra 1:1–4). Cyrus of Persia has conquered Babylon, and has allowed the exiles to return to Judah. They have two major tasks ahead of them: to rebuild the Temple (*Ezra*), and reconstruct the city's broken walls (*Nehemiah*). These books remind us of the importance of divine guidance, sacrificial teamwork and persistent continuance, despite opposition and frequent discouragement. God is on the side of his people, even when things seem most against them.

Ezra is in two parts, and deals with two distinct returns: one party led back by ZERUBBABEL, the Governor, and another, later, by EZRA, the teacher, who does not appear until chapter 7, in spite of the book's title.

1. CHAPTERS 1–6
BUILDING GOD'S HOUSE

This summary of the opening chapters suggests six principles for Christian service:

a. ACKNOWLEDGE PROVIDENTIAL DIRECTION (1) It all begins with God (1:1). The Lord moves the heart of the king (1:1), the hands of the people (1:5) and even their neighbors, who reach for their purses (1:4, 6). An inscription on a cylinder of baked clay, found at Ur, comments on Cyrus' conquest of the near eastern world, and goes on to say that he "returned the gods to their shrines." Jews obviously have no images, but Temple treasures are certainly returned (1:7).

b. OBEY KNOWN INSTRUCTIONS (2) Obedience to God's word is of supreme importance in all forms of service. Chapter 2 is a list of the 42,360 people who returned, together with their 7,337 servants (2:64–65). Look at 2:59–63—some are of doubtful parentage, and God's word has clear instructions on this matter (see Num. 16:39–40), as it has about food reserved for priests (2:63; see Lev. 2:3, 10). Every believer must honor God's word by obedient submission to its precepts.

c. IGNORE INEVITABLE DISCOURAGEMENT (3) When seeking to work for the Lord initial difficulties often come from *within* the company of God's people rather than outside it. 3:12 records what is probably the melancholy despondency of some of the people. The tears may have been tears of joy, but Haggai 2:3 suggests that the people were weeping because of the reduced size of the Temple. Within the Church depressed people have always sighed for the past, neglected the opportunities of the present and feared the perils of the future. Do not be swayed by them.

d. AVOID SERIOUS COMPROMISE (4) Discouragement from inside now gives way to opposition from outside. The colonists offer to help (these are the Samaritans, descendants of immigrants who had been settled in the area by the Assyrians), but here again, God's word is remembered (2 Kings 17:24–41). Over the years the Samaritans have practiced idolatry of many kinds and the builders want *holy* service, unmixed with degrading religious practices and beliefs. This leads to active opposition, which certainly proves that the offer of service was insincere.

e. RECOGNIZE FELLOW WORKERS (5) The opposition results in the delay of the rebuilding program (4:24) but God raises up two courageous and outspoken prophets, Haggai and Zechariah (5:1–2). These two men are entirely different in their approach but both are used. The supreme importance of teamwork is emphasized in 5:1. We cannot achieve everything on our own and Zerubbabel is delighted to have these two dedicated preachers by his side.

f. FINISH ALLOTTED TASKS (6) Although serious objection has been raised to the building work, God is on the side of the returned exiles, and Cyrus' decree permitting the work is found (6:2). The king's instructions to those who oppose the work are unmistakable:

- Keep off (6:6)
- Pay up (6:8–9)
- Be warned (6:11)

The work is finished and the people rejoice (6:22). So much Christian work is left incomplete. Ventures are begun but not continued, a sad reflection on our powers of endurance and devotion to the Lord.

2. CHAPTERS 7–10
PURIFYING GOD'S PEOPLE

a. THE LEADER The Temple is finished, but it is not enough to have a building in which to worship if the people are impure and disobedient. Ezra is the main figure in these remaining chapters, in which a favorite phrase is "the hand of God." It is:

- a bountiful hand (7:6: "The king had granted him everything he asked, for the hand of the Lord his God was on him.")
- a sustaining hand—they were kept safe on their long journey of four months because: "the gracious hand of his God was on him"(7:9)

- an empowering hand (7:28: "Because the hand of the Lord my God was on me, I took courage . . .")
- a protecting hand (8:22, 31)

Note Ezra's ambition: to *study,* to *do,* and to *teach* (7:10). Is that our aim with God's word: to know it, to show it and to share it?

b. THE TRAVELERS 8:1–14 lists the returning exiles. These details are recorded with loving care: *facts* were important to the Hebrew people. Do we pay attention to detail in our service for our Lord, or will almost anything do?

c. THE MINISTERS 8:15–20 record details about the provision of servants for the newly constructed Temple.

d. THE TREASURERS 8:24–34 tell about other forms of work. All kinds of gifts are needed. Are you doing *your* part?

The final chapters raise the problem of national impurity—the question of mixed marriages leading to apostasy, idolatry, low standards of conduct, and spiritual rebellion, etc. Here again it is a case of cooperation in service: Ezra repents for the people (9), and SHECANIAH initiates the reform among the people. These two men have different personalities. Ezra sits appalled (9:3), and then prays; his colleague says, "*Rise up;* this matter is in your hands. We will support you, so take courage and do it." Shecaniah is the encourager behind Ezra: he has *hope* (10:2), *resolution* (v. 3), and *compassion* (10:4: "we are with you," RSV).

The story of disobedient husbands, unbelieving wives, damp spirits and wet clothes is recorded in 10:9–15. What a pathetic sight it must have been. It is sad that so many religious leaders (10:18–44) were offenders—they ought to have known God's word on this important matter.

Nehemiah

his fascinating book continues the story of resettlement in Judah. The exact dates are difficult to determine with accuracy, but if ZERUBBABEL returned in 536, and EZRA in 458 BC, then NEHEMIAH's journey to Jerusalem was probably twelve years later (445 BC).

The Zerubbabel party, aided by the vigorous prophetic ministry of HAGGAI and ZECHARIAH, accomplished the rebuilding of the Temple. The task assigned to Nehemiah is the rebuilding of the walls of Jerusalem, a city constantly exposed to cruel attacks from its heathen neighbors.

The book can be divided into three main sections:

1. CHAPTERS 1–7
REBUILDING THE WALLS

The first two chapters deal with God's selection of the right man for leadership at this critical time. In chapter 2, his helpers are described, and in chapters 4–7 their difficulties are explained. We might summarize the story of Nehemiah's work in this way:

a. HOW HE IS PREPARED (1–2) He has:

- concern (1:3–4)
- faith (1:5)
- repentance (1:6–9)

- reliance on God (1:11–2:4)
- confidence (2:5–8)
- discretion (2:9–18)
- self-control (2:19–20).

b. How he is assisted (3) Chapter 3 is an account of the people employed on different sections of the wall. At first it appears to be just a list of names, but when you look more closely you see that this chapter can be instructive, and even exciting.

God's work starts near home (10, 23, 28), but it is often not easy to get "nobles" to work (5)! The work is supported by sacrificial women (12), even though they are wealthy and can be done *zealously* or just done (20). Our service should not be undertaken for selfish reasons: verses 2, 7, and 13 record work done by people whose home is not in Jerusalem—they have nothing personal to gain from the refortified city. Some people do more than their fair share, and are glad to do so: Meremoth repairs one section of the wall (4), and then works on another section (21)—and so do the Tekoites (5, 27).

c. How he is opposed (4–5) When you start God's work, adversities come from all sides! In Ezra we noted that difficulties came first from inside, and then from outside (Ezra 3:12; 4:1–5). In *Nehemiah* the order is reversed. Direct opposition comes from without (4), before serious difficulties arise from within (5). Chapter 4 deals with external rogues, and the following chapter with internal robbers—ruthless Jews, who in earlier years of poverty had grasped property and slaves as "interest" on money loaned by them. Nehemiah is a good example of frugal living (5:14–18).

d. How is he equipped (6–7) When their direct attack proves unsuccessful, the enemy resorts to more subtle temptations, but Nehemiah has:

- resolution (6:3–4)
- discernment (6:5–13)
- prayerfulness (6:9, 14)

- patience (6:17–19: though surrounded by spies and traitors)
- sensitive obedience (7:5)

2. CHAPTERS 8–12
RENEWING THEIR FAITH

Ezra reappears (8:1), once again as teacher and reformer. There are three sub-sections:

a. EXPOSITION (8) What a superb congregation he has: united (8:1); attentive (8:3); reverent (8:5); responsive (8:6a: "Amen"!); submissive (8:6b); enlightened (8:8). The proclamation of the word of God should lead to a response from those listening.

The Feast of Tabernacles (Booths) is held again. It has the elements of *thanksgiving* (for the exodus), of *remembrance* (because they were pilgrims), and *testimony* (to their heathen neighbors).

b. CONFESSION (9) To God, they confess their sins (9:2–3); to men, they confess God's goodness and mercy as they pray (9:5–37).

c. DEDICATION (10–12) The people first dedicate themselves to God (9:38; 10:1–12:26), and then they dedicate the newly constructed wall (12:27–47).

Once again, the lists are instructive. Note that the people who dwell in Jerusalem are:

- willing (11:2)
- brave (11:6, RSV)
- orderly (11:16)
- thankful (11:17)
- lowly—the gate-keepers are not ashamed of their lowly work (11:19); we all have a part to play.
- joyful (11:22–23)

3. CHAPTER 13
REFORMING THEIR CONDUCT

Nehemiah goes away for a while, and things get very slack (13:6). It is to this period of spiritual carelessness that the ministry of Malachi belongs.

On his return, Nehemiah makes sure that the following reforms are carried out:

a. THE HOUSE OF GOD IS CLEANSED (13:1–14) Tobiah has turned up again (13:4; see 2:10, 19; 4:3, 7; 6:1, 14, 17). Imagine it, the enemy of God right inside the Temple. It still happens (2 Cor. 2:11; 1 Pet. 5:8; 2 John 7). Note that when Satan comes in, the song goes out (13:10).
b. THE DAY OF GOD IS HONORED (13:15–22) The Sabbath day has become the shopping day. Nehemiah is practical as well as prayerful: he orders the porters to shut the gates at dusk so that no trader can come in (v. 19). But commercially-minded traders are not to be hindered by that—they set up their stalls outside the gates so that anyone who wants to buy can come and do so. They only try it once or twice, though (v. 20). Nehemiah isn't the kind of man you can twist around your little finger. His active zeal is a tonic to see (vs. 8, 21, 25, 28).
c. THE LAW OF GOD IS OBEYED (13:23–31) The "mixed multitude" has always been a snare (Deut. 7:3–4). Notice the difference between Ezra and Nehemiah. When Ezra had this problem he pulled his own beard in grief (Ezra 9:3); Nehemiah is an extrovert—he pulls theirs (Neh. 13:25)!

The words, "Remember . . . O *my* God" conclude each section (13:14, 22, 29) and close the book. They indicate Nehemiah's deep *personal* faith and absolute reliance on God.

Esther

his amazing story continues to illustrate the theme of God's *gracious protection* of his people. *Ezra* emphasized protection on a *journey* (8:22–23, 31); *Nehemiah* in the city (4:9, 14, 17, 20); *Esther* in a *foreign land*. The name of God is not mentioned at all in *Esther,* but careful study of the Hebrew text has revealed a number of acrostic features in which the divine name Y-H-W-H (Yahweh) occurs, the idea being that God's name is secretly hidden within the text just as his ways are often hidden in history. The book has not always gained acceptance; Martin Luther wished it had not been included in the Canon! Its message, however, is important, assuring and relevant. The purpose of the book is twofold:

a. To EXPOUND A TRUTH God is fully in charge of his world and carefully orders the affairs of his children. It is Romans 8:28 in the form of an historical narrative (see, particularly, 4:14).

b. To EXPLAIN A FEAST After the miraculous deliverance told in the book, the Hebrew people had an annual commemoration of this gracious act of mercy: the feast was called *Purim* (9:19, 26–28).

The events of this story are set in the historical period between Ezra 6 and 7. The outline of the book can take the following form:

1. CHAPTERS 1–2
GOD'S SOVEREIGNTY IS DEMONSTRATED

It all begins with QUEEN VASHTI'S refusal to obey KING AHASUERUS (Xerxes, 484–464 BC). Who can blame her? Her sense of purity and dignity in refusing to attend this drunken orgy is used by God to cause the king to look for another Queen. ESTHER, a Jewess, is chosen: it is essential for the Lord's purposes that one of his own people should have the ear of this pagan monarch.

Character studies are of special interest in this little book. Note MORDECAI'S qualities:

- sacrificial compassion (2:7: "Mordecai had taken her as his own daughter when her father and mother died.")
- continuing protection (2:11)
- immense discretion—Mordecai is convinced that Esther should not tell all and sundry that she is of the Jewish race (2:10). Note, too, his wisdom in telling the assassination plot to Esther so that *she* can relate it to the king (2:21–23)—thus strengthening the royal bond of loyalty as well as affection. All this is by way of introduction to the drama, yet *God is in it all:* in Vashti's disobedience, in the king's annoyance, in Esther's appointment, in Mordecai's alert observations (2:21–23).

2. CHAPTERS 3–8
GOD'S JUSTICE IS MANIFESTED

At this point the real story begins to emerge. It focuses on the jealous and small-minded HAMAN the highest court offi-

cial in the Persian empire, a man full of his own importance
(3:2)—though Haman might never have known of Mordecai's refusal to reverence him had not an equally small-
minded group of servants spent their time gossiping (3:3–4).
Three features are worthy of note:

a. HAMAN'S PLOT (3) Haman takes an instant dislike to all
Jews because of the spiritual principles of Mordecai: note
that Mordecai did not lack respect, but he refuses to offer
to Haman the reverence and adoration which was due to
God alone. Haman asks that all Jews should be slain.

b. MORDECAI'S PLAN (4) But this is why Esther is in the
palace. Now the Jews have someone at the king's right
hand who can appeal for their deliverance. Mordecai discerns a pattern in all these happenings (4:14). There are
some practical as well as spiritual issues here:

- Be thorough (4:8) Esther is given a copy of the decree
  so that she has written proof of their sentence and
  threatened doom.
- Be sensitive (4:14: "for such a time as this")—
  Mordecai urges Esther to see that God is behind all
  this. Can she not see his hand in her appointment and
  elevation to the royal palace? Do we always discern
  God's hand in the "ordinary" affairs of everyday life?
- Be dependent (4:16: "fast for me"). This is so that her
  fellow-Jews can pray for her. The prayers of our
  friends are of immense comfort and help in times of serious trouble, but Esther is relying entirely on her God.
- Be courageous (4:16: "if I perish, I perish") If Mordecai's plan fails Esther will not only lose her crown,
  she will forfeit her life. To go into the presence of the
  king without invitation is a brave thing to do; it is
  completely alien to their tradition and acceptable
  court practice.

c. ESTHER'S PLEA (5–8) Notice how carefully, calmly and
decorously she approaches this problem. Although the

days are precious, she does not rush into the matter. God
is at work in it all, of course. He gives the queen favor
(5:2), and gives the king insomnia (6:1)! As a possible
cure for his sleeplessness he orders that the state records
be read: surely they will send anyone off to sleep! By this
means he hears of Mordecai's kindness and alert, speedy
handling of the assassination affair, and realizes that the
loyal Jew has never been rewarded. Events move swiftly
after this. At the banquet Haman is exposed as the origi-
nator of the unjust plot against all the Jews (7:3–6) and the
judgment is reversed so that Haman is hanged from the
very gallows he had hoped to use for Mordecai. Sometimes God so orders the affairs of men that evil designs,
meant to create havoc in the lives of others, are turned on
those who plan them.

3. CHAPTERS 9–10
GOD'S GOODNESS IS COMMEMORATED

Such a mighty act of deliverance and sovereign protection
must not be quickly forgotten. The Feast of Purim is insti-
tuted (9:17–19). Do we quickly forget God's mercies?

The final comment on Mordecai is a portrait of a godly
man in his relationship with God's people (10:3):

- He is widely accepted
- He is deeply respected
- He is actively concerned for his people's welfare.

The Bible tells us of another Prime Minister (also a Jew
in a foreign land) who had similar qualities: Joseph. Wherever we are placed we should glorify God and serve others.

Job

ob is widely acknowledged as a literary masterpiece. Try reading it aloud: just to hear it will do something for you. Luther said it is "magnificent and sublime as no other book of Scripture." The work of a genius, it records a story from the earliest period of Hebrew history. Its theme is the bewildering problem of undeserved suffering. We are reminded that suffering is part of the fabric of human existence; we can either complain bitterly, blaming God for it, or trust God in it, making new discoveries of divine resources and present help.

1. CHAPTERS 1–2
JOB AND HIS ADVERSARY

JOB, a wealthy landowner (29:6; 31:20, 31) with numerous servants (compare 19:14, 15), has an established place of respect in the community (29:8, 16, 21, 24) and is generous to those in need (31:17, 19–20, 32). His word is important in discussions (29:22, 25). But the book begins with his standing *before God* rather than before men (1:1–5). It is this evidently *good* man who is to be the sufferer in this highly important test case. It is those who already bring forth fruit who are purged (John 15:2) and those God loves are the ones he corrects (Heb. 12:6). H. Wheeler Robinson *(The Cross in the Old Testament)* rightly reminded us that both

Job and his friends are ignorant of this part of the drama (1:6–12): "To understand what they say and think, we must try to stand where they do," that is, in utter ignorance of the importance and significance of this time of testing.

Satan argues that nobody on earth loves God *for his own sake,* and if God takes gain out of religion, then even the "perfect" will forsake him. Satan is permitted to test his theory and reduce Job to destitution. The final test is loss of health, the most precious of life's good gifts. At this point, even Job's wife loses her faith. Chapter 2:10 does not imply that Job sinned in his heart; it expresses the contrast between Job and his wife. She sins with her lips (2:9) and begs him to curse, but he refuses.

When people are in great trouble, there is a deep healing ministry in *silence* (2:13).

2. CHAPTERS 3–37
JOB AND HIS FRIENDS

The friends fall into two groups:

a. THE THREE FRIENDS (3–31) ELIPHAZ, BILDAD and ZOPHAR speak in turn and each time Job replies. There are three cycles of speeches through to chapter 31. The friends, who represent different approaches to Job's problem, are important though mistaken in their views (42:7–8).

Eliphaz has been described as the *mystic.* He tries to help you in your troubles by telling you about *his* experiences. He is the "never mind *your* problems, you listen to *mine*" type (e.g., 4:12–16)! H. L. Ellison says of this approach, "There is a very real danger that where there is experience it may be equated with religion . . . the victim of this delusion thinks there is little more to be reached, and that his experience is an infallible yardstick by which he may measure the religion of others" *(From Tragedy to Triumph).*

Bildad comes next. He has been described as the *traditionalist,* the champion of orthodoxy. He is the "look to the past" type (e.g., 8:8–10). As Ellison says again, "We can ill do without him and he has a rare gift of recognizing the first insidious roads of false doctrine . . . But when men are sore, tired and distressed, and the landmarks of life are hidden, it is seldom to Bildad that they turn." Bildad seems to infer that Job has sinned (8:3, 6, 13, 20) and he is pitiless in his approach (he is the only one to mention Job's children, 8:4). He considers the truth his private possession and woe betide you if you don't agree with him.

Zophar cannot wait to speak next (11). He is the impatient *dogmatist,* who lacks compassion (11:5–12). Note how sure he is that God is *against* Job, when actually he couldn't be more *for* him.

The three visitors think that they are offering constructive help, but Job laments their harshness (16:1–4); the agony is that these cold, unsympathetic, sometimes cruel words are from *friends* (19:21–22). Yet exactly at this point of loneliness and despair comes the triumphant cry of trust and hope (19:23–27).

The *Hymn to Wisdom* (28:1–28) emphasizes the inaccessibility of wisdom to man without God. Metals can be found in the rocks (28:1–2) but wisdom cannot be discovered so easily. In chapter 29 Job thinks of the past; in chapter 30, the present; and in chapter 31 he makes what has been called his "final oath of innocence."

b. THE YOUNG FRIEND (32–37) Now ELIHU speaks (32:4, 6). He believes that without "the breath of the Almighty" (32:8) man cannot understand any deep problem. He is on better ground than the other friends, but even he is misled about Job, seeing him as a sinner under punishment (32:2). Elihu has some fine insights though, especially into the *disciplinary value of suffering* (e.g., 36:8–10). Suffering can have *teaching* value. (36:22), and also it teaches us the *limitations of our knowledge* (37:14–19,

23). However, Elihu is not really adding much to what the sufferer himself has been saying (9:4–10; 12:13–25; 26:6–14).

3. CHAPTERS 38–42
JOB AND HIS CREATOR

God hurls a seemingly endless series of majestic questions at Job concerning the wonders of creation. The main idea is that if God controls the intricate orders of creation which Job cannot fully perceive, then Job ought to be able to *trust him* with every single part of his life, even though mysterious things often perplex him. God makes the great things (40–41), but he also makes a snowflake (38:29). Job's reaction is important:

- he seals his lips (40:4–5)
- he reaffirms his faith (42:1–3)
- he confesses his sin (42:4–6)
- he pardons his accusers (42:7–9)

POSTSCRIPT

The book emphasizes the right attitude to suffering and adversity: acknowledge our limited understanding, surrender ourselves to him who has done everything well (Mark 7:37), believe that a greater plan is being unfolded than we can ever fully grasp, and realize that our present suffering is a magnificent opportunity for courageous witness.

Psalms

The Hebrew title to the book means "Praises." It is from the Greek translation of the Old Testament that we get our title *Psalms,* from the Greek word *psallo,* "to play an instrument."

Here, then, is a magnificent collection of Hebrew songs. Several people, including David, are named as authors, but many psalms are anonymous. Several of the writers experienced grave troubles and were not afraid to express their doubts and fears. They also proved God's nearness in dark times, and expressed their gratitude and penitence in these magnificent hymns of adoration, thanksgiving and dependence.

Their date of composition also varies: some psalms recall early songs of the Hebrew people, stemming from just after their deliverance from Egypt, while others lament the adversities of the exile, and even later. Several include precise historical references in their titles (e.g., 3, 7, 30, 34, 51, 52, 54, 56, 57, 60, 63), and others provide details in the text which enable us to give some approximate date (e.g., 137:1).

The contents of the book of Psalms cannot be analyzed briefly without considerable danger of over-simplification, but they can be looked at under the overall subject of *the doctrine of God*. Some psalms naturally move from one aspect of God to another, while others are given over entirely to the development of one theme.

In this marvelous hymn book God is:

1.
THE CREATOR WHO DESERVES OUR PRAISE

A vast number of psalms are devoted to the theme of worship. The English word "worship" derives from "worthship," that is, the one who is *worthy*. The Greek word *axios*, meaning "worthy, estimable, deserving," was the cry of the spectators at the Greek games when the victor appeared: "You are worthy" (compare Rev. 5:9). In these "worship" psalms the theme of *praise* is usually introduced by referring to God's goodness in:

    a. creation (e.g., 8, 24, 29, 33, 65, 67) or,
    b. history—what he has *done* rather than what he has *made* (77:5, 14–20; 87: God established the city of Jerusalem; 105, 106, 107: where the Exodus and desert wanderings are a key theme) or,
    c. experience (84: a man who has proved in his own experience the value of worship with God's people; 89, 90, 92, 94).

Other psalms which roughly fall into this main category of worship psalms are 93, 95–97, 99, 100, 104, 113, 115, 117, 122, 134–6, 145–50.

2.
THE TEACHER WHO DEMANDS OUR OBEDIENCE

God is not only one who created the world and man but one who addresses man continually. Many psalms deal with this great theme of *revelation*, of God making his will known to his people. This kind of psalm stands right at the beginning of the psalter (Psalm 1). Psalm 19 is a magnificent portrayal of God speaking generally through nature (19:1– 6), and directly through his word (19:7–14). Further examples of this type of psalm are psalms 50, 78, 95, 128, but the supreme example is the unique psalm 119.

3.
THE LOVER WHO EXPECTS OUR PENITENCE

God has created us and speaks to us—but man is rebellious and sinful. Many of the psalms are *psalms of confession.* They deal with the universal problem of man's sin and the broken relationship to which it leads. Man in his sin cries to God for pardon, but only because God has already pleaded with man to return. God only does this because he is merciful (a favorite theme with the psalmists) and he is merciful because he loves us intensely and persistently. Examples of psalms of penitence are: 32, 39, 51, 101, 103, 123.

Psalm 32 was written long before men talked about psychosomatic medicine, yet that is what 32:3–4 are about. People who are troubled about their guilt often become physically ill. The psalmist also recognizes that *all* sin is sin *against* God, before it is sin against our fellows (e.g., 51:4).

4.
THE JUDGE WHO EXAMINES OUR MOTIVES

Although he is the Great Lover, we must not get a distorted or one-sided portrait of God. He is holy *and just,* seeing and understanding everything about us. This theme of God as "the one who sees all our lives" is often found in psalmody and is always used to great spiritual effect (e.g., 7, 12, 14, 15, 26, 44, 53, 58, 60, 139).

5.
THE HELPER WHO REWARDS OUR TRUST

It is in this final category that most of the psalms can be placed, though one must hasten to add that many of the above four elements come into these psalms as well. It would be such a mistake to think that a psalm must fit neatly into *either* one group *or* another, in fact an occasional psalm has all five aspects of truth in it. However, the majority deal with this theme of God as a helper in time of suffering, adversity, persecution or trouble. Sometimes the trouble is *personal*, sometimes *national*. The key idea is that of deliverance, and here again (as in the first group) the psalmists appeal to both *national history* and *personal experience*, for example, 2 (2:2: "kings of the earth"); 27 (27:3: "war . . . against *me* "); and 37 (37:35–36: *"I* have seen a wicked and ruthless man . . . but . . .").

Examples of this type of psalm are 3–6, 9–11, 13, 16–18, 20–23, 25, 28, 30–31, 34–36, 38, 40–43, 45–49, 52, 54–57, 59, 61–64, 66, 68–76, 79–83, 85, 86, 88, 91, 98, 102, 106, 108–112, 114, 116, 118, 120–121, 124–127, 129–132, 137–144.

Clearly some psalms do not fit naturally into any of these categories, for example, psalm 133, which extols the benefits of *unity* among God's people, but most of the psalms focus the praying man or woman on one or more of these great themes. The book which begins with blessings on the man who listens to God (1:1) ends with praises offered to the Lord who has done so much for his people (150). This final psalm is a summons to everyone: it invites us *all* to worship: "Let everything that has breath praise the Lord" (150:6) for his "surpassing greatness" (150:2). The psalmists believe not only in the necessity of worship *to God*, but also in its importance *for us* (92:1: "It is good").

Proverbs

ike *Ecclesiastes* and the *Song of Solomon, Proverbs* belongs to the *Wisdom Literature* of the Old Testament. The *wise man* was as distinct and important a figure in Hebrew religious life as the priest and prophet; Jeremiah 18:18 mentions all three. It would seem that these wise men specialized in the preservation and communication of important sayings about God and life. They have been called "the *interpreters* of Hebrew religion."

In the early period of Hebrew history, the sayings were passed on by word of mouth, but later they were committed to writing, hence the emergence of "the scribe": that is, the wise man who wrote out the sayings (compare Jer. 8:8).

The Hebrew word *mashal,* "proverb," literally means "likeness" or "comparison," and so came to denote a popular saying. We have such sayings, too ("a rolling stone . . ."; "too many cooks . . ." etc.). Like our proverbs, many of the Hebrew proverbs deal with the practical aspects of life. This is of immense importance, of course. The Bible saves us from a belief which does not result in better behavior, but as well as easily-memorized teaching about human behavior and social conduct, the biblical proverbs also teach spiritual values.

A variety of themes emerge again and again and the compiler(s) of this collection of sayings have special interests and ideals. Certain types of people are highly objectionable, for example, the nagging woman (19:13; 21:9; 25:24; 27:15); the lazy man (6:6–11; 13:4; 20:4); the dangerous gossiper (6:12–14; 11:9); the dishonest tradesman (16:8–11; 20:10, 23).

The first nine chapters contain teaching in blocks, each passage dealing with one idea. The tendency of the later chapters is to group together short sayings on a variety of themes, with each saying following a similar literary structure—initially an aid to memorization—for example, "A wise son brings joy to his father, but a foolish man despises his mother"(15:20).

The book can be summarized under the following injunctions:

1.
SEEK TRUE WISDOM

The Prologue to the book introduces this wisdom theme. Chapter 1:7 is a key saying, which recurs in this book (9:10; 15:3) and also in Job (28:28). "Wisdom" is a key virtue (3:13; compare Eccles. 9:13–18 for a parable-illustration on the subject of the supreme importance of wisdom. Remember that *Ecclesiastes* is another "wisdom" book). *Proverbs* stresses the importance of *seeking* wisdom (1:1–7; 2:1–9; 3:1–12; 4:1–13; 18:15; 22:17–21; 28:4–9). Now and again the wise men personify wisdom as an *attractive person,* greatly to be desired and sought for, who offers many benefits (1:10–33; 3:13–26; 8:1–9:6). In the New Testament, wisdom is a gift of the Holy Spirit (1 Cor. 12:8); it is ours in Christ (Col. 2:3), and is imparted liberally to those who ask for it believingly (Jas. 1:5).

2.
WELCOME GOOD ADVICE

The wise man recognizes that though true wisdom comes from God alone, he should value the good advice of trustworthy and godly friends, and should ignore the bad advice of those who are not concerned about his highest spiritual and moral welfare. This is a favorite theme in *Proverbs,* for example, children should take the advice of parents (1:8–9; 6:20–22), and the theme is expounded in various ways at 9:7–12; 10:8, 17; 12:1; 13:1, 18; 15:32–33; 19:20; 21:11; 23:12–25; 28:23; 29:17–18. It will be seen from these passages that the wise man has a particular dislike of people who cannot be told when they are in error or danger.

3.
SHUN CORRUPT FRIENDS

It is clearly perceived that bad companionships lead to debased behavior. Chapters 1:10–19; 2:12–22; 4:14–19; 5:1–23; 6:23–29; 7:1–27; 9:13–18, read like the advice of an affectionate father to his son before he goes up to the wicked city. Similar themes, gathered around the "bad friends" idea, are expounded at 13:20; 22:24; 23:6–8, 26–35; 28:10–18; 29:3.

Paul knew how badly his church members could be led astray by unhelpful friends (see 1 Cor. 15:33, where Paul quotes from Menander, a Greek playwright, 320 BC).

4.
HELP NEEDY PEOPLE

There is more to life than protecting yourself—we move on now to man's responsibility to care for those who need his help in the community. Relevant passages here are 3:27–35; 14:21–22, 31; 19:17; 21:13; 22:9; 28:27; 29:7. Of course, all this goes back to the Deuteronomic Law (see Deut. 15:7–8, 11). This appeal is continued in the New Testament, for example, in Galatians 6:10.

5.
AVOID IMPROPER SPEECH

We have observed that *Proverbs* deals with *community* life as well as *personal* life. Much unhappiness in communities is caused by careless talk. The theme of the harm done by gossiping, and evil chatter, etc. is found throughout this very practical book, for example, 4:20–27; 6:1–5 (which deals with *hasty unreliable talk:* the kind of person who glibly says, "Yes, I'll be surety for you!" when all the time he lacks the means to give such backing); 6:12–19; 10:11–14, 18–21, 31–32; 11:9–14; 12:17–23; 13:3; 14:3–7, 25; 15:1–7, 23, 26; 16:10, 13; 21:21, 27–33; 17:7, 20, 27–28; 18:1–8; 19:1, 5, 27–29; 20:15–20; 21:6, 9, 19, 23–24; 22:10–11; 24:28–29; 25:8–28 (which is a loosely arranged collection of sayings about *speech,* both good and bad); 26:17–28; 27:1–6; 29:5.

6.
ENJOY HARD WORK

The wise man knows the supreme value of the diligent, reliable worker in the community. The idle man or woman is despised (6:6–11). *Proverbs* says much that is of value about the importance of a good standard of work. Do we bring our *best* to our daily work? Look at 10:4–5, 16, 26; 13:4, 11; 18:9; 19:24; 20:4, 13; 21:17, 25–26; 22:13; 24:27, 30–34; 26:13–16. How can these important sayings be meaningfully applied in communities where large numbers of people are unemployed through no fault of their own?

POSTSCRIPT

The contemporary relevance of *Proverbs* can hardly be exaggerated. Look at 30:11–14 for a striking commentary on our own generation. In a day like ours when one marriage in three is said to end in divorce we do well to read the wise man's account of a good wife (31:10–31). It is with this superb portrait that the book closes.

Ecclesiastes

rom *Proverbs* we turn to another book in the *Wisdom Literature* of the Old Testament. It is quite different from *Proverbs;* in that book there are serious warnings, but the underlying spirit is bright and joyous. *Ecclesiastes* is marked by a strain of morbidity and pessimism: we are in a totally different world. Graham Scroggie describes this book as "the most mysterious in all the Bible." "The Preacher" offers an honest though occasionally bewildering meditation upon life. The main theme is that of our common humanity, its perplexities, ambitions, quests and frustrations. In arresting language *Ecclesiastes* shows how utterly futile it is to live without God in the center of our lives. The book might well be described as a mirror, showing us ourselves, and, more particularly, ourselves without the unique transformation wrought in human experience by Christ.

Like *Proverbs, Ecclesiastes* deals with a variety of themes, and a chapter by chapter analysis is not possible without oversimplification. The leading ideas can be summarized under the following divisions:

1.
OUR LIMITATIONS

The aim of the Preacher is to investigate life and its meaning (1:13), and he is deeply frustrated because at times he finds it difficult to imagine that there is any meaning to life. Things just happen; even in nature there is a continual round of events (1:1–11). Men and women might try to use their intellectual powers to reason things out, but they are bound to be frustrated (1:12–18). The author fears that it is not specially helpful even to be wise (2:12–17) because death awaits the wise and foolish alike (2:15–16). His bitter conclusion is that he *hates* life. It is this limited vision which makes this book such a sad work, and nowhere is this more noticeable than in the author's attitude to death. For him, there is little joy after the grave (3:16–4:3): in that uncertain world beyond, men and women seem no better off than beasts!

Chapter 6:1–12 is similarly pathetic because of its determinism: "Whatever exists has already been named" (6:10). There is no sense of wonder and awe at the idea of God as the Controller of human destiny, and the Sustainer of our lives, as there is in so many other parts of the Old Testament. Chapters 8:6–9:6 also consider the futility of life, and when the afterlife is viewed with the grim pessimism of 9:5, what is there left?

Chapter 11:1–8 dwells similarly on our limited understanding but this time looks at the world of nature and is more optimistic; we do not know how everything works in nature (11:5), but we do know that generous sowing leads to bountiful reaping.

2.
OUR PLEASURES

Because human life has such serious limitations, the Preacher suggests that it is natural for men and women to try to forget themselves by enjoying life whenever they can. These passages often come alongside those we have just considered. It is as if the author cannot bear thinking too long about life, and so suggests that it is better simply to enjoy it. The trouble is that his pessimism continues to control his thinking, for he honestly admits that even pleasures do not really satisfy. Chapter 2:1–11 is an example of this approach, ending, as it does, with the familiar lament "all was vanity" (RSV), "everything was meaningless" (NIV). In 2:18–3:15 the Preacher is filled with despair (2:18) but he begins to cheer up a little (2:24) when he advises his congregation to enjoy their work; it is a kind of "make the best of things" philosophy.

Chapter 3:11 offers a rare moment of insight into the magnificent work of God as Creator.

3.
OUR NEIGHBORS

Under this heading we should include passages like 4:4–16; 7:1–10; 9:7–18; 10:1–20. Various themes are discussed here. Some of the more important are:

- the value of companionship (4:8–12)
- a good name (7:1)
- wise correction (7:5–6)
- patience (7:8–9)
- obedience to the king or ruler (8:1–5)
- contentment in the home (9:7–10)
- wisdom (9:11–18)

Chapter 10 is a collection of short sayings about good and bad behavior in the community and is similar in style to *Proverbs*, for example, in its exhortations to avoid gossip (10:11–14); to beware of ignorant people who are suddenly promoted to positions of authority (10:5–7, 17); in its condemnation of laziness (10:18); and its warning to be careful what you say about other people, because it usually gets back to them (10:20)!

4.
OUR MAKER

Ecclesiastes has more to say about men and women than about God. Throughout the book one hears more of what Wordsworth called "the still, sad music of humanity" than majestic chords and uplifting cadences about God. But here and there we come across a superb passage about men and women in their relationship to God. The teaching in these passages might be classified under five simple headings:

    a. HONOR HIM (5:1–8)—teaching about the keeping of vows made to God.

    b. TRUST HIM (7:11–29)—with its immensely encouraging statement about God's goodness in *balancing* the experiences of life so that it is not *all* adversity for anyone (7:14: "God has made the one as well as the other").

    c. REMEMBER HIM (11:9–12:7)—especially in youth (11:9–9:1) and in view of the approaching end (12:3–7). Both the beginning and ending of life are mentioned in this section.

    d. WORSHIP HIM (12:13)—"fear" God means reverence him. The same idea is found in Psalms 15:4; 22:23; 25:14; 66:16. This theme appears in several places in *Ecclesiastes* (3:14; 5:7; 8:12).

    e. OBEY HIM (12:13)—"keep his commandments" (compare John 15:10–14; 1 John 3:22).

The Song of Solomon

The meaning and purpose of this book is not immediately obvious, and its interpretation has puzzled Christian people for centuries. The divines who met at the Westminster Assembly in the seventeenth century remarked on "the obscurity and darkness of this book." One is therefore naturally cautious about rigid or dogmatic assertions about its precise meaning. The *dramatic* interpretation of the Song understands it as a play which is not always easy to interpret in detail because the parts taken by various actors in the drama have to be inferred from the text; sometimes this is straightforward, but at other times one cannot be sure of the precise identity of the speaker.

The central theme is "*true* love," what Shakespeare described as the "ever fixed mark, which looks on tempests and is never shaken," a love which will stand up to all lands of tests and remain completely loyal. Human love is a major factor in happy and healthy living and this book is a moving portrayal of loyal love, its joys, testings and security.

The following is offered as a *possible* interpretation of this intensely moving drama. It is not without its problems; it has to allow (as do other interpretations) for occasional interjections by other speakers. A different interpretation is suggested in the NIV which rightly indicates that in some instances its divisions and titles are debatable.

1. Chapters 1:1–3:5
ACT ONE: TRUE LOVE DEPICTED

    a. Introduction of the Shulammite Maid (1:2–2:7) in which she describes herself (1:5–6) and longs for her lover, a shepherd from her home territory. The setting of the drama suggests that she is away from home, probably among the women ("daughters of Jerusalem," 2:7) at Solomon's court.

    b. Introduction of the Shepherd Lover (2:8–3:5) in which the youth comes to plead with her to leave the court (2:10–13). It would seem that she asks him to give her time to think (2:17: "turn" can mean "come again"). During the night she cannot sleep (3:1) and then wishes she had left with him. It is possible that the encounter in 3:1–5 describes a dream.

2. Chapters 3:6–6:13
ACT TWO: TRUE LOVE TESTED

    a. The arrival of the Wealthy King (3:6–4:16)—a vivid description of Solomon's royal caravan (3:6–11), and possibly the King's eulogy on seeing this beautiful Shulammite Maid (4:1–15). But the Shulammite wishes that her "beloved," the Shepherd, were with her (4:16).

    b. The return of the Shepherd Lover (5:1–6:3)—though, once again, this could be a dream (5:2). This time, instead of finding him, she meets with opposition (5:6–8). Her companions at Court are puzzled by her persistent loyalty to the Shepherd. What is so special about him (5:9)? When they realize how much he means to her, they offer to help search for him (6:1), possibly in Jerusalem and its environs, but she explains that he has returned to the country (6:2).

    c. The plea of the Wealthy King (6:4–13) It seems at this point that the King has an interview with her and tells her that she means more to him than all others (6:8–9).

The other women envy her for this (6:9b) but it means nothing to her. Chapter 6:11–12 seems to describe her exit from the court with 6:13 the appeal of her companions for her to return.

3. CHAPTERS 7:1–8:14
ACT THREE: TRUE LOVE PROVED

a. THE WELCOME OF THE SHEPHERD LOVER (7:1–9) He is so thrilled to see her back.

b. THE FIDELITY OF THE SHULAMMITE MAID (7:10–8:14)— a passage in which she gives expression to many thoughts that have been on the lips of all lovers from the beginning of time. She wants to spend every moment of the day with him (7:11); he has made everything else in life so much more wonderful (7:13); she wishes she had known him all her life (8:1a); and she is so proud of him when she is with him in the company of others (8:1b). She affirms her loyal love for the Shepherd (8:6–7) and says that her younger sister, an immature girl, might later be in danger of following her steps to Jerusalem (8:8). The Shulammite Maid only hopes that her young sister will be loyal and true in love—like a wall—as she has been (8:10).

WHAT IS THE VALUE OF THIS BOOK IN OUR TIME?

a. IT HAS MORAL VALUE Campbell Morgan used to say that the repeated appeal in 2:7, 3:5 and 8:4 is a *warning*. "That love is so sacred a thing that it must not be trifled with. To trifle with the capacity for it, is to destroy that very capacity. This is the evil of all philandering." The *Song* has a word to the flirt, and to the sexually permissive society of our time.

b. IT HAS SOCIAL VALUE With its appeal for loyalty in love it has a clear message for our generation, when marriage breakdown is so common. E. J. Young has said that the book "comes to us in this world of sin . . . where fierce temptations assail us and try to turn us aside from the God-given standard of marriage. And it reminds us, in particularly beautiful fashion, how pure and noble true love is."

c. IT HAS LITERARY VALUE Although the terminology in the book sounds strange to our western ears, the literary beauty of many of its passages cannot be questioned. In contrast, much modern literature about love is just dirt.

d. IT HAS TYPOLOGICAL VALUE Although this approach has its danger, it also has profound insights. The Jews have always considered that the book has some allegorical value (as a description of the love of their God, etc.) and Christians have seen it as a portrayal of the loving appeal of Christ (e.g., 2:10; 5:2–8) and the attractiveness of other lovers in our lives.

e. IT HAS SPIRITUAL VALUE Let this be our last word. Without confusing the book by resorting to highly imaginative typological explanations by allegorizing every detail, does it not say something about our own love for Christ? For example, in 5:2–8 we see the appeal of the one who comes to our door (compare Rev. 3:20), but is often met by excuses (compare Luke 14:16–24). Do we *love* him (Jer. 2:2; Matt. 24:12; Luke 7:44–47; John 21:15; Rev. 2:4)?

Isaiah

saiah, of Jerusalem, has been well described as "the evangelical prophet." His ministry belongs to the eighth century, a period rich in forceful prophetic activity (Amos, Hosea and Micah also belong to this century) and marked by traumatic historical events. Isaiah is called to service at a time when the throne of Judah is vacant (Isa. 6:1). But the throne of God is never unoccupied; the Lord God, who calls us to his work, is sovereign (6:1), holy (6:3) and merciful (6:7).

The book is fascinating in that its three main sections appear to address their message to three specific periods in the history of God's people. The word, directed primarily (but not exclusively) to later periods of history, may have been copied, preserved, treasured, edited and interpreted by Isaiah's prophetic school, a group of disciples specifically mentioned in 8:16, and 18; such groups of dedicated students and followers may not have been uncommon. Earlier, Elisha had such a group around him who even had their own theological college buildings (2 Kings 6:1–2)!

Three great "evangelical" themes emerge in the teaching of this book:

1. Chapters 1–39
CONDEMNATION

The "evangelical" message cannot be fully appreciated and applied until sin is exposed for what it really is (chapter 1):

- sin is rebellion (1:2)
- sin is disloyalty (1:4)
- sin is sickness (1:5–6)
- sin is disobedience (1:19–20)
- sin is injustice (1:21–23)

Isaiah's ministry is to Judah, the southern kingdom, during the reigns mentioned in 1:1. These are difficult times, with the nation exposed to internal spiritual apostasy and external military oppression.

The eighth century prophets only speak *against sacrifice* (1:12–15) because they know that God prefers righteous behavior to ceremonial ritual (1:16–17, 21–23; compare Hos. 6:6; Amos 5:21–24). Similarly, they speak *against foreign alliances* because these indicate the people's loss of faith in God and their failure to rely utterly upon him. This is a key theme in Isaiah (30:2; 31:1–3; 36:6).

The opening section of the book can be divided as follows:

a. National judgment (1–12) The southern kingdom is condemned for religious apostasy and reliance on political solutions to their problems. They are a disappointment to God. He intended them to be fruitful (5:1–4) but they have brought forth wild grapes (5:4–7). In the reign of Ahaz, the armies of Israel (under Pekah) and Syria (under Rezin) unite against Judah, but the prophet assures the people that before his child has grown up these two nations will have been subdued (8:3–4).

b. Universal judgment (13–23) These chapters comprise a series of oracles against the self-sufficient and over-confident surrounding nations. God does not confine his judicial activity to Judah alone. He is sovereign, and rules over all the kingdoms. He is far from being a merely "national" God, like some of the deities in which their neighbors trust.

c. ETERNAL JUDGMENT (24–27) The scene changes, and the reader is taken from Judah's condemned neighbors to the scenes of ultimate judgment, when it is not one nation (e.g., Babylon, Tyre, Philistia) who mourns, but the entire human race (e.g., 24:4, 21). Similarly, *hope* is extended beyond the boundaries of the Jewish race (25:6–7). Isaiah's teaching here anticipates not only the judgment of godless kings (24:21) but of *the* worst enemy (27:1; compare Rev. 12:3–9).

d. IMMINENT JUDGMENT (38–39) The chastisement of Judah is beginning. Besieged by the Assyrian army (36:1–20), Hezekiah prays and the Lord delivers Jerusalem (37:33–37). But the impending disaster is only postponed; the Babylonian invasion is on the horizon (39:5–7).

2. CHAPTERS 40–55
CONSOLIDATION

The judgment threatened in 39:6–7 has actually happened. 2 Kings 24–25 records the details. Isaiah 40–55 presents a magnificent portrayal of *hope*. The Babylonian captivity is almost over and Babylon herself is about to be captured by Cyrus, the king of Persia (41:2, 25; 44:28; 45:1–4). Chapter 46 is a superb account of the Babylonians leaving their capital city with their gods packed on their backs (they are carrying their gods to safety, compare 46:4: *our God carries us!*). Now the judgment is over (40:1–2; 54:7–8) and God is preparing a highway for his people to return across those desert wastes (40:3–4). Here is the good news of a promised return (40:9) under the leadership of a Shepherd God (40:11) who cares for his people because he created them (40:12–14). Three figures emerge in this second main section of the prophecy:

a. THE OMNIPOTENT DELIVERER—God. The prophet is at pains to show how God has acted *in history as Creator* (a favorite theme in Isaiah 40:12–31; 45:9–12, 18–19) and the *Conqueror* who saved them (the exodus story is re-told as an encouragement that he can do the same again: 43:15–21; 48:20–21; 51:9–11).

b. THE MILITARY DELIVERER—Cyrus, a Persian prince. God is pleased to use human instruments to achieve his purposes. Although Cyrus does not know God (45:4–5) he becomes their deliverer (46:8–11).

c. THE SPIRITUAL DELIVERER The really magnificent por-traiture of this section is that of the *Servant of the Lord.* The prophet refers to a "servant" who will fulfill God's purposes for his life and so bear the iniquities of many. Four special passages, the "Servant Songs," are found at 42:1–4; 49:1–6; 50:4–9 and 52:13–53:12. Their precise fulfillment is only to be found in the Lord Jesus (compare Acts 8:30–35).

3. CHAPTERS 55–66
CORRECTION

The final section seems to envisage the Israelite people just back in their own land, and observing the usual feasts, and religious ceremonies (58:3–5) though the Temple does not appear to have been rebuilt (63:18; 64:11; 66:1). Three themes are developed here:

a. GRIEF (56–59) Religious leaders are selfish and greedy (56:10–12), idolatry has crept back (57:9, 13) and the peo-ple are more concerned about making money than helping others (58:13; compare 58:6–9). God is grieved about them (59:2, 15).

b. GLORY (60–62) This is a key word in these three chap-ters (e.g., 60:1, 2, 7, 9, 19, 21; 61:3; 62:2, 3). Things might be so different: God could be glorified.

c. GRACE (63–66) The theme in these final chapters is *hesed*—God's steadfast love, kindness and grace (e.g., 63:7, where it is translated "steadfast love" in RSV, and "kindnesses" in NIV; 66:12–14). The book ends on a note of rich expectation; it anticipates a time when people of all nations shall come to the purified Jerusalem in order to worship the Lord (66:18–21).

Jeremiah

EREMIAH was a unique spiritual leader, and one of the most outstanding of the Old Testament personalities. His prophetic ministry covers forty years, from the thirteenth year of King Josiah (626 BC) to the fall of Jerusalem in 587 BC. God called him at a time when spiritual apostasy sought to cloak itself with ardent, but hypocritical, religious activism: zeal for the *Temple* (7:1–4); *sacrifice* (7:21–22); *prophetism* (2:8, 26; 4:9; 5:30–31; 6:13–14; 8:10–11; 23:11–12; compare Lam. 2:14). These prophets are *false,* but it is because they say the wrong things about the true God, not because they serve other gods. Alongside this spiritual apostasy there is *moral and ethical apathy:* the poor are neglected and there is no sense of justice (5:1, 27; 7:5–6; 9:2–6; 22:3); Judah is a backsliding nation (2:19; 3:8).

The book does not lend itself to a chapter by chapter analysis, but three great subjects demand our attention:

1.
THE PEOPLE GOD CORRECTS

This sin cannot be left unpunished: the nation has to be purified and purged. Jeremiah's message is one of *ultimate and inevitable judgment* and it is this which causes him to be so unpopular and leads to his persecution. People like to be told nice things, even if they are not true (compare 6:13–14; 8:11)! Ezekiel will encounter similar difficulties (Ezek. 33:30–32). Judah can be described as:

a. A PRIVILEGED PEOPLE The prophet looks back to days when the people were utterly devoted to the God who had been so good to them (2:1–3). If only they could realize the generosity of his love and return to him (3:4).

b. A DISLOYAL PEOPLE Key words in *Jeremiah* are *forsaking* and *forgetting* (2:13, 17, 19, 32; 3:20, 22; 4:1; 5:7, 19; 9:13; 13:25; 16:11; 18:15; 19:4). The *covenant* is of supreme importance to Jeremiah; Judah is a nation bound in covenant love to God, and they have left him and broken their promise of loyalty (3:6–5, 20).

c. A MISGUIDED PEOPLE The land is full of false prophets and blind leaders (14:13–16; 23:9–11). Hananiah is an example of the type of prophet who offers false security without either divine revelation or approval (compare 28:1–17).

2.
THE PROPHET GOD USES

When called, Jeremiah, who is deeply sensitive, shrinks from the task, pleading his social unacceptability (1:6–7, "child" means unmarried youth). He is called to deliver:

a. A PAINFUL MESSAGE—judgment is coming (1:14; 4:6; 11:11–12; 12:14; 15:1–9; 16:11–13), and it is inevitable. Jeremiah is regarded as treacherously unpatriotic when he tells the people that they had better submit to their punishment and give themselves up to the Babylonian invaders who have been raised up by God to correct them (21:3–10; 25:9–11)! Jeremiah insists that Nebuchadnezzar is God's servant in this matter (25:9; 27:6). This is why Jeremiah is imprisoned: the authorities think he is bad for national morale in time of invasion (32:1–5).

   Of course, the message is not only painful to the hearers but also to Jeremiah, and he wishes he could keep silent (20:7–9).
   b. A HOPEFUL MESSAGE Jeremiah knows that Judah cannot escape the chastisement of the exile experience, but he also knows that God is a Father (3:4, 19; 31:9) who is correcting them because he knows it is for their good. Therefore Jeremiah looks forward to a time of restoration and return. Chapters 29–33 record this message of hope, and 32:6–14 tells the story of Jeremiah's purchase of land as a *sign* that after the exile the people will return (32:15–25).

Jeremiah's is probably the most costly ministry of any Old Testament prophet. Obedience to the call of God involves him in:

   a. SPIRITUAL SUFFERING (36:5)—he is not allowed to worship God in the Temple.
   b. SOCIAL SUFFERING (16:2)—God does not allow him to marry; by his enforced single state he is saying to the people that there is no point in settling down to a comfortable life because judgment is near.
   Similarly, as an indication of the seriousness of the times, Jeremiah is told not to attend festive occasions (16:8), nor to mourn with the bereaved (16:5), because the dead are better off.
   c. PHYSICAL SUFFERING (11:21; 20:1–2; 26:7–9; 30:1–2; 37:11–16; 38:1–13). His life is frequently in danger, and he is often imprisoned (there were spies, even in those days, see 38:24–28).
   d. EMOTIONAL SUFFERING Some passages, known as the "Confessions of Jeremiah," record something of his mental anguish and emotional distress (8:18–9.6; 10:19–25; 11:18–20; 12:1–4; 15:10–18; 18:19–25; 20:7–18). From the start God has warned Jeremiah that the people will fight against him (1:19) and that they will not obey God's

word (6:17; 25:4), but Jeremiah is still grieved (compare 13:15–17).

3.
THE NATIONS GOD JUDGES

In the call narrative, Jeremiah is described as "a prophet to the nations" (1:5) and it emphasizes the sovereignty as well as the justice of God. Although he speaks primarily to apostate Judah, Jeremiah has a word from the only God for other countries too (25:15–31; 27:1–11). In the closing chapters of the book, in particular, there are messages for Egypt, Philistia, Moab, Ammon, Edom, Damascus and Elam, as well as Babylon (46–51).

The final chapter (52) provides historical detail of the exile judgment. Jeremiah's immense breadth of vision and world outlook is illustrated not only by his messages to other countries but also in his continuing concern for those Jews who have been sent to Babylonia (Letter to the Exiles, 29) and also for those who have gone to Egypt for refuge, even though Jeremiah had warned them not to go (42–44). Against his will they take him with them (43:6–7).

Lamentations

W e have just been considering the sensitivity of the prophet JEREMIAH (4:19; 9:1–2; 13:17; compare also, 2 Chron. 35:25). *Lamentations* is a series of laments by Jeremiah for the fallen city of Jerusalem. The poems follow an alphabetic acrostic form in chapters 1–4, and though this is not continued in chapter 5, that chapter does have as many verses as there are letters in the Hebrew alphabet. Knox's translation of *Lamentations* is a brilliant example of the style. This literary device may have been used to aid memorization.

It is possible to discern four themes in this group of laments.

1. CHAPTERS 1–2
THE ANGUISH OF THE PEOPLE

The first two poems focus attention on the distressed nation and the desolate city. The Jews were intensely proud of Jerusalem (Ps. 48), and its destruction is not only a political grief but a spiritual agony: God had set his name there (Deut. 12:21; 16:2; Jer. 6:1–8). Four aspects of their condition ought to be noticed:

a. THEIR LOSS OF PRECIOUS THINGS (1:7, 10 see RSV; 2:5–7) Gentiles are not allowed into the sanctuary, yet foreign soldiers have trampled through the sacred Temple courts (1:10).

b. THEIR NEGLECT OF HOLY THINGS (1:8–9, 18; 2:14) "She took no thought of her doom" (1:9, RSV) and those who should have exposed the sins of the people only utter pleasantries (2:14; compare Jer. 6:14; 8:11–12; 23:25–29; 29:8–9).

c. THEIR NEED OF ESSENTIAL THINGS (1:11) Many are dying of starvation in the besieged city (Jer. 52:6). Chapter 4 comments further on this terribly distressing theme (see 4:4–5, 9–10).

d. THEIR LOVE OF WORTHLESS THINGS (1:19, "allies" means any merely human aid). All too often in our trouble we turn to those who cannot help us (compare Lam. 1:2; Jer. 2:25; 22:20–22; Hos. 2:5, 7, 10, 12–13). In this prophetic context the "lovers" are both religious (priests, false prophets, etc.) and political (foreign alliances, see 4:17).

2. CHAPTER 3
THE HOPE OF THE PROPHET

This next lament is phrased in more personal language and gives vivid expression to the prophet's deep agony of soul:

- he is affected spiritually (3:3, 8: "He has turned his hand against me . . . he shuts out my prayer.")
- he is affected physically (3:4)
- he is affected socially (3:14; compare 20:7)
- he is affected emotionally (3:17: "I have been deprived of peace")

But at 3:21 there is a magnificent transition: "Yet this I call to mind . . ." What should *we* call to mind in times of adversity and personal distress?

- his steadfast love (3:22: "The steadfast love of the Lord never ceases," RSV)

- his unfailing mercies (3:22: "His compassions never fail")
- his great faithfulness (3:23) He is not a God who will let you down (compare Jer. 17:7).
- his promised deliverance (3:25–26) His saving help will come but not always at the moment *we* feel we must have it.
- his tender compassion (3:33: "He does not willingly bring affliction . . .")
- his providential control (3:37: ". . . if the Lord has not decreed it?")

3. CHAPTER 4
THE SCENE OF THE PLIGHT

This poem seems to take the reader right into the streets of the grief-stricken city. In a series of contrasting pictures the reader is made to see *the Jerusalem that was* and then *the city in its present plight*.

The beautiful Temple is a heap of worthless ruins (4:1); hungry animals are more kind to their young than are the distressed citizens (4:3–4); those who attended lavish banquets now hunt for food in refuse-heaps (4:5); the once wealthy princes are now pitiful paupers (4:7–8); those who died an immediate death by the sword are better off than those who suffer the lingering death of starvation (4:9); compassionate mothers have become heartless cannibals (4:10); the "impregnable" city has collapsed (4:12) because of the sins of the "impeccable" priesthood (4:13–15).

4. CHAPTER 5
THE CRY OF THE PENITENT

The final lament looks away from the tragic circumstances of the fallen Jerusalem to the unshaken throne of God. Here the people are heartbroken, not only because of the

disaster but because of what has caused it: *sin.* The guilty
are pleading:

- REMEMBER US (5:1)
- PARDON US The penitent confesses both the sins of
  his ancestors (5:7) and his own sins (5:16). Both are
  mentioned together in Jeremiah 14:20.
- COMFORT US (5:19)—that is, with the great fact of
  God's sovereignty. Since God controls all life, even
  this tragedy can be used for good.
- RESTORE US (5:21: "Restore us to yourself, O Lord,
  that we may return.")

Ezekiel

e have now come to the outstanding personality who ministered to the exiled people in Babylon, Ezekiel. As a priest, Ezekiel communicates his message in images and symbols which would be particularly meaningful to someone trained in priestly circles.

EZEKIEL THE PROPHET

a. WHAT HE DOES As well as the oracles there are several "dramatic-presentations" of truth (known as prophetic symbolism). Here the prophet does not merely speak but does something to illustrate his message. We should observe, however, that for the Hebrew this was something more than an illustration: his action was regarded as an *initiation* of the events which were being described in this symbolic form. This method of prophesying was used by earlier prophets (e.g., Isaiah 20 where the prophet assumes the guise of a captive, and Jeremiah 13, where the prophet's marred girdle symbolizes the nation which should have cleaved to God), but it is seen in its most pronounced form in Ezekiel (e.g., 4:1–3, 4–8; 9–13; 5:1–4; 12:3–7, etc.).

b. WHAT HE SEES Ezekiel is a visionary as well as a missionary. God reveals himself to the prophet by means of these highly colorful visions. He is "taken to see" things by God (e.g., the magnificent *call vision* in ch. 1; compare also 8:3–16; 9:2–11; 10:1–22). As well as the visions, he is made to *see* a number of magnificent parables, and his eye is directed to vivid imagery (15:1–5; 17:1–8; 19:1–14).

c. WHAT HE HEARS Ezekiel is admitted to the audience-chamber of the sovereign God (compare 1:28–2:10). He is told that the people will not want to hear his message (2:5; 3:7) but he is to be like the watchman of a city (3:17–21) who warns the people of the approaching danger. Because God knows their rebellious spirit he makes Ezekiel *hear* the truth in unmistakably clear statements, warnings, metaphors and images (3:27; 14:1–11, where Ezekiel hears God's word for the elders as they are sitting in front of him). Notice that hearing and communicating the word is not a static thing: see chapter 18.

Any attempt at a simple analysis of this book is bound to have an element of artificiality but it is possible to discern the following main divisions in the prophet's message to the people of God:

1. CHAPTERS 1–3
THE GOD BESIDE THEM

The exiles have to be encouraged to believe that even though their nation has been conquered by Babylonian soldiers Yahweh is still the omnipotent sovereign God who has not been left behind in Jerusalem, but is with them. The opening vision (1) is of the chariot throne of God. The cherubim of glory which feature in the attractive furnishings of the Temple are there in the call vision to emphasize the continuing sovereign presence of the invincible God.

Chapters 2–3 record the circumstances of Ezekiel's call and indicate the reticence of the prophet as well as the rebellion of the people.

2. CHAPTERS 4–24
THE INIQUITY WITHIN THEM

Although the prophet ministers in Babylon, much of what he has to say concerns Jerusalem in the period between JE-HOIACHIN'S captivity (597 BC) and the final collapse of the city. In that period ZEDEKIAH was left as a puppet king and some so-called prophets predicted a free Jerusalem and a return of the first exiles within two years (Jer. 28, 29:8). Both Jeremiah and Ezekiel know this is not to be (Jer. 29; Ezek. 4). But why is Ezekiel's word *about* Jerusalem addressed to the *exiles* in Babylonia? H. L. Ellison (*Ezekiel, the Man and his Message*) makes the helpful suggestion that Jeremiah 24 is the clue: "The message of Jeremiah that the exile was an act of grace on the part of God, and that the real sinners had been left in Jerusalem for dire punishment, was one that was hard to accept both in Jerusalem and in Babylon." Ezekiel's message is not intended for those left in the city of Jerusalem, but for those in Babylon who have to understand that the judgment of Jerusalem was inevitable. The main burden of this section is that of Judah's sins. Three themes can be traced in Ezekiel's message:

a. THEIR INIQUITY WILL BE PUNISHED (4–7) Details of the siege (4:1–17) and the desolation (7) are given.
b. THEIR INIQUITY MUST BE EXPOSED (8–17) Much of the iniquity goes on in secret (8:3–18). The offenders are marked out by the fact that God's sign is *not* upon them (9:4–6) and the wicked are clearly pointed out to the prophet (11:2–3). Ezekiel exposes:

- the sins of their king (12)
- the sins of the prophets (13)
- the sins of the elders (14)
- the sins of the citizens (15–17)

c. THEIR INIQUITY SHOULD BE CONFESSED (18–24) Details of the coming judgment continue but there is also a winsome note of appeal in these chapters (e.g., 18:21–23,

30–32; 20:41–44). However, judgment is inevitable and the section closes with the moving story of Ezekiel's bereavement (24:15–27) symbolically used to emphasize that such grief will be as nothing compared with the grief they feel when they hear of Jerusalem's desolation at the hand of the Babylonian armies.

3. CHAPTERS 25–32
THE NATIONS AROUND THEM

Oracles like these are found in many prophetic writings (Isa., Amos, Jer.). In Ezekiel they are specially meaningful, for the exiles are now living in a heathen country and are in danger of imagining that God is not concerned about, or is unaware of, heathen tyranny. These passages would be of immense comfort to Jews in Babylonia at this time and underline the message with which *Ezekiel* opens: God is sovereign Lord of the universe.

4. CHAPTERS 33–48
THE PROSPECT BEFORE THEM

These chapters urge the exiles to look to the future. Here is a new stage in Ezekiel's work: his message is now of *hope*, not doom. Many arresting messages follow:

- the accountable watchman (33)
- the unfailing shepherd (34)
- the iniquitous enemies (35)
- the reviving Spirit (37)
- the coming oppressors (38–39)
- the future Temple (40–46)
- the fruitful river (47)
- the promised land (48)

Daniel

n our study of *Ezekiel* we looked at the exiled people of God in Babylon (first deportation 597 BC, second 586 BC). *Daniel* is also set in the exilic period. It clearly divides into two sections; the first is mainly historical (1–6) and the second primarily prophetical (7–12). It presents us with a magnificent portrait of God. He is in full control of world history (7–11) and yet he takes care of individuals who are in danger (1–6). He is as concerned about solitary individuals in serious trouble as he is about vast nations in deadly conflict.

1. CHAPTERS 1–6
GOD'S SERVANTS AND THEIR EXEMPLARY LOYALTY

Chapters 1–6 introduce us to a group of faithful Hebrew loyalists who refuse to compromise their faith just because they are in an alien environment. These four devout heroes (1:6–8) are able to maintain their integrity not because of natural endowments but because of confidence in God. They know Yahweh to be:

a. THE GOD WHO REWARDS LOYALTY (1) The first chapter tells the story of their refusal to eat food offered to Babylonian deities. DANIEL is recognized as a gifted wise man and his services are used throughout the exile (1:19–21).

b. THE GOD WHO PROVIDES WISDOM (2) Their heathen employer is baffled by a mysterious dream and Daniel relates the dream to him and unfolds its meaning. Daniel believes in a God who reveals secrets (2:28).

c. THE GOD WHO EFFECTS DELIVERANCE (3) Our attention is now turned to Daniel's three companions (2:49) who refuse to worship a heathen idol (3:12–18). Notice:

- what the opponents said—"they do not serve your God" (3:12, RSV)
- what the loyalists said—"the God we serve is able to save us . . . But even if he does not . . . we will not serve your gods" (3:17–18)
- what the onlookers said—"four men walking around in the fire, unbound and unharmed, and the fourth looks like a son of the gods" (3:25)

Is our witness so definite? Do our opponents know and understand our convictions? Is our confidence in God as deep as the trust of the three loyalists? Are people aware of Christ's presence with us when we are in the furnace of affliction?

d. THE GOD WHO ABHORS PRIDE (4) From the three Hebrews, back to Daniel—and courage is required once again, for the king has had a dream which portrays the judgment of God upon him for his arrogance. Daniel warns the king that he will become mentally sick (4:25), and pleads with him to abandon his sin (4:27). But a year later pride takes hold of him (4:29–30) and in that very moment he is changed from a haughty monarch to a helpless maniac (4:33).

e. THE GOD WHO PUNISHES EVIL (5) After the story of Nebuchadnezzar's pride comes the account of Belshazzar's doom. He uses the sacred Temple vessels from

Jerusalem at a state banquet and during the orgy God writes a message of judgment upon the wall. Daniel is once again called upon to interpret, and before the next morning the king is killed.

f. THE GOD WHO GUARANTEES PROTECTION (6) The famous lions' den story emphasizes yet again the sovereign power of God. The Lord who can bring an arrogant monarch to the dust can close the jaws of lions (6:22).

These stories are historical events belonging to the exile period, but they were widely circulated during the Maccabean revolt in the second century in order to encourage Jews who were in similar danger of compromise and disloyalty, cowardice and corruption.

2. CHAPTERS 7–12
GOD'S WORLD AND ITS APPOINTED DESTINY

At this point in the book, the subject matter changes dramatically; from contemporary events, the mind is diverted by a series of dramatic visions to future conflicts. The *individual* believer, so important in chapters 1–6, is made to realize that God is in control of the *nations*. With this type of apocalyptic literature the interpretation of symbolism can lead to wide divergence of opinion, and every interpretation needs to be maintained with charity and meekness. It is possible to divide this fascinating second half of the book into three sub-sections:

a. THE BEASTS AND THEIR BATTLES (7–8) Four beasts emerge in chapter 7, typifying the powers which will trouble the earth (probably the lion represents Babylon; the bear, Medo-Persia; the leopard, Greece, which later split into four divisions; and the fourth beast, Rome).

In chapter 8 a conflict is portrayed between a two-horned ram (Medo-Persia, 8:20) and a he-goat (Greece, 8:21, which, as we have seen, was divided into four sections, 8:22–23). During the period of the Maccabean revolt, Antiochus Epiphanes certainly persecuted God's people (8:23–25), but the vision may well point ahead into the future as well. In other words, Antiochus is also a type of the evil ruler who will persecute the saints.

b. THE PENITENT AND HIS VISITANTS (9–10) Daniel is bewildered (8:27), but he is a man of prayer. He knows that the people of God have sinned (9:3–4, 20), and he confesses those sins: disobedience (5), inattentiveness (6) and stubbornness (13). God sends his angel to Daniel with:

- immediate help (9:21: "in swift flight")
- sympathetic help (10:10: "touched me")
- fortifying help (9:23: "I have come to tell you")

Daniel is to be given insight into the future and is to see their present trouble against the background of a wider conflict. The *seventy weeks* (9:24, RSV) are variously interpreted but they certainly outline a dramatic future. Possibly 9:25–27 describes the coming of the Messiah (the Anointed One), with the words "cut off" (9:26) referring to his crucifixion, which takes away the need for the Jewish sacrifices (compare Heb. 8:13). However, there are other interpretations.

c. THE CONFLICT AND ITS CONSUMMATION (11–12) The final visions reveal a panorama of the centuries. Chapter 11 is a prophetic account of the conflict between Syria and Egypt and the scene is set for the last act in the drama of world history. Chapter 12 prepares us for the future "distress" (12:1). The book closes by indicating the importance of having our names in "the book" (12:1; compare Luke 10:20; Rev. 3:5; 20:12); by announcing the fact of the resurrection (12:2); and by defining the difference between those who are *wise* (12:3, 10) and those who are *wicked* (12:4, 10).

Hosea

OSEA was an eighth century prophet who ministered to the northern kingdom (Israel) shortly after the prophetic work of Amos, and prior to the Assyrian invasion. The moving and eloquent appeal of Hosea to the unfaithful people of God is against the background of his own unfaithful wife's desertion and their bitterly disappointing marriage relationship. She left him for other lovers (1, 3) and "his grief became his gospel." Just as he bought her back, so Yahweh yearns for the renewed love of his people who are bound to him by a covenant relationship.

A great Hebrew word, *hesed,* meaning loving-kindness, mercy, loyal love, is a key term in this book (e.g., 2:19; 4:1; 6.6; 10:12). The teaching of Hosea roves widely over a series of themes which are all closely related to this "forsaken covenant" idea. The subjects he develops cannot be outlined in a chapter-by-chapter type of analysis as he keeps on returning to them all, and they are found throughout the book, but the following outline focuses attention on the leading ideas:

1.
FAITHLESS LOVERS

Like Hosea's wife, God's people have "played the harlot" (2:5, RSV; 3:3; 4:15; 9:1). They have pursued other gods and forgotten the covenant they made with Yahweh when he brought them out of Egyptian bondage (2:15; 11:1; 12:9, 13; 13:4–5). As in *Jeremiah,* the "wilderness wanderings" are, by comparison, regarded as a time of early devotion and loyalty to God (2:15; compare Jer. 2). But Israel has forsaken her covenant-keeping God and gone after other lovers (2:5–7), the idols of Baal. In their folly the people of the northern kingdom have come to believe that Baal is the god of their land and that fruitful seasons are the result of Baal's help. God will punish them for failing to recognize that their agricultural prosperity is due to his goodness alone (2:8–13). This theme of the unfaithful lover appears throughout the book (e.g., 4:1–3; 7:4–7; 9:1–2; 11:1–7).

2.
USELESS SERVANTS

Hosea has the same trouble as many of his prophetic successors—the land is full of false prophets and corrupt priests. These men ought to be the guardians and heralds of the truth, but instead they use their office to improve their own standing in society and increase their financial assets (4:4–10; 6:9; 9:7–9). We have already seen this grave problem in our study of *Jeremiah.*

3.
GODLESS KINGS

For Hosea, the northern kingdom is a ghastly mistake. He realizes that the breakaway under Jeroboam has been spiritually disastrous (8:5–6; 13:2; compare 1 Kings 12:28–30 which tells the story of the manufacture of these golden calves). Hosea longs for the unification of the land under a Davidic monarch (3:4–5) and he refuses to recognize the Israelite kings as men appointed by God (7:3–7; 8:4; 9:15; 10:7, 15; 13:10).

4.
HELPLESS FRIENDS

The great ancient trade routes passed through Israel and
Judah, and the two countries were consequently the storm
center of near-eastern politics. Instead of relying upon God,
both countries turn to their neighbors for help, and, as in
Isaiah the making of foreign alliances becomes a spiritual
issue. These international treaties demanded the recognition
of each other's gods, and their covenants were often agreed
and sealed in religious/sacrificial settings. In other words,
Yahweh just becomes one of the pantheon of near-eastern
deities. The prophets despise this kind of reliance and regard
it as the act of a traitor, of someone who no longer relies on
a God who is able to keep him through every difficulty. The
theme emerges in 5:13–14; 7:8–16; 8:8–10; 12:1; 14:3. Do
we turn to people and things for help in *our* trouble instead
of to God himself?

5.
LOVELESS WORSHIPPERS

The greatest agony is that in all this apostasy God's people
are keeping up appearances by continuing with all the tradi-
tional ceremonies and rituals. But, as in *Jeremiah* and *Isaiah,* the sacrifices are obnoxious to God. He only longs for
their love and loyalty (6:4–6: "What can I do with you,
Judah? Your love [*hesed,* covenant love] is like the morning
mist, like the early dew that disappears . . . For I desire
mercy [*hesed*], not sacrifice."). Sometimes they offer their
sacrifices to Yahweh but sometimes to Baal (2:11–13; 4:13;
8:11–14; 9:4) and they are so indifferent to the Law (part of
the covenant terms) that they make use of idols, something
which is expressly forbidden in the covenant commandments (Exod. 20:3–4; see 2:8; 4:11–19; 8:4; 10:8; 13:1–2).
Do we have idols? Anything is idolatrous if it comes between us and God.

6.
CARELESS CITIZENS

People who are disobedient to God are in grave danger of becoming indifferent to men. Although Hosea does not say as much about *social* crimes as, say Amos and Micah, he is deeply aware of these serious community problems. The covenant commandments are not only about man's attitude to God, but also about man's concern for his fellow men (see 4:1–2, which is almost a summary of the social demands of the Ten Commandments; and also 7:1; 10:4, about false witness; 12–13). A man whose heart is in love with the Lord will not neglect the needs of his fellows, and he will do nothing to cause another to stumble.

The final appeal of the prophet (14) is for the *lovers* to return to the one who truly loves them (14:1, 4). They must not heed the word of useless servants, nor rely on the protection of godless kings and helpless friends (14:3). He urges the loveless worshippers to abandon their idolatry and take *sincere* words into the presence of their God (14:2, 3b, 8).

Joel

his vigorous and arresting book cannot be dated with precise accuracy because there is nothing in it about contemporary rulers and events except the reference to a locust plague, which could have been at any time. It is probably of early date, possibly during the reign of Joash of Judah. Its message, however, is relevant for all time: God must punish sin, but he always pleads with the sinners, and longs to pardon those who genuinely turn from their evil ways.

1. CHAPTERS 1:1–2:11
THE DIVINE PUNISHMENT

Joel firmly believes in the sovereignty of God; the Lord is in control of the forces of nature: he sends the locust plague to bring his people back to their former faith and reliance upon him. Notice, however, that the punishment is not vindictive but corrective. God knows it is the *only* effective way of bringing the people back to him. Sometimes God does this with us in order to bring us to our senses (John 15:2; Heb. 12:5–11).

a. EDUCATIVE PUNISHMENT (1:2–3) The story of this punishment will be passed from one generation to another. People over the centuries will learn by it.

b. INESCAPABLE PUNISHMENT (1:4–13) Possibly 1:4 describes the different stages in the growth of a locust, or it could refer to various types of locust; the former is more likely. The point of these verses is that people cannot get away from this act of judgment. Whatever their position in society, whether they be religious leaders (1:9–10, 13) or agricultural workers (1:11–12), it will reach them and seriously affect them.

c. JUST PUNISHMENT (1:14–20) And it is deserved! There is nothing unfair about it at all. God did it and he knew it to be necessary (1:15: "as destruction from the Almighty it comes," RSV).

d. ANTICIPATED PUNISHMENT (2:1–11) These verses record the note of *warning.* This is "the day of the Lord" and the people have expected it. The only thing is, as Amos observes in the next prophetic book, "the Day" is not quite what they had anticipated! They had expected the day of the Lord to bring punishment on their enemies, but the prophets also see it as the punishment of their own iniquities (compare Amos 5:20). We see other people's transgressions so much more clearly than we discern our own.

2. CHAPTER 2:12–27
THE DIVINE PLEA

We have just seen that *sin is punished;* here Joel rejoices in the complementary truth that *pardon is offered.* God begs his people to come back to him (2:12: "Even now . . . return to me"). Note the prophet's magnificent portraiture of God in action, longing for renewed fellowship with his beloved people. Joel emphasizes:

a. GOD'S COMPASSIONATE APPEAL (2:12) It is God who takes the initiative (see Ezek. 33:11; 1 John 4:9–10).

b. GOD'S MERCIFUL NATURE (2:13–14: "for he is gracious and compassionate"). It is God's nature to forgive and restore us to fellowship with himself. God loves like that!

c. GOD'S UNIVERSAL HONOR (2:17) "God's honor is at stake," the penitents say. If the devastation and anguish continue, the unbelieving nations will say, "Where is their God?" The Hebrews were often concerned about the effect these disasters could have upon the minds of the heathen who, generally speaking, regarded prosperity as a sign of divine favor and disaster a token of disapproval, or, far worse, of the inability of their God to cope with difficult situations (Isa. 37:18–20)! The theme often occurs in psalmody (e.g., Ps. 44:13; 74:10; 94:2–7; 115:1–2).

d. GOD'S UNGRUDGING GENEROSITY (2:25) "I will restore to you the years which the swarming locust has eaten": this is a text full of hope, certainty, *and grace!* God never deals with us as we deserve. He often uses harsh circumstances in life to bring us back to himself, but it is only to hedge us in with our selfishness, disobedience and resistance, and to show us that we cannot be truly happy unless we put him absolutely first in our lives (Matt. 6:33).

e. GOD'S PROMISED COMPANIONSHIP (2:27) "You shall know that I am in the midst of Israel" (RSV). In their anguish they felt that God had left them. Here he assures them that once forgiven he will be in their midst.

f. GOD'S UNCHALLENGED SOVEREIGNTY (2:27: "There is no other") Out of this time of chastisement and correction came a new sense of God's total sovereignty. There must be no other gods in the nation; there must be no idols in our lives, either.

The divine plea is made first to the *individual* (2:12–14), then to the *nation* (2:15–16) for the sake of the *world*. But the repentance must be:

- sincere repentance (2:12)
- united repentance (2:15)
- immediate repentance (2:16)

3. CHAPTERS 2:28–3:21
THE DIVINE PROMISE

Future blessing is here assured. The key word is "afterward" (2:28). God promises that "afterward" there will be:

    a. SUPERNATURAL EVENTS (2:28–32) We are familiar with this passage because of its use in Peter's sermon at Pentecost (Acts 2:16: "this is what was spoken").
    b. UNIVERSAL JUDGMENTS (3:1–16) The sins of the nations against God's people will all be punished. Men cannot persistently sin against the chosen of God and hope to get away with it (compare 3:19).
    c. NATIONAL RESTORATION (3:16b–21) The prophet points to a time when his people shall once again enjoy the peace and prosperity (3:18) that has for so long been denied them.

Some think that the reference to Edom (3:19) indicates a late date: the Edomites were particularly cruel to those who remained in Judah during the Babylonian exile, but there had been more or less constant hostility between Jews and Edomites.

Amos

robably the best known of the minor prophets, Amos lived in the eighth century, and was a shepherd in Judah until he received a clear call from God (7:14–15) to go and prophesy to the northern kingdom (Israel). He obeyed God, but found that some people resented this outspoken missionary from the south (7:12).

The book is packed with vivid imagery. In its rich language and arresting ideas we see something of the gigantic personality of Amos. He is not an innovator, but is railing the vast crowds in the busy market towns of the north back to the true religion of Moses (compare 2:6–7 with Exod. 22:26–27; 5:12 with Exod. 23:1–3; 6–7).

1. CHAPTERS 1–2
THE WORLD GOD CONTROLS

This section contains *eight songs* (the Doom Songs) and they concern the sins of Israel's near neighbors. The cruelty, arrogance and injustice of these surrounding countries are brought under serious review and the crowds in Israel's markets love to hear about this threatened judgment—until it's their turn (2:6–16)! The songs perfectly express the convictions of this courageous prophet about:

a. GOD'S SOVEREIGNTY God is not a territorial God; he is not only the God of Israel and Judah but of the world, and he is just as concerned about the sins of Edom as about Israel's transgressions.

b. GOD'S OMNISCIENCE He is not a God "out there," entirely unmoved and unconcerned about what is happening on earth. He *knows* everything about everybody; nothing can be hidden from his view. For thinking people in the crowd listening to Amos this will have disturbing implications. If God knows about the injustice that is going on in Gaza, he doubtless knows all about the daily robberies in the marketplace at Bethel and elsewhere (8:5).

c. GOD'S COMPASSION God is not only disturbed by sins against his chosen people, but by sins against *anybody*. (e.g., 2:1–3: an act of vindictive cruelty that did not affect the Israelites. 1:6–8 and 1:9–10 may also refer to sins against other nations. These verses do not say that the people carried off as slaves were Israelites.) After speaking of the sins of the neighboring countries, Amos launches forth into an attack on the evils to be found in both Judah (2:4–5) and Israel (2:6–8): sins of greed (2:6); indifference (2:7); immorality (2:7); disobedience (2:8); ingratitude (2:9–10); and rebellion (2:11–12). These are not just remote problems of the past: similar sins can still be found today, even among God's people.

2. CHAPTERS 3–6
THE TRUTH GOD DECLARES

This section contains *three oracles,* which begin at 3:1, 4:1, and 5:1. They each open in the same way: "Hear this word . . ." These three sermons declare:

a. THE TRUTH ABOUT RESPONSIBILITY (3:1–15) The Hebrews are rejoicing in their privileges (3:1–2) and hold that God says, "You only have I known, therefore I will *prosper* you." But look what God really says (3:2). They are neglecting their responsibilities. God reveals the *truth* that because of their refusal to show his love toward others by caring for them, the nation will be judged (3:11).

b. ABOUT DISOBEDIENCE (4:1–13). There is a five-fold repetitive plea: "Yet you have not returned to me" (6, 8, 9, 10, 11). God has been using various means to correct his people (as we saw in *Joel*). Here Amos notes that the people have ignored God's repeated warnings and their lives are characterized by total disobedience.

c. ABOUT WORSHIP (5:1–6:14) The people imagine that they are pleasing God with their meaningless sacrifices. God pleads with them to abandon the empty ritual in which he takes no pleasure (5:4–6, 21–27), preferring right living (5:24). He knows that the wealth of these insincere worshippers has been obtained at the expense of the poor and needy (6:3–6).

3. CHAPTERS 7–9
THE FUTURE GOD UNVEILS

This section contains *five visions:* locusts, drought, plumb line, basket of summer fruit, and a vision of God himself. From our study of *Joel* we know the locust plague (7:1–3) to be a terrifying threat; the scorching heat of the sun (7:4–6) could burn up all their crops; the plumb line depicts the accuracy of God's judgment (7:7–9). In the vision of the summer fruit (8:1–2) there is a magnificent play on words. The Hebrew for "fruit" is *qayits,* and the Hebrew for "end" is *qets.* In other words, Amos is saying, "We have reached the harvest, the end" (compare 8:9–12). The final vision portrays:

- the inescapable God (9:1–4)
- the omnipotent God (9:5–7)—active both in nature and history (9:5–6, 7)
- the righteous God (9:8–10)
- the merciful God (9:11–15)

Just as the book opens with magnificent statements about God (1, 2), so it closes with these arresting sayings about the only true God. Have these truths become part of our own experience? Do we know him as:

a. the God who pursues us (9:2–4)
b. the God who corrects us (9:8)
c. the God who restores us (9:11)?

The short biographical passage at 7:10–15 records a conflict between prophet and priest and tells us a good deal about the immediate obedience of Amos (7:14–15) and the arrogant disobedience of Amaziah. Like so many others since the eighth century, Amaziah did not mind the truth being preached (7:12) but he did not want it preached *at him* (7:13)!

Obadiah

he book of *Obadiah* is the shortest of the prophetical books, being contained within the compass of twenty-one verses. It expounds the judgment theme in respect of the Edomite brigands who had often made life intolerable for the people of Judah. The date generally accepted is after 586 BC. It would seem that OBADIAH prophesied very early in the exilic period, and in *Judah* itself. If so, this would make him the *only* prophet delivering a clear message from God on Judean territory during the period of the exile. H. L. Ellison (*Men spake from God*) suggests that the Judah's sinfulness is not mentioned by the prophet because Judah is in exile and so is already under Yahweh's judgment. This would also explain the reference to the later time when "the house of Jacob shall possess their own possessions" (17). The name *Obadiah* means "Servant of Yahweh"; just as *Ezekiel* was charged with the task of bringing hope to the Jewish exiles in Babylonia, so Obadiah has the responsibility of delivering a similar message to those dispirited and harassed people who have been left behind in Judah. Notice that many of the ideas in *Obadiah* are also found in Jeremiah 49:7–22.

1. Verses 1–14
THE REPUDIATION OF GOD EXPRESSED

Although Obadiah's message seems to relate to Edomite cruelty during the exilic period, the feud between the two nations had a long and sad history. It started during the wilderness wanderings, when the Edomites (the descendants of Esau) refused to grant the Hebrew people permission to pass through Edomite territory to safety (Num. 20:14–21; compare Deut. 23:7–8). The bitterness increased in the pre-exilic period (2 Sam. 8:13–14; 1 Kings 11:14–25; 2 Kings 8:20–22; 14:7–10; 2 Chron. 28:16–17). But it was during the exile that the Jewish people were most hurt by Edomite mockery and cruelty (compare Lam. 4:21–22; Ezek. 35, Mount Seir stands for the land of Edom). It is for this reason that some of the Psalms also expound this Edomite judgment theme (compare Ps. 60, 137). It also appears in the teaching of other prophets (see Isa. 34, Ezek. 25:12–14; Joel 3:19; Amos 1:11; Mal. 1:2–5). In view of their persistent cruelty and bitter hostility toward Judah, the prophetic word of Amos (2:1–3) that Moab would be punished for cruelties *against* Edom, is even more remarkable.

In the teaching of Obadiah, God's judgment will come upon this cruel nation not only because of their *hostility toward the Jews* but because of their *pride before the Lord,* Obadiah emphasizes four Edomite sins which have grieved God:

- military arrogance (1–6)
- political cunning (7–9)
- humanitarian indifference (10–12)
- materialistic greed (13–14)

2. Verses 15–16
THE RETRIBUTION GOD ORDAINED

The Edomite hordes swept down on the poor and crushed Jewish communities. Any kind of strong military and political leadership had been removed to Babylon (2 Kings 24:14–16;

25:12) and those who were left were utterly helpless against such cruel invaders. But the word of Obadiah brings comfort to the wounded, the hungry, the bereaved and the spiritually bewildered remnant: "God is still sovereign; he reigns. These are grim days but do not forget *the* day of the Lord."

The judgment theme is not mere vindictiveness; it is a necessary reminder of God's rule over the world. Many Jews were in danger of abandoning their faith because God's people seemed to be at the mercy of the heathen. The gods of Babylon and Edom appeared to have triumphed, but Obadiah points out that the promised judgment is:

a. IMMINENT (15)—"The day of the Lord is near";
b. UNIVERSAL (15)—it is for "all the nations." Not the Edomite oppressor only, but all who have caused others to suffer, will be punished;
c. JUSTIFIED (15)—"As you have done, it will be done to you . . ." There is nothing improper or unjust about the coming doom. God is not only merciful, he is righteous.

3. VERSES 17–21
THE RESTITUTION GOD PROMISED

As this brokenhearted minority bathe their wounds and bury their dead, they hear this word of radiant hope from the prophet Obadiah: "But on Mount Zion will be deliverance . . ." He helps them to see themselves as God's people, still in his sovereign care despite their present adversities. Obadiah believes them to be:

- the people God spares (17)
- the people God empowers (18)
- the people God rules (20–21)

The final word of the prophet offers hope and peace to those pathetic groups who gather around him in dark days: "The kingdom will be"—not the Edomites, but—"the Lord's." These are words for our time, too, when all too often evil not only abounds but seems to triumph over good.

Jonah

*onah* has suffered more at the hands of critics than almost any other Old Testament book. Concern about history and the swallowing of Jonah by "a great fish" (1:17) has tended to direct interest away from the theological content of the book. *Jonah* differs from other Old Testament prophetic books in that it is mainly biographical, whereas the others generally contain little biographical detail.

The prophet is mentioned in 2 Kings 14:25, indicating that he exercised his prophetic ministry in the northern kingdom during the reign of Jeroboam II. This means that Amos, Hosea and possibly Joel were his contemporaries.

Dr. Graham Scroggie says: "Its subject is not a 'whale' but Foreign Missions." Campbell Morgan gives the following words as the only appropriate title to Jonah's message: "Condemnation of exclusiveness." The main theme, admirably and forcefully told, is that the good news of God's generous love is not to be protected but proclaimed. It is strange how right through religious and Christian history there seem to have been two types of believers: guardians and heralds. Of course, even the heralds must be sure that they declare the *truth*.

The book can be divided into four sections:

1. CHAPTER 1:1–17
DISOBEDIENCE

If Jonah had been told to pronounce *doom* over Assyria, like
Nahum, he would have obeyed immediately. It was not cowardice that sent him in the other direction, but bewilderment and
disappointment. Are you ever like that? When circumstances do
not work out exactly as *you* think they should, when they baffle
you, are you tempted to feel that God has become unjust? This
is exactly how Jonah felt, and he did the kind of thing that we
sometimes do—he tried to get away from God. Like Jonah, we
also find that every escape route turns out to be closed; wherever
we go, God is waiting to receive us (compare Ps. 139:7–12).

Are we ever guilty of accusing God (perhaps not in
words, but by a resentful attitude) of being unjust or unreasonable? These thoughts were in Jonah's mind when he
heard the divine call to go and preach. He thought:

a. GOD WAS UNJUST The Assyrians were terribly wicked
and were well known for their heartless atrocities and
Jonah thought that they deserved only the grim punishment of the divine wrath. Do we ever accuse God of being
unjust in the ordering of our circumstances? Psalm 73
deals with this complaint that the godless seem to do well
while the righteous suffer.
b. GOD WAS UNREASONABLE—Jonah was not merely baffled by God's command to him, as if this were just a theological mystery, but he found it intellectually
astonishing. Like his prophetic contemporaries, Jonah
may well have realized that the Assyrians were going to
be "the staff of my fury" (Isa. 10:5, RSV). He obviously
shrank from going on a mission which would result in
saving his hearers from doom only so that they could later
inflict grief on Israel: which they ultimately did! It
seemed to him that if he went he would be *against* his
people and *for* the heathen. *Jonah* is a very *human* story;
it reflects something of our own reactions when life does
not work out for us in exactly the way we had hoped.

2. CHAPTER 2:1–10
DESPAIR

When we get rebellious, God has his own way of bringing us to our senses, as we saw in *Joel.* Jonah thought that by leaving the country he was getting away from God, but God is inescapable (Jer. 23:23–24). Some people try to do a similar thing by staying away from church, and avoiding the company of Christians, etc. In this case, God in his mercy as well as his omnipotence prepares an experience of the *deep* (2:3). The message of Elijah and Elisha, Jonah's immediate prophetic predecessors in Israel, was frequently attested or accompanied by supernatural events (1 Kings 17:3–7, 14–16; 18:13–39; 2 Kings 2:11–12, 19–22; 3:16–20; 4:1–7; 5:1–154). Jonah came from the Galilean town of Gath Hepher (2 Kings 14:25), less than an hour's walk from Nazareth. This story of the "great fish," uniquely "provided" (1:17) for this specific purpose, and Jonah's admittedly miraculous deliverance by a God who is in sovereign control of his creation, was clearly treasured by our Lord Jesus. Christ's deliverance from actual, rather than potential, death by his resurrection was an even greater miracle (see Matt. 12:40–41, where the two events are linked).

Observe that in his despair:

a. JONAH RECALLED GOD'S WORD The whole of chapter 2 is a selection of verses from the Psalms. Do you know God's word well enough to recall it when you are in dark circumstances?

b. JONAH REMEMBERED GOD'S MERCY (2:4) He had not been cast out, he had run away! But he looked to the place of mercy. Do we need to say, "I will look again"?

c. JONAH RECOGNIZED GOD'S SOVEREIGNTY (2.9) "Salvation comes from the Lord." It is his prerogative to save, and he saves those he will, whatever their cultural or racial background. Jonah had yet to learn this.

3. CHAPTER 3:1–10
DELIVERANCE

The chastised prophet went on his way in *obedience* but not, it would seem, in *compassion* (3:10–4:2). He obeyed but in the spirit of cold duty. Our *attitude* is as important as our *activity* in service. What counts is not the quantity we get through but the quality we bring to it. Note the *response* of the Ninevites to Jonah's preaching; it was:

- comprehensive (3:5)
- public (3:16–7)—nothing secret about it, every penitent became a witness
- genuine (3:7–8)—their sincerity was expressed in their refusal to eat and drink
- prayerful (3:8) "Let everyone call urgently on God"
- practical (3:8) "Give up . . . evil ways"
- believing (3:9) "God may yet . . ."

Is this how people respond to the preaching of the word today?

4. CHAPTER 4:1–11
DISAPPOINTMENT

The chapter records Jonah's disappointment, but more importantly *God's disappointment* with Jonah. Jonah was willing to do what God wanted (preach) but he wanted to deny God his right to do what he wanted (forgive). Jonah said he would rather die than see the Ninevites live (4:3)! He could grieve over the withering of the gourd, just because it had given him shelter; but he was not at all grieved at the possibility of the destruction of the Ninevites, including children (4:11). God has to break down our exclusiveness and our selfishness. Note that as Creator, God is also concerned about animals (4:11b) as well as men and women. Conservation had a prominent place on God's agenda long before it found its way on to ours (Deut. 20:10–20; 22:1–7).

Micah

ICAH is one of the eighth century prophets. AMOS and HOSEA preached to the northern kingdom, while Micah's (and ISAIAH's) ministry in that same period was directed to the southern kingdom. Like Amos, Micah was nurtured and employed in a rural community, though, unlike Amos, he was not a desert shepherd. Moresheth (1:1) was green and fertile, surrounded by rich cornfields and fine olive groves. Micah proclaims the judgment of God upon the rich, who have made their money at the expense of the poor. All life belongs to God, says Micah, he is not just interested in religious activities. J. B. Phillips says of Micah, "He is horrified at the luxurious and degenerate life of the city, and realizes that he and his fellow-peasants are paying for it. In another age he might have led a Peasants' Revolt, although he was no mere political agitator. It is justice between men and a right attitude toward God which are his concern." (The Four Prophets). Judgment is very near for Israel, and it will not be long before the invaders also sweep over the rich fertile countryside of Judah (1:5–7 and especially 8–16).

The book does not yield easily to neat analysis. H. L. Ellison observes that the "transition of thought is often violent, and in many cases the only connection between sections will be that of later juxtaposition because of spiritual connection." However, the book can be divided into *two main* sections:

1. CHAPTERS 1–3
JUDAH'S CORRUPTION

Two main themes are expounded in these opening chapters:

a. DESTRUCTION FROM OUTSIDE 1:1–16 is concerned with the "march of God" (1:3–7) across the territory of Israel. He comes in judgment, and that judgment reaches Judah (1:9). Then in a series of compelling puns (probably to attract the attention of an unconcerned and spiritually apathetic audience) Micah portrays the invading armies sweeping south over Judah, especially over the fertile Shephelah which Micah knew so well. It is a rich play on words ("verbal fireworks" says H. L. Ellison, *Men Spake from God).* Moffatt and J. B. Phillips bring this out well in their translations, for example:

". . . In Gath where tales are told, breathe not a word!
In Acco, the town of Weeping, shed no tear!
In Aphrah, the house of Dust, grovel in the dust!"
J.B.Phillips, Micah 1:10

b. CORRUPTION FROM INSIDE (2:1–3:12) The next two chapters give the reason for the judgment that is threatened. It is the *leaders* who are so sinful. Micah knows that the leadership is corrupt in three particular areas:

- commercial—the landowners strive to get hold of more fields and thereby oppress the poor (2:1–5)
- religious—the false prophets who, as later in Jeremiah's time, preach only of pleasant things and lull the rich into careless lethargy by their false optimism: "Do not prophesy about these things; disgrace will not overtake us" (2:6, see also 2:7; 3:5–7; compare Jer. 6:14; 8:11–12)

 • legal—the judges are equally self-seeking and greedy. Jerusalem, the center for all this corruption and vice, will be utterly destroyed (3:9–12).

2. CHAPTERS 4–7
YAHWEH'S COMPASSION

This also divides into two sub-sections:

a. HE DETERMINES THEIR DESTINY (4–5) From all the distressing corruption outlined in the earlier chapters, the prophet moves to a portrayal of truth on a wider canvas and the faithful in Judah are reminded of a better Day (4:1–5). Three distinct themes can be discerned in these two chapters:

 • the Kingdom (4:1–5)
 • the remnant (4:16–5:1, 7–9)
 • the Messiah (5:2–6)

Notice that the prophet looks to the distant horizons; he knows that the nation will go into captivity, but he rejoices in the prospect of an established and purified Kingdom in the future (4:10–11).

b. HE DESIRES THEIR DEVOTION (6–7) From the vision of the future, Micah returns to the agonies of the present. The opening chapters condemned the sins of the people; now the prophet appeals for their repentance. God has a controversy with them (6:2) and begs them to observe:

 • His former goodness (6:3–5) Yahweh has been active in the salvation-history of his people.
 • His present demands (6:6–8) The prophet here expounds a familiar prophetic theme: God is not at all interested in the multiplication of their sacrifices if their heart is not right before him. This subject recurs throughout the Hebrew prophetic tradition (compare Isa. 1:11–16; Jer. 14:12; Amos 5:21–27). The refer-

ence in 6:7b has led many scholars to suggest that Micah's prophetic ministry went on into the evil reign of Hezekiah's son, Manasseh, with its offering of human sacrifices (compare 2 Kings 21:6; Jer. 7:31). God does not want this sort of sacrifice; he longs for justice, mercy and humility (6:8)—mercy is *hesed,* the word we noted particularly in *Hosea.* What is the use of making elaborate sacrifices when these are presented by thieving hands (6:10–11); or of offering high-sounding prayers with deceitful lips (6:12–13)? The Lord demands sincerity.

- His future plans (7) Judah's doom is vividly portrayed, as if it had actually happened. This is a favorite prophetic device (see Jer. 6:1–5; 14:1–6). Notice how acutely they fear the reproach of the heathen (7:8–10; compare Obad. 12). But although Yahweh's purpose is to purify and refine them through the painful experience of exilic-judgment, they retain their belief in him as:

- the God who answers their prayers (7:7)
- the God who illumines their darkness (7:8–9)
- the God who directs their steps (7:14–15)
- the God who pardons their sins (7:18–19).

Do we have such a lofty view of God when things are against us? Or is he a "fair-weather God" only?

Nahum

onah delivered his message to the people of Nineveh, Assyria's capital. NAHUM'S message is also addressed to the Ninevites, and, like Jonah, his theme is judgment. But there the similarity ends. For Nahum, who came after Jonah, the opportunity for repentance is over and the Assyrians must face the consequences of their sins and evils. The date is probably around 625 BC. Their last leading ruler, Ashurbanipal, died in 626. The Babylonians and the Medes joined forces to conquer Assyria, and Nineveh fell in 612.

The word of the prophet here seems harsh and pitiless, but one must remember the agony caused throughout the near-eastern world by the Assyrian invaders. They have been described as "the most brutal empire which was ever suffered to roll its forces across the world." The book is about the utter justice of God, and, as such, it has an *essential* place in the Bible. Men must be reminded not only of the goodness, but also of the severity of God (Rom. 2:1–4; 11:22).

The message of *Nahum* can be simply analyzed, and the book can be viewed almost as a Court scene. First, we have a portrait of the One who judges in Court: God. This is followed by a declaration of the sentence, and a final chapter outlines the reason for such a heavy sentence.

1. CHAPTER 1:1–15
NINEVEH'S JUDGE

The opening chapter compels the Assyrians to look at Yahweh, the Judge. They have repeatedly ignored his warnings and they have ruthlessly persecuted his people. Now he reveals himself to them. It is a magnificent portrait of God. We see:

a. HIS JEALOUSY (1:2–3) This word often baffles us. Remember "that when God is described as jealous (Exod. 20:5; 34:14; Deut. 4:24; 5.9; 6:15), it is his demand for the exclusive worship of his people that is in mind. When he is jealous for his land or for Jerusalem (Joel 2:18; Zech. 1:14), he is concerned for their honor and inviolability" (H. H. Rowley, *Dictionary of Bible Themes*). Here Nahum insists that God is deeply concerned for the honor of his name (the heathen would regard the Assyrian domination of Israel as a sign of Yahweh's impotence), and for the welfare of his people.

b. HIS MAJESTY (1:3b–6) Here is one of the Bible's superb pictures of God revealing his majesty in nature. These portraits are often found in psalmody (e.g., Ps. 89; 93; 97; 104) and in prophecy (Isa. 19; 10:2–8; Amos 9:5–6; Mic. 1:2–4). The prophets had a huge conception of God. Is our God too small?

c. HIS RELIABILITY (1:7) Yet this same God is a refuge to his people. His goodness and strength never fail ("stronghold," RSV, means "a fortified place"), and his compassion never wavers. "In times of trouble" he feels for us, for "he *knows* those who take refuge in him." He is a God who both establishes and enjoys a personal relationship with his people.

d. HIS EQUITY (1:8–14). The God who is a refuge to his people, will break down the fortifications of those who think they are stronger than he is. The Assyrians tried to use their wisdom against him and his people: what folly (9)! Their strength will count for nothing when God attacks them (12). Their international supremacy and religious pride will be utterly broken.

e. HIS SOVEREIGNTY (1:12–13) Nahum recognizes that God has used the Assyrians for the chastisement of his people: "though I [not they] have afflicted you." Isaiah knew that the Assyrians were "the rod of my [God's] anger" (Isa. 10:5). These nations were all in his hands. The Babylonians were to overthrow Nineveh, but they in turn would be overthrown when God had used them for his refining purposes (Isa. 40:15, 23; Jer. 10:10).

f. HIS MERCY (1:15) There is a picture here of the herald who announces the coming of peace. It is a picture which is found also in Isaiah 40:9. God has heard the sighs of his people. He feels for them in their anguish and his merciful deliverance is at hand.

2. CHAPTER 2:1–12
NINEVEH'S PENALTY

The herald of peace to God's people is quickly followed by the harbinger of war. Here is a vivid account of siege-warfare (1–10).

In verses 11–12 Nineveh's fall is compared to the destruction of a pride of lions: those who bring terror are themselves destroyed. This doom will come upon Nineveh because the Lord is against her (13). God's concern for justice will mean *restoration* (2:2) and *retribution* (2:13).

3. CHAPTER 3:1–4
NINEVEH'S CRIMES

The transgressions of Assyria are noted in this short passage: the judgment is justified. Nahum remembers:

- **THEIR CRUELTY** (3:1) The bloodthirsty Assyrians were noted for their terrifying atrocities. Wherever they went, they were merciless and vicious.

- THEIR LYING (3:1: "full of lies"; compare Prov. 12:22) The word of Assyria was not to be trusted.
- THEIR STEALING (3:1: "all full of booty")—their wealth was built up on robbery and violence.
- THEIR IDOLATRY (3:4)—this is probably what is meant by *harlotry*, the prophets often speak in this way of false gods (compare Ezek. 23:30).
- THEIR IMMORALITY (3:4)—note that the harlot imagery is not merely figurative. The religious ceremonies and commercial transactions of many of these near-eastern nations were marked by wild orgies and corrupt behavior.
- THEIR INSINCERITY (3:4–5: "graceful and of deadly charms," RSV)—Assyria seemed to be dependable, but lured nations to their doom. God will show her as she really is (5) and treat her as she has treated others (6).

4. CHAPTER 3:5–19
NINEVEH'S END

The inevitable collapse of the city is vividly portrayed. Once danger is near their leaders will desert them (3:17–18). Nahum recognizes that all the known world has suffered at Assyrian hands (3:19) but now the Assyrians feel deep anguish at the hands of a just God (Rom. 12:19 is relevant here).

Habakkuk

he book of *Habakkuk* deals with the prophet's difficulties rather than his discourses. He is confronted by an immense problem which has disturbed many people since his day: the frequently intense suffering of the righteous and the apparent prosperity of the wicked. The same theme is found in the psalms (e.g., Ps. 37, 73). The prophet expresses his triumphant faith in a sovereign God, a God he is determined to love and obey, even when things go against him.

The date of the prophecy has been variously assessed by scholars, but it probably belongs to a period just prior to the exile. The background, therefore, could extend from, say, 626–586. If this dating is correct, Habakkuk was a contemporary of Jeremiah.

1. CHAPTER 1
THE PROPHET'S ANGUISH

To this sensitive prophet it seems as though the Babylonian (Chaldean) armies are conquering everywhere, while the people of Judah groan under their tyranny. He asks where God is in all this? Is he in control of the world, or is that just a common religious cliché with no basis in fact? These are the prophet's difficulties.

a. DOES GOD HEAR? (1:2) Prayer seems to be useless. Is it
of any real value at all? Habakkuk is not the only character in the Bible to give expression to this kind of doubt, for
example, there are David (Ps. 13:1–3) and Jeremiah
(14.8).

b. DOES GOD RULE? Habakkuk wonders who is in charge
of the world. God speaks and assures him that *he* is "rous-
ing the Chaldeans" (1:6, RSV). He is the Power behind all
national strength and military prowess (1:11: "whose own
strength is their god").

c. DOES GOD CARE? 1:12–17 marks a transition. God has
been speaking (1:5–11) and now the prophet expresses his
concern and bewilderment. Once again he is distressed
about God's apparent silence and seeming indifference
(1:13). The prophet wonders whether God is as troubled
about all this injustice and ruthless oppression as he is!

2. CHAPTER 2
THE PROPHET'S ANSWER

The vivid prophetic imagery of the *watchman* (2:1) features
here, as in *Ezekiel* during the exilic period (compare Ezekiel
3:17–21; 33:1–9; see also Isa. 21:8). The word comes from
God and the prophet is instructed to declare it plainly and urgently (2:2). The message is about:

a. RESPONSIBILITY (2:4–5) The key verse is 2:4: "The
righteous will live by his faith" (or "faithfulness," see NIV
margin). H. L. Ellison notes that "the Hebrew in his con-
crete thinking did not speak of faith, but of *faithfulness* toward God, and this in turn implied *faith,* i.e. trust—where
faith in God does not lead to faithfulness it is vain. The
promise through Habakkuk is that the man who shows his
trust in God by his faithfulness to God will find God faithful in keeping him" *(Men spake from God).* This saying is
later to assume great importance in Christian thought (see
Rom. 1:17; Gal. 3:11). Initially this word pointed a con-

trast between the heathen (so "puffed up," 2:4a; compare 1:11; 2:5) who seemed to prosper but were doomed to destruction, and the godly, who would live because of their reliance upon an ever faithful God (2:4).

b. ACCOUNTABILITY (2:6–20) God has declared what man must do if he is to "live"; now he announces what happens to those who are not faithful to him. Five woes are pronounced upon the enemies of God's people:

- upon the greedy (2:6–8)
- upon the selfish (2:9–11)
- upon the cruel (2:12–14)
- upon the corrupt (2:15–17)
- upon the godless (2:18–20)

Such people are accountable to God himself. Habakkuk's message is of a God who is *faithful* (2:3–4), *just* (2:8, 16), *living* (2:18–19) and *sovereign* (2:20).

3. CHAPTER 3
THE PROPHET'S AFFIRMATION

The closing chapter is a triumphant psalm. It is another prophetic picture of *God on the march* (compare Mic. 1:3–4). Habakkuk has confidence in:

a. THE GOD OF NATURE (3:2–6) The created world is in his hand. He measures the earth (3:6, RSV). Mountains and seas are part of his dominion.

b. THE GOD OF HISTORY (3:7–15) The scene changes from the created world to the populated world, to nations, empires and thrones. God's control over the forces of nature was demonstrated at the Red Sea and the victories of his people indicate his power in plotting their destiny (see especially 3:12–15).

c. THE GOD OF EXPERIENCE (3:16–19) This God who rules the world in majesty and might is concerned about individuals as well as empires. The prophet fears that even greater troubles may come to him later (3:16), but he firmly resolves that whatever the adversity he will trust and rejoice (3:17–18). Habakkuk does not believe in God just for what he receives from him. Whatever the nature of the trouble, the prophet believes that man must *rejoice* (3:18) and *rely* (3:19): God is his strength and will enable him to endure and conquer.

Zephaniah

he prophecy of ZEPHANIAH is precisely dated in 1:1. It belongs to the reign of JOSIAH, and Zephaniah's preaching may have played a significant part in initiating Josiah's desire for a national reformation. 1:4–9 may well be a summary of the prophet's message to the pre-reformation situation; it reflects something of the distressing moral and religious conditions of the preceding reign of MANASSEH. During that reign prophecy had been silenced; Manasseh preferred wizards (2 Kings 21:6). Zephaniah was probably the first prophet to break that silence with a clear, direct word from God.

1. CHAPTERS 1:1–2:3
JUDAH'S SINS

The sins are those of Jerusalem, the capital city. The prophet is well acquainted with its streets and markets. George Adam Smith said, "In the first few verses of Zephaniah we see almost as much of Jerusalem as in the whole book either of Isaiah or Jeremiah."

Notice how seriously Zephaniah regards the sins of the citizens:

a. THEY DO NOT HONOR GOD'S NAME (1:4–5) God is a jealous God; he will not tolerate "mixed" worship. The citizens tried to compromise by worshipping false gods alongside Yahweh. This clearly recalls Exodus 20:3–4 (compare 2 Kings 21:3–4 and especially 2 Kings 23:5, 12; Matt. 6:24).

b. THEY DO NOT SEEK GOD'S FACE (1:6) One of the most disastrous of their sins is prayerlessness. They do not bother to seek God. Are we guiltless in this respect?

c. THEY DO NOT OBEY GOD'S WORD (1:9) God had clearly declared that they should not do these things: their sins are sins of *cruelty* ("Violence," 1:9), and *covetousness* (1:11), a craving for things, instead of love for people. This was in complete disregard of the Law of God given through Moses (Exod. 20:17; Deut. 15:7–11).

d. THEY DO NOT ACKNOWLEDGE GOD'S RULE (1:12) There are those who suggest that God is not concerned about all this sinful behavior.

Zephaniah's word to this tragic situation is clearly one of *warning*. He tells his fellow citizens of the coming *Day of the Lord* and as he develops this impressive, majestic theme he makes careful mention of three great things about that Day. It is a day when:

- God searches (1:12)—nothing is hidden from him. This is a familiar theme in prophecy (Jer. 16:16–17; Ezek. 9:4–11; Amos 9:1–3; compare Ps. 7:9; 26:2; 139:1–16; Prov. 17:3).
- God judges (1:13–18)—the judgment is near (1:14) and inescapable. No amount of wealth will be able to purchase protection (1:18).
- God pardons (2:3)—for some that day will hold no terrors; those who have sought him in repentance will be hidden by God himself.

2. CHAPTER 2:4–15
JUDAH'S NEIGHBORS

The prophets were not locked up in a limited conception of a merely tribal, local or national God. That is why they could not tolerate idolatry. They knew that these idols were meaningless and empty. There was only God, and he ruled over the entire universe and shaped the destiny even of those who did not believe in him. This second main passage in the book turns to the sins of Judah's neighbors over whom God rules. Dr. Graham Scroggie notes that the prophet points to nations in the *West* (Philistia, 2:4–7); *East* (Moab and Ammon, 2:8–11); *South* (Ethiopia, 2:12); and *North* (Assyria, 2:13–15). Possibly these are chosen to illustrate the *universal* rule of God.

3. CHAPTER 3:1–7
JUDAH'S LEADERS

Here attention turns from the godless nations to the unspiritual leaders in Judah itself. The city of Jerusalem is probably in the prophet's mind here (3:1) even though it is not mentioned by name.

- The city is rebellious (sin against God)
- The city is defiled (sin against their better selves)
- The city is oppressive (sin against others)

This is a further picture of their self-reliance, unbelief and prayerlessness (3:2; see 2:4–6).

In this section different groups of citizens are brought before God for judgment: officials, judges, prophets and priests. The language and ideas are similar to Jeremiah, Zephaniah's contemporary (see Jer. 6:13–14; 8:8–12). Zephaniah is astonished that the people of Jerusalem can go on sinning in the light of:

a. GOD'S HOLY PRESENCE (3:5: "The Lord within her is righteous") How can the people be so evil when the Temple constantly reminds them of his holiness and righteousness amongst them?

b. GOD'S UNFAILING MERCY (3:5b: "Morning by morning he dispenses his justice") Even though they sin he goes on revealing his just concern and his generous goodness (compare Matt. 5:45–47).

c. GOD'S FORMER DELIVERANCES (3:6–7) In times of invasion, God has helped them and given them victory: yet they will not turn to him (3:7).

4. CHAPTER 3:8–20
JUDAH'S HOPE

Here is Zephaniah's teaching about a righteous *remnant*. In the future God will clearly separate those who truly believe in him from those who merely mention his name. The prophet discerns a number of things about that day of restoration and blessing. He asserts that:

a. GOD'S PEOPLE MUST BE PATIENT (3:8: "wait for me"; compare Hab. 2:3). To the righteous, the ultimate deliverance seems a long time in coming but true believers must learn to wait for God's time.

b. GOD'S PEOPLE WILL BE MULTIPLIED (3:9–10). There is a real missionary note here.

c. GOD'S PEOPLE WILL BE PURIFIED (3:11–13) The arrogant will be removed and the lowly will be left.

d. GOD'S PEOPLE CAN BE JOYFUL (3:14) The sighs of the vanquished will be changed to the songs of the victor.

e. GOD'S PEOPLE MAY BE CONFIDENT (3:15–17) He is in the midst to deliver them (17), renew them (17, RSV), and transform them (19). These promises may still be appropriated by true believers.

Haggai

I n our study of the last three books of the Old Testament we move on to the post-exilic period. Some of the exiled Jews have returned to the city of Jerusalem and the first task is to rebuild the Temple, burned down by the soldiers of Neb-uchadnezzar. This reconstructed Temple will be an outward symbol of the people's devotion to God and their determination to put him first. But that was not as easy as it sounds. The returned people think first about themselves and their own material interests. They spend their time earning and saving, not serving and worshipping.

Two prophets are called by God to meet this situation—HAGGAI and ZECHARIAH (compare Ezra 6:14). Although contemporaries, these two men have vastly different ways of presenting the same message. Haggai delivers his message in down-to-earth, matter-of-fact prose; Zechariah is a, possibly youthful (Zech. 2:4), visionary and the truth is conveyed by means of vivid word-pictures and symbolic scenes. God is not confined to one type of ministry and approach; all are his (see 1 Cor. 3:21).

The divisions in *Haggai* are given for us by the prophet himself. He dates each prophecy precisely; the record of the ministry only extends to a brief period of about three months. The four "addresses" cover four distinct but closely related themes:

1. CHAPTER 1:1–15
THE PRESENT TASK

The majority of the people believe that the Temple ought to be rebuilt, but "not yet" (1:2). "Some time" is a phrase which wrecks many ambitious plans and enterprises. We think something ought to be done, but we push it away into the distant future. Haggai says, "No! 'Some time' will not do; we must build *now*." The building program is an immediate opportunity for the people to show how much God matters in their lives. Nebuchadnezzar had burned the Temple (2 Kings 25:9), so it is possible that much of the essential stonework remained; Haggai stresses the need for timber (1:4, 8).

The prophet clearly asserts that when we honor God—by putting him first—everything else will fall into its rightful place (1 Sam. 2:30; Matt. 6:33). If we ignore this divine precept, then nothing will bring satisfaction (1:6, 9–10; compare Deut. 28:15, 38). Notice the changed situation within the chapter. God's word does alter lives, attitudes, and circumstances. At the beginning of the chapter:

- they ignore God (1:3–4); then:
- they hear God ("thus says the Lord of hosts": 2, 5, 7, 9, 13); then:
- they obey God (12); finally:
- they reverence God (12).

2. CHAPTER 2:1–9
THE FORMER GLORIES

After a few weeks the workers become despondent. Some remember, or have heard about, the old Temple and their work seems nothing by comparison. Solomon's Temple took over seven years to build (1 Kings 6:37–38); they have only been working seven weeks (at the most!). The depressives in the team become vocal (2:3 reflects their despondent attitude). But God's word comes to them again in clear, practical terms: "Don't fret, I am with you. Don't waste your time by rehearsing the wonders of the past: believe in the greater glories of the future" (4–5, 6–9).

Do we ever sin in this way? A fascination with the past can be a means of escaping the grim realities of the present. Some people are always talking about their former experiences. But what is God doing for you *now?* Some sense of history is both necessary and profitable (for example, see Ps. 44:1–2) but a constant preoccupation with the past is almost a sickness (see Phil. 3:12–14).

3. CHAPTER 2:10–19
THE CONSTANT NEED

God does not only demand that we serve him (1:1–15) but that *our service be unspoiled by sin.* This is the theme of Haggai's third address to the people. Holiness is always essential. Some people are working on the building assignment with impure motives, grudging spirits and resentful attitudes. Priestly imagery is used to illustrate this truth: they are, after all, laboring on the Temple site (2:11–14). They have expressed some devotion to God by the outward building program, but God is looking into their sinful hearts. Haggai's colleague, Zechariah, gives expression to a similar truth at this time (Zech. 1:2–6).

Do we mar our service to God by secret sins and unconfessed transgression (Ps. 19:12–14)? It is far easier to be a sinner than to be a saint, and Haggai emphasizes how immediately contagious sin is. Possibly there are corrupt workers on the Temple site, who, by their own low standards, are spreading evil, bringing great grief to God. The Lord tells them that as they offer purified service, he will bless them with all their material necessities (2:16–19).

4. Chapter 2:20–23
THE FUTURE PLAN

Haggai does not have as much to say about the future as Zechariah, but in this final address he does look to the future, and his word is addressed to the man who has been the main drive behind the rebuilding program: Zerubbabel (2:21; see Ezra 5). Note that Zerubbabel's leadership might have involved him in difficulties with King Darius. Haggai's promise to Zerubbabel from God is that the Lord will protect him. The final lesson to the leader is the lesson God brings to all of us: put God first, and all other things will work out right.

Zechariah

aggai's contemporary declares similar truths but uses other arresting thought forms and a different method of presentation. The post-exilic community has to be awakened not only to an outward indication of their loyalty to God (rebuilding the Temple), but to a purified life within. Both Haggai and ZECHARIAH are concerned about the *immediate needs* of God's people but Zechariah places a greater emphasis on the *ultimate destiny* of God's people. There are passages here which are not easy to interpret because they make vivid use of symbolic language, but the book has some great truths to present to us.

1. CHAPTERS 1–6
VISIONS ABOUT VICTORY

Although the prophet has an optimistic view of God's kingdom, he constantly urges the people to realize the seriousness of sin as a *delaying factor* as well as a degrading factor in history. "The day of Jehovah, which will bring the promised triumph, may be delayed by Judah's sin; so the visions and oracles of Zechariah are interspersed with stern warning, but the predominant note is promise" (J. I. Brice, *The Book Supreme*). This first main section opens with a *Plea*

(1:1–6) and closes with a *Promise* (6:9–15). Within this section there are eight visions. These are:

a. THE VICTORIOUS RIDER (1:7–17) God knows of his people's former distresses and he is among them as their protector.

b. THE FOUR HORNS (1:18–21) "Horn" is a symbol of strength and aggression. God will destroy these hostile powers from the four corners of the world.

c. THE MEASURING LINE (2) God's plans for his people completely exceed their expectations.

d. THE UNCLEAN PRIEST (3) The iniquity of the people which must be removed if they are to serve God acceptably.

e. THE LAMPSTAND AND THE TREES Man is absolutely dependent on the Holy Spirit.

f. THE SCROLL AND THE OFFENDERS (5:1–4) Judgment is inevitable.

g. THE WOMAN AND THE BUSHEL (5:5–11) Sin must be entirely removed from the land.

h. THE CHARIOTS AND THE MOUNTAINS (6:1–8) God is sovereign over the entire world, as the first vision. "The mountains of brass" (6:1, RSV) were interpreted by Calvin as "the providence of God or his hidden counsel . . . they cannot be broken."

In the closing promise Zerubbabel is to be honored for his leadership; he is regarded as the foreshadowing of the Messiah.

2. CHAPTERS 7–8
FACTS ABOUT FASTS

The inquiry, "Ought certain fasts to be maintained?" is here answered in four statements:

a. Examine what is meant by fasting (7:4–7).

b. Remember that God looks for righteous living rather than ceremonial observances (7:8–14).

c. God presents his people with a picture of a future bright with promise (8:1–8).

d. In this glorious future, fasts will be changed to feasts of joy and Jerusalem will be the missionary center of the world (8:8–23).

3. CHAPTERS 9–14
DISCOURSES ABOUT DESTINY

The closing section of the book is not easy to analyze. Our attention is turned to the future and Israel's destiny is the central theme. H. L. Ellison rightly reminds us that ". . . these chapters are apocalyptic and, as is usual in such prophecies, the general drift is clear enough but detailed interpretation is impossible—he who thinks otherwise should learn humility from those as good as he who have interpreted them otherwise" *(Men spake from God)*. There are three main divisions:

a. THE COMING OF THE KING (9–10) The passage announces the arrival of a peaceful King (9:9–10); the nation will no longer be under heathen domination (9:11–17) though God in his sovereignty, will raise up heathen rulers and use them for his purpose in restoring Israel to their land (10:3ff).

b. THE REJECTION OF THE SHEPHERD (11) The imagery changes here from king to shepherd, though remember that the term "shepherd" meant any ruler or leader. This reliable Shepherd assumes full responsibility for the care and protection of the flock and his concern for them is expressed symbolically in the *two staves* (11:7–9, RSV): "Beauty," or more correctly, "Grace," and "Bands" (that is, bound together, "Union," NIV). But his ministry is not valued (11:8) and the people return his kindness with enmity. The low view they have of him is further symbolized as they pay him the price of a slave (11:12–13; see Exod. 21:32).

c. THE DELIVERANCE OF THE PEOPLE (12–14) The final chapters turn our gaze from the Leader (King and Shepherd) to the people. Four clearly defined themes are expounded:

- CONQUEST (12:1–9) The nations around about Judah gather together to besiege the city but they are frustrated by God. Jerusalem is as safe as a very heavy stone, deeply embedded in the soil, which tears the hands of those that seek to remove it (12:3).
- CONTRITION (12:10–14) "They will look on *me.*" The Lord God is the speaker. The Jews pierced him metaphorically by their rebellion and ingratitude, then literally in the crowning act of rebellion, Christ on the cross (see John 19:37; Rev. 1:7).
- CLEANSING (13:1–9) Repentance (12:10–14) is followed by pardon (13:1–2). There is a fascinating reference to prophetism in 13:2–6: prophetism became degraded in this period. Note the return here to the earlier prophets like Amos who refused to call himself a prophet (compare 13:4–5 with Amos 7:14).
- CONSUMMATION (14:1–21) The Lord appears as the Great Deliverer of his people and, in that day, holiness will be evident not merely in the Temple or among spiritual leaders but in every sphere of life: everything and everybody will belong to God (14:20–21).

Malachi

he name MALACHI means "my messenger" (see 3:1). Possibly it is a pen name which the writer gave to himself because he did not wish to draw attention to himself, but only to his message. This final book of the Old Testament belongs to the post-exilic era. The Temple has been rebuilt and the sacrificial system is in operation, but the spiritual life of the nation is terribly low and depressing. "Malachi" is called by God to confront the spiritually indifferent masses with the clear challenge of God's demands. God does not change (3:6) but *they* have certainly changed (1:6–8). The book can be divided into three unequal parts.

1. CHAPTER 1:1–5
A NATION WHICH HAS FORGOTTEN GOD'S LOVE

The opening of the book is extremely important. It sets the scene for all that follows. The prophet expounds the immense theme of God's *electing love*. Possibly the returned community is discouraged. They may have imagined that once the Temple was rebuilt everything would go wonderfully well with them. This kind of optimism may have been the result of some of the things said by Haggai and Zechariah. The people may have looked for the immediate fulfillment of sayings like Haggai 2:6–9; 2:21–23; Zech. 2:11–13; 8:22–23; 12:1–5; 14:20–21. Ellison says, "In the difficulties of the post-exilic community, which were so contrary to the high hopes with which they had returned, and which had decreased but little after the rebuilding of the Temple, in spite of the glowing promises of Haggai and Zechariah, it was easy to doubt the love of God" (*Men spake from God*). "Malachi" urges them to see from the start that God does love them deeply and intensely and that love can be proved by:

a. THEIR ELECTION: God chose them (1:2–3). This is the greatest proof of his love for them as a people. The election love of God is a major theme in the Old Testament, and this clear note, sounded at the beginning of the eighth century prophetic movement by Amos (3:2), continues through to Malachi. Although God owned everything, yet he chose his people because he loved them so much (Deut. 10:14–15)—and his people's gratitude for his love ought to be expressed in their love for others (Deut. 10:17–19). His love was not deserved or merited. It was due neither to their goodness (Deut. 9:4–6) or greatness (Deut. 7:7–8) but just because he loved them. The Old Testament writers sometimes say God acted in a certain way "for his name's sake" (2 Kings 19:34; Isa. 48:9; Jer. 14:7, 21, etc.)—they mean "according to his nature," that is, because "that is what he is like." God's love is like that.

b. THEIR PROTECTION God had further revealed his love in saving them from *their* enemies. Esau (Edom) "I hated," means "I did not set my love on them" (1:3–4). As we have seen in our earlier studies, Edom constantly tried to oppress the people of God (Ps. 137:7; Isa. 63:1–6; Ezek. 25:12, 14; Obad. 8–19). God can protect them in his love because he rules over the whole earth (1:5: "Great is the Lord—even beyond the borders of Israel!"); he expresses his love by his sovereign control over them (see 1:11, 14).

2. CHAPTERS 1:6–3:15
A PRIESTHOOD WHICH IGNORES GOD'S LAWS

God loves the nation, but the people do not love him in return. Their lack of loving response is given its most pathetic expression in the poor offerings which they present to him. God is the disappointed Father (1:6), and his disappointment is due to the failure of the religious leaders to set a rich and noble example of loving obedience to him. Three main themes emerge in this section:

a. GOD'S GRIEVANCE "Malachi" mentions the failure of *the priests.* God is sad about:

- their unacceptable offerings (1:7–8, 12, 14; 3:8–9).
- their unloving service (1:13: "What a weariness is it!," RSV). There is no love for God in their meaningless ritual.
- their unfaithful teaching (2:8–9, 17; 3:13–14). They have not faithfully and accurately expounded God's law.
- their ungodly behavior (2:13–16). God treasures the marriage bond, yet both priests and people are ignoring its serious responsibilities and loving demands. Doubtless people other than priests were guilty of this breakdown in home and family life, but the priests were the pastors in Israel (see 2:5–7), and they should have disciplined offenders while being at the same time a good example to others.

b. GOD'S PATTERN The passage in 2:5–9 portrays the *ideal* priest. This is how God intended him to be. Note the priorities: worship, holiness, pastoral concern, evangelism, fellowship. These verses ought to be uppermost in our minds when we talk about "the priesthood of all believers."

c. GOD'S REMEDY God is going to send one who will be used to put all these things right (3:1, see Mark 1:2). Chapter 3:1–12 foretells a time of purifying judgment: the priesthood will be cleansed (3:3–4), offenders will be punished (3:5) and the backsliders will return (3:6–7).

3. CHAPTERS 3:16–4.6
A REMNANT WHICH HONORS GOD'S NAME

Although God has ever been grieved by those who have deliberately disobeyed him (3:7), he has always rejoiced in the faithfulness of a minority: the Remnant. These people are always distinguished by their deep reverence (3:16; 4:2): reverence is a major theme in this book (see 1:6, 14; 2:2, 5).

Malachi ends by pointing the reader to two great figures, Moses and Elijah (4:4–6). Possibly we are intended to look back to Moses (the giver of the law) and forward to Elijah (John the Baptist, Matt. 11:13–14), the exponent of "inner" religion and moral faithfulness. A great prophet was to appear in John the Baptist (Luke 7:28), but the greatest Prophet would follow (see Deut. 18:15; John 1:21, 25; Acts 3:22–23).

Matthew

he Gospels present us with four portraits of Christ, the one who is himself the good news:

- MATTHEW—Christ the King
- MARK—Christ the Servant
- LUKE—Christ the Man
- JOHN—Christ the Son of God, emphasizing his unique deity and essential humanity.

In about 130 AD Papias, the Bishop of Hierapolis, wrote that he had received from John the Elder that: "Matthew composed the oracles in the Hebrew tongue and everyone translated them as he was able." It is likely that the sayings and teachings of Jesus which had been collected together by Matthew were then incorporated into our present Gospel either by Matthew himself or by another early Christian. Certainly written accounts of Jesus' life were drawn upon when *Matthew* was compiled, for almost the whole of *Mark* is in *Matthew*, and in the same order.

Like the other "evangelists," Matthew has special themes which are of particular interest to himself:

a. THE JEWS He wants to convince Jewish readers that Christ is their true King and Messiah (2:2). The Gospel genealogy begins with Abraham, father of the Jewish race, whereas Luke begins with Adam. (See also, 10:5–6 and the emphasis on the failure of the Pharisees in 23:1–39.)

b. THE SCRIPTURES Matthew is concerned to explain that Christ's coming fulfills Old Testament prophecies (see 2:15, 17, 23; 3:3; 4:14; 8:17; 12:17; 13:35; 21:4; 22:31; 24:15; 27:9; sometimes called "Testimonies"). Some commentators have noted that Matthew has *five discourses* (5:1–7:29; 10:5–42; 13:1–52; 18:1–35; 24:1–25:46), just as the Pentateuch, or "book of the law" (the first section of the threefold Jewish canon) has five books (Genesis, Exodus, Leviticus, Numbers, Deuteronomy). Matthew's choice of *five* may not be accidental if he wrote for Jews.

c. THE CHURCH More is said here about the *believing community* than in any other Gospel (see the teaching in passages like 18:1–35, and particularly 16:18; 18:17; 28:18–20).

d. THE FUTURE We see this especially in the parables of the kingdom (chapter 13) and the teaching on Christ's return in chapters 24–25 and 26:64.

Our main interest focuses on Matthew's exposition of the kingship of Christ.

1. CHAPTERS 1–4
THE KING'S ADVENT

Right at the beginning some wise men ask: "Where is the king?" (2:2), but the king they have come to worship is quickly opposed by a godless king (2:8, 16–18). The King's herald (John the Baptist) prepares the way for Christ's coming (chapter 3), and the devil does his utmost to destroy the King by offering the kingdoms of the world (4:1–11). The King begins his earthly ministry by urging the people to repent because "the *kingdom* of heaven is near" (4:17) and, after calling his disciples (4:18–22), preaches "the good news of the *kingdom*" (4:23), proving his kingly power by miraculous signs.

2. CHAPTERS 5–7
THE KING'S DEMANDS

The famous "Sermon on the Mount" focuses the attention of Christ's disciples on the *royal law* of love, and reminds us of the Christian's:

  a. happiness (5:3–12)
  b. witness (5:13–16)
  c. holiness (5:17–37)
  d. compassion (5:38–48)
  e. generosity (6:1–4)
  f. prayerfulness (6:5–15)
  g. sincerity (6:16–18)
  h. priority (6:19–24)
  i. trust (6:25–34)
  j. sensitivity (7:1–6)
  k. faith (7:7–12)
  l. commitment (7:13–20)
  m. obedience (7:21–29)

No believer can afford to neglect or minimize these themes, least of all to make them marginal by relegating them to some future date, calling them rules or regulations for Christ's future reign; this is to use an artificial interpretive device to escape the word of God's *present* spiritual demand.

3. CHAPTERS 8–9
THE KING'S POWER

The Lord Jesus was not merely a teacher, his *deeds* revealed his power and confirmed his unique authority. Christ's healing miracles do not follow an identical pattern. There is no rigidly defined formula. He deals with us all in different ways. The leper made his own request (8:2), the centurion spoke on behalf of someone else (8:6–13, and see also 9:2) and Peter's mother-in-law was healed without a request from anyone (8:15). The Lord works as he wills (Ps. 115:3; 135:5–6). The miracle stories in these two chapters illustrate his compassion as well as his power both for individuals and crowds (9:36).

4. CHAPTERS 10–17
THE KING'S TEACHING

Here is a detailed account of Christ's teaching ministry to his people. Chapter 10 contains a record of his teaching to his disciples (see 11:1) and this is followed by his teaching about:

a. John the Baptist (11:7–19)
b. judgment (11:20–24)
c. rest for the humble (11:25–30)
d. the Sabbath (12:1–14)
e. blasphemy against the Holy Spirit (12:24–32)
f. careless talk (12:33–37)
g. signs (12:38–42)
h. the kingdom (13:1–52)
i. purity (15:1–20)
j. Messiahship (16:13–20)
k. suffering (16:21–23)
l. discipleship (16:24–28)
m. faith (17:14–21)

He taught not only in word but by signs (for example, 14:13–21, 35–36; 15:21–39; 17:1–9).

5. CHAPTERS 18–23
THE KING'S SUBJECTS

The shadow of the cross has already fallen across the earlier chapters (17:12, 22–23) but Christ now prepares his men for the future by giving them clear instructions about the new community that he is to form. This next group of chapters expounds what is expected of a Christian, not only in his personal life but within the fellowship of his Church (18:17). There is much here about our spiritual responsibility to others (18:5–6) and the need for personal discipline (18:7–14). Christ expects the members of his Church:

- to correct one another (18:15–18)
- to pray for one another (18:19–20)
- to forgive one another (18:21–35)

He expects his subjects to have high standards (chapter 19) yet they must realize that their acceptance is all of grace (chapter 20). They must be challenged by Christ's humility (21:1–11, see 20:20–28) and his sacrifice (21:33–42), but once again the message of grace is clear (chapter 22). It is not by merit that men enter the kingdom (chapter 23). All the works of the Pharisees, done in order to impress men, will not impress God.

6. CHAPTERS 24–25
THE KING'S RETURN

The previous section closed on a note of sorrow and rejection (23:37–39) but these two chapters expound some aspects of his triumphant return. Jesus is coming again. The facts are declared in chapter 24, and three practical implications are mentioned in chapter 25:

- watchfulness (25:1–13)
- service (25:14–30)
- compassion (25:31–46)

7. CHAPTERS 26–28
THE KING'S VICTORY

The final chapters open and close with moving stories of the devotion and eager service of grateful women (26:6–13; 28:1). They stand in sharp contrast to the greed, cruelty and suspicion of those who are merely religious, like Caiaphas and his colleagues (26:3–5), Judas (26:14–16) and the frustrated priests (28:11–15). To trust in Christ's redemptive work is to respond to his evangelistic commission (28:18–20). Those who obey his word enjoy his presence (28:20).

Mark

he stories and teaching of Jesus became well known throughout the early Church long before they were committed to writing. There is little doubt that Mark's Gospel was the first to be written, probably about thirty years after the ascension of Christ, about 65–67AD. Papias recorded a tradition about it: "Mark, who became the interpreter of Peter, wrote accurately as far as he remembered the things said and done by the Lord, but not in order." A. M. Hunter describes the Gospel as "The reminiscences of Jesus as told by Peter to his friend John Mark." Notice that Peter is hardly mentioned except in terms of rebuke or disgrace (see 8:29–33; 14:29–30, 37, 66–72). Peter must have repeated the details of these episodes but when the Gospel was written his shame had been overshadowed by the glory of his subsequent ministry and martyrdom (John 21:18–19).

Mark has many attractive characteristics, for example, the vivid attention to detail (compare 5:1–20 and 9:14–29 with the accounts given in Matthew and Luke). It is a breathtaking account of Christ's life: notice the recurrent "immediately" and "straightaway." The humanity of the Lord is portrayed throughout: see the references to Christ's anger (3:5); his astonishment at the unbelief of the citizens of Nazareth (6:6); his amazement and fear in Gethsemane (14:33–40); his limited knowledge about the End (13:32).

In this study we use *Mark* 10:45 as our key verse, looking at the Gospel's portraiture of Christ as the *servant*. The "ransom saying" (10:45) has echoes of the Suffering Servant of Isaiah (see Isa. 53:11, 12) and it may not be fanciful to see echoes of the Servant Songs of Isaiah throughout the five sections of this Gospel.

1. CHAPTERS 1–5
A MINISTRY OF UNFAILING MERCY

The introductory section relates how the Servant-Messiah is:

- welcomed by the herald (1:1–8)
- acknowledged by the Father (1:9–11)
- tested by the enemy (1:12–13)

In subsequent narratives:

- he announces his message (1:14–15)
- he chooses his friends (1:16–20)
- he proves his authority (1:21–34)
- he shares his secret (1:35–39)
- he reveals his compassion (1:40–2:5)
- he encounters his opponents (2:6–3:35)
- he instructs his followers (4:1–34)
- he demonstrates his power (4:35–5:43)

These chapters portray one who possesses all the compassionate qualities and gracious attributes of the *gentle Servant* of Isaiah's first servant-song (Isa. 42:1–4, note especially Mark 1:11 and Isa. 42:1).

2. CHAPTERS 6:1–8:30
A MINISTRY OF WIDENING INFLUENCE

These chapters can be read against the background of the *missionary Servant* of Isaiah 49:1–6 (the second servant-song) which predicted one who would "bring back" his people and extend the knowledge of God to "the ends of the earth" (49:5–6).

They begin with the "offense" of his own people at Nazareth (6:1–6), followed by a clear indication of the Servant's missionary zeal. Christ refuses to be daunted by the unbelief of the people in his hometown and sends out his men on a highly successful mission to the villages (6:7–13). We are then reminded that an attempt to present truth exposes the messengers to the opposition both of godless unbelievers (see 6:14–29) and of religious traditionalists (7:1–23).

The missionary emphasis reaches a climax with the cry for help from the Syrophoenician woman (7:24–30). It is the first stage of a movement which will take this good news to "the ends of the earth" (see Isa. 49:6). In Mark the story is immediately followed by a brief account of a further missionary tour through Gentile territory, the cities of the Decapolis (7:31–37).

Readers are men reminded that Jesus fed a hungry multitude on more than one occasion (8:1–9, 19–21) and this section concludes with Peter's magnificent testimony to Christ's messiahship (8:27–30).

3. CHAPTERS 8:31–13:37
A MINISTRY OF STEADFAST PURPOSE

Following Peter's confession, Christ tells his men that he must die, but they will not accept the truth. He also makes it plain that his followers must also tread the way of hardship and sacrifice. The main theme of the remaining chapters is the Servant's "steadfast, high intent," and it reflects the teaching of the *determined Servant* of Isaiah 50:4–9, who set his face as a flint, and gave his back to the smiters. It can be divided into four parts:

a. JESUS AND THE DISCIPLES (8:31–9:50) The disciples are baffled about his cross, but are privileged to witness Christ's glory (9:1–13). They are unable to utilize his power (9:14–29); and are slow to apply his teaching about humility (9:30–37), love (38–41) and discipline (42–50).

b. JESUS AND THE INQUIRERS (10:1–52) We see the cynical questioner (10:1–12), the wealthy inquirer (10:17–31), the selfish seekers (10:32–45), and the persistent beggar (10:46–52).

c. JESUS AND THE OPPONENTS (11:1–12:44) We move from seekers to enemies (see especially 11:18, 27–33; 12:12).

d. JESUS AND THE FUTURE (13:1–37) In this famous discourse we read both of the fall of Jerusalem, and the return of Christ.

4. CHAPTERS 14–15
A MINISTRY OF SACRIFICIAL SURRENDER

The Passion story is again introduced by the moving account of the anointing at Bethany (14:3–9), deliberately set alongside the greed of the priests for his blood (14:1–2), and of Judas for their money (14:10–11). But Christ is not without his friends. The unnamed householder is glad to place a room at his disposal (14:12–16)—are we? And the disciples are eager to have fellowship with him (14:17–25).

The rest of the story recalls the *Suffering Servant* of Isaiah 52:13–53:12, despised and rejected of men; even Jesus' followers reject him (14:50–72). But there are those who emerge as bold helpers, for example Simon of Cyrene and Joseph. Like them, we need to "take up the cross" (15:21), openly confess Christ's deity (15:39), and "take courage" (15:42–46, RSV).

5. CHAPTER 16
A MINISTRY OF TRIUMPHANT CONTINUANCE

a. THE GARDEN (16:1–11) Verse 8 (where some versions of Mark finish) indicates two of the Church's greatest problems: silence and fear.

b. THE ROAD (16:12–18) Another weakness—unbelief— is added (see also verse 11).

c. THE ROOM (16:14–18) Christ rebukes their lack of faith and orders them to break this unbelieving and cowardly silence.

d. THE THRONE (19–20) Our Lord is at the right hand of God, victorious, vindicated and enthroned. Because of this we can obey the summons to share with everyone the great message of salvation and life.

Luke

riting for Gentiles, Dr. Luke (Col. 4:14) traces Christ's lineage back to Adam (3:38); one of his aims is to portray the Lord Jesus as the perfect Man. This Gospel is the first part of a two-volume work on the ministry of the victorious Christ, before and after Pentecost (see Luke 1:1–4; Acts 1:1–2). The Man Christ Jesus is for *all* men and the missionary appeal to Gentile readers is never far away (see 2:10, 32; 3:6; 13:29). It is to Gentiles that blessing comes in Old Testament times (4:25–27), and the message of repentance is to be preached "unto all nations" (24:47). We shall summarize Luke's record of Christ's ministry under seven headings:

1. CHAPTERS 1–2
THE UNIQUE CHILD

The virgin birth emphasizes that, although Christ is perfect Man, he is no ordinary man; his entry into this world was of a unique character (1:26–35). The opening chapters give man's response in the form of exultant songs (1:46–55, 67–79; 2:13–14, 28–35). Even as a child, Christ longed to discern more of God's word and will (2:46, 49).

2. CHAPTERS 3–4
THE RESOLUTE MAN

After a detailed account of John's preaching (3:1–20), we read of Christ's baptism (3:21–22). The voice from heaven (3:22) unites two great Old Testament themes: Christ is the messianic Son of Psalm 2:7 and the Suffering Servant of Isaiah 42:1 ("in whom my soul delights," RSV). A genealogy follows (notice, "so it was thought," 3:23) which, as we have seen, goes back to Adam, "the son of God." Then there is another temptation story, set this time not in a delightful garden (Gen. 2:15) but in a bleak wilderness. The devil comes, as at that first temptation, to cast doubts on God's word and authority (Gen. 3:1), but Jesus replies, "It is written" (4:4, 8).

With strong resolution the perfect Man emerges victorious from the conflict only to discover that, although some were glad to hear him (4:22), the unbelieving world is as hostile as the devil himself (4:29–30). But he can silence the cries of the demons (4:32–35), rebuke the fevers of needy men and women (4:38–41), and hear the call of other areas of equally urgent opportunity (4:42–44).

3. CHAPTERS 5–9
THE ATTRACTIVE LEADER

Jesus introduces some disciples to their better work by a miraculous catch of fish which illustrates their uselessness without him and their need for utter reliance upon him (5:1–11). He leads them to

- unclean people like lepers (5:12–16)
- helpless people like paralytics (5:17–26)
- unpopular people like tax collectors (5:27–32)
- unattractive people like Pharisees (5:33–6:11)

The leader prays fervently all night before he chooses his men (6:12–16) and then spends some time teaching them

(6:17–49). They have much to learn not only from his words but also from his deeds. A series of miracles, interviews and parables present them with some immense truths about:

- authority (7:1–10)
- power (7:11–17)
- perception (about John, 7:18–23, and those who opposed him, 7:24–35)
- compassion (7:36–50)
- the message—it grows (8:1–15) and shows (8:16–18)

His friends do his will (8:19–21); his followers receive his peace (8:22–25) and witness his power in the realm of mental (8:26–39) and physical illness (8:40–48), and even death (8:49–56).

The Leader sends out his twelve disciples on a preaching tour (9:1–9), feeds the hungry multitude with food (9:10–17), and gives his intimate group of followers some important teaching about *his cross* (9:18–22) and *their own* (9:23–37). Then three of his disciples witness his transfiguration and see Moses (the Law) and Elijah (the Prophets) talking with Christ about his *exodus* (9:28–36; exodus is a significant word in the light of the tremendous importance of the exodus in Jewish history).

A passage follows which focuses on some of the failings of the disciples; what an honest record this is! They are shown to be ineffective (9:40), unperceptive (9:45), proud (9:46), censorious (9:49) and loveless (9:54). Some would-be disciples make a merely emotional response (9:57–58); others lack a sense of urgency (9:59–60) and resolution (9:61–62).

4. CHAPTERS 10–14
THE DISTURBING TEACHER

This section contains Christ's teaching about:

- MISSION (10:1–20)
- PRIVILEGE (10:21–24)

- LOVE (10:25–37)
- PRIORITIES (10:38–42)
- PRAYER (11:1–13) The Teacher's own example communicates much about prayer, and Luke records numerous details (3:21; 5:16; 6:12; 9:18, 28; 11:1; 22:32, 41; 23:34).
- THE HOLY SPIRIT Luke gives us important and extensive teaching about the Holy Spirit (1:35, 41–67; 2:25–27; 3:16, 22; 4:1, 14; 10:21–24; 11:13; 12:10, 12; 24:49).

In these chapters Christ is portrayed as the strong man (11:21); the one greater than the great king Solomon and Jonah the prophet (11:29–32); the discerner of hearts (11:33–12:3); the Lord who cares for his people in this life (12:4–31) and prepares them for the next (12:32–40). Christ tells his disciples about their stewardship (12:41–48), and illustrates his teaching by reminding them of his own (12:49–50). He urges their repentance (13:1–5) while there is opportunity (13:6–9).

Those who are healed adore God (13:10–13), but those who are challenged murmur (13:14–17; see also 14:1–6). His blessings are for all who respond to his gracious invitation (14:15–17), but the majority do not wish to dine with him, so make lame excuses (14:18–20). Jesus emphasizes the cost of discipleship (14:25–35) as strongly as he emphasizes the loving invitation of free grace.

5. CHAPTERS 15–18
THE COMPASSIONATE FRIEND

T. W. Manson describes this section as "the gospel for the outcast." The *prodigal* is loved by the Father (15:11–24); the *pauper* at the rich man's gate is received into glory (16:19–31), and the only *leper* to offer thanks is a *Samaritan* (17:11–19). It was the *tax-collector* who went home justified (18:9–14; see also 19:1–10). Christ is a friend to all:

the *wealthy ruler* (18:18–30) and the *penniless beggar* (18:35–43).

6. CHAPTERS 19–23
THE REJECTED SON

The work of saving the lost (19:10) was to be costly. Men did not want him (19:14), and though a multitude sing their songs about him (19:37–40), he weeps over them, knowing their blindness and insincerity (19:41–47). Scribes, priests and Sadducees all long to trap him (20:1–47). He foretells the ultimate future (21:5–38) and courageously faces the present (22:1–71). Luke's account of the cross assures the *outcast* of a better future (23:39–43).

7. CHAPTER 24
THE VICTORIOUS LORD

The resurrection narratives vividly illustrate man's unbelief (v. 11), despair (v. 21), ignorance (v. 25), fear (v. 37), doubt (v. 38) and bewilderment (v. 41), but:

- he teaches them (vv. 26–27)
- he encourages them (vv. 39–43)
- he sends them (vv. 47–48)
- he equips them (v. 49)
- he prays for them (vv. 50–53)

Renan calls *Luke* "a book full of joy"; it ends as it began (compare v. 24, 52 with 2:10).

John

ohn's Gospel was the last of the four to be written; its author had access to a considerable amount of material but was highly selective in his choice (see 20:30; 21:25). Clement of Alexandria said, "Last of all, John, perceiving that the *bodily* facts had been set forth in the Gospels, being urged by his friends and inspired by the Spirit, composed a *spiritual* Gospel." We divide this majestic account into four main sections.

1. CHAPTERS 1–11
SIGNS

The Prologue to the Gospel (1:1–14) contains some intended reminiscences of Genesis 1. It assures the reader that from the beginning of Christ's pre-incarnational glory he was the agent in the work of creation (v. 3; see Col. 1. 16; Heb. 1:2), and he is still at work recreating men and women who believe in him (12–13; 3:3).

The ministry of John the Baptist is given in some detail (see 1:15–37; 3:22–36; 5:33–36). The Herald is portrayed as a convinced evangelist, an obedient servant, and a self-effacing saint.

The dominant theme in these opening chapters, however, is not the ministry of John, but the miracles of Christ. Seven signs are described here. They are:

a. WATER INTO WINE: the power to transform the ordinary into the special (2:1–11), and the reward of obedience.

b. HEALING OF THE NOBLEMAN'S SON: the power of the authoritative word (4:46–54) and the response of faith (4:50).

c. HEALING OF THE PARALYTIC (5:1–9): Christ, the answer to human despair ("I have no one to help me," v.7).

d. FEEDING OF THE MULTITUDE (6:1–14): Christ, the bread of life has abundant satisfaction to offer to "the world," a favorite Johannine phrase (see 1:29; 4:42; 6:33; 8:12).

e. WALKING ON THE SEA: Christ, the answer to human fear (6:16–21).

f. SIGHT TO THE BLIND MAN: Christ, the light of the world for those who are spiritually blind and ignorant (9:1–7; 9:40–41).

g. RAISING OF LAZARUS: Christ, the giver of life (11:17–44).

The miracles are described by John as "signs" (20:30); they are ways of manifesting Christ's glory (2:11) and, as such, will be used to create faith in him (2:11; 20:31). Through these seven signs the opening chapters expound *what Christ does*.

2. CHAPTERS 12–16
TEACHING

This section preserves a unique account of Christ's teaching on some highly important themes, and emphasizes *what Christ expects*. The teaching is set within the context of the Passion and the Passover (12:1;13:1): as Christ's parting words, their value is greatly increased. He focuses his disciples' attention on five great priorities of the Christian life:

a. A LIFE OF SURRENDER This is typified in Mary's sacrificial gift (12:1–8), and exemplified in Christ's own sayings about his sacrificial death (for example, 12:23–26).

b. A LIFE OF SERVICE The feet-washing is a clear demonstration of this vital principle; it is John's way of presenting a truth such as Mark 10:44–45. Disciples are servants (13:14–16) who do not only *know* their Master's wishes but do them (13:17). This service should arise out of love (13:34–35), the true test of discipleship.

c. A LIFE OF OBEDIENCE This theme constantly emerges in chapter 14 (for example, vv. 15, 21, 23, 24). In stressing the importance of obedience, Christ does not ask us to do anything he did not do himself. He was utterly obedient to the will of his Father (14:31).

d. A LIFE OF COMMUNION The vine imagery in chapter 15 has a rich Old Testament background (Isa. 5; Jer. 2:21; Eze. 15), but now the vine is no longer the Jewish nation but the Lord's people, joined inseparably to him as branches. This communion—abiding in him— brings immense blessing: cleansing (v. 3); fruitfulness (vv. 4–5); love (vv. 9–10); joy (v. 11); and insight (v. 15); but it also provokes opposition (vv. 18–25).

e. A LIFE OF WITNESS The witness theme is prominent in *John* (1:7–8; 3:11, 26, 28; 5:31–37; 8:18; 9:24–34; 15:27; 18:37). LAZARUS is a faithful and highly effective witness (12:9–11), but, by contrast, some of the chief rulers who had believed in Christ were cowards (12:42–43); so was Joseph of Arimathea until after Christ's death (19:38).

Christ expects his followers to be courageous witnesses (15:26–27), and the ministry of the Holy Spirit makes this witness possible in a hostile society (16:1–6). The Spirit will use our witness, awakening conviction of sin (16:7–11) in those who listen, and unfold the truth to those who wish to speak (16:13–15). Christ knows that the days ahead are going to be difficult (16:20), but his disciples will also have:

- joy (16:21–22)
- love (16:27)
- peace (16:33).

3. CHAPTERS 17–19
SACRIFICE

The next section focuses on *what Christ achieves*. The high priestly prayer in chapter 17 reminds us that although his teaching ministry is of immense importance, we need something more than instruction. If we are to win through we also need his intercessory prayer ministry: and it is promised (Heb. 7:25). Christ delights to pray for his own on the basis of his finished work (17:4): because he can be glorified in us (17:10); because he knows how fiercely the world opposes us (17:14); because his followers are united with him eternally (17:21–22); and supremely because he loves us (17:23–26).

The story of the cross in *John* makes frequent mention of Christ as *King* (18:33, 34–37, 39; 19:3, 12, 15, 19, 21). The Gospel began with this affirmation on the lips of a disciple (1:49; see 6:15). Note also John's insistence that Christ really died (19:31–37). This is because in the first century some Docetists (from the Greek *dokein* "to appear") suggested that Christ did not really die but only appeared to be dead. As well as denying the reality of his death, they also denied his humanity. John's Gospel also constantly asserts Christ's deity (1:1, 14, 18, 17:1; 20:28–31).

4. CHAPTERS 20–21
COMMISSION

This final section is concerned with *what Christ demands*. The resurrection narratives lay a special emphasis on *service*. The risen Christ meets his men that he may thrust them out into the world of vast opportunity: evangelism (20:21–23) and pastoral care (21:15–17).

But personal commitment matters most, whatever the cost (21:18–19).

Acts

his thrilling account of early Church pastoral life and missionary enterprise is the second part of Luke's two-volume work (1:1; see Luke 1:1–4). The book reminds its readers that the Holy Spirit empowers individual lives and believing communities, equipping them for teaching, evangelism, corporate care and social service. The figure of PETER dominates the first half of the book (chapters 1–12), while that of PAUL occupies the second (chapters 13–26).

1. CHAPTERS 1–3
THE CHURCH AND ITS POWER

Three dominant themes are clearly introduced in this first main section of the book:

a. WAITING (chapter 1) The prayerfulness of the early Christian community is demonstrated from the start. The Lord Jesus, through the Holy Spirit, gives his "instructions" to them all (1:2), but the Church has to pray in order to discern what those orders mean in practical response. "Wait" is the key word here (1:4; see Luke 24:49). This exciting book begins with passivity, not activity; it presents us with a pattern for Christian service.
b. WITNESSING (chapter 2) The Spirit manifests his pres-

ence in a remarkable way, enabling a vast multiracial congregation to hear the gospel in their own language. It is a clear reversal of Babel (see Gen. 11:1–9). Man is not now seeking to exalt himself (Gen. 11:4); he desires only to exalt his God. It is not his own name that matters (Gen. 11:4) but Christ's (3:6, 16; 4:10; 5:41). Notice, however, that the theme of their witness is not their ideas, nor even their experience, but the mighty acts of God. Peter's message is:

- biblical—the Old Testament quotations attest the truth of the gospel from prophecy
- Christocentric (2:22–36)
- convicting ("whom you crucified" v. 23, 36–37)
- appealing (vv. 38–40)
- effective (v. 41)

Be sure not to miss Luke's insistence that worshipping is a vital aspect of witnessing (2:46–47; see also Luke 24:48, 52).

c. WORKING (chapter 3) Lest we should imagine that the Lord is only concerned about the conversion of multitudes (2:41), we are soon reminded of the *personal* nature of our work for him. It is "love to the loveless shown, that they might lovely be" (3:2–10). Every individual is important.

The key theme in chapters 1–3 is the Holy Spirit's power: power expected (chapter 1), power manifested (chapter 2), power demonstrated (chapter 3).

2. CHAPTERS 4–12
THE CHURCH AND ITS PROBLEMS

There can be no work for God without some opposition. These chapters relate the initial hazards of the early Church.

a. EXTERNAL TROUBLE: persecution. We read of the interrogation of Peter and John (4:3–22); the arrest of the apostles (5:17–18); the martyrdom of Stephen (7:54–60), the persecution campaign of Saul (8:3); the death of James (12:2). Right from the beginning the believers realize that they are working in a thoroughly hostile society.

b. INTERNAL TROUBLE: this is far more serious.

- Insincerity and hypocrisy soon raise their ugly heads (5:1–10), but when this unclean element is removed, immense blessing follows—miracles (5:12), conversions (5:14), healings (5:15–16), exorcisms (5:16)—*and* trouble (5:17–18), but only to be turned to triumph (5:19).

- Difficulties in relationships is the next internal problem (6:1), though it is soon used of God to institute the diaconate (6:3). Notice particularly that spiritual qualities are essential for practical tasks (6:5) and that at least one deacon not only waits at tables (6:2) but also preaches (7:2–54).

- Theological tensions: one of the greatest problems for the Church in the first few centuries was the relationship between Christians and Jews. Here is the first attempt to grapple with some of these thorny issues (chapter 10): the first step in the reconciling process of Christian love. Jews were not allowed to eat with Gentiles, or even come under their roof (11:3). No wonder Cornelius kneels when Peter comes in (10:24–28). But these are difficult days (see 11:2). Some insist that meticulous Jewish observances should be zealously maintained. The matter will be raised again (see chapter 15; Gal. 2:11–14; 5:1–6).

3. CHAPTERS 13–28
THE CHURCH AND ITS PASSION

The book now turns from internal difficulties to external opportunities, telling of Paul's three missionary journeys and his later experiences at Jerusalem, Caesarea, Malta and Rome. We might summarize them under these seven headings:

a. PAUL THE MISSIONARY First journey (13:1–15:35); second (15:36–18:22); third (18:23–21:16): nobody can deny the extraordinary courage (15:26) and sensitivity (16:6–10) of Paul and his companions.

b. PAUL THE PREACHER We have magnificent summaries of the apostle's preaching ministry, for example:

- to devout synagogue worshippers (13:16–41)
- to superstitious philosophers (17:22–31)
- to spiritual leaders (20:18–35)

Notice the difference of approach each time: no stereotyped sermons!

c. PAUL THE APOLOGIST Chapters 22–28 record several speeches during which the apostle seeks to defend the faith and declare the gospel (for example, 22:1–22; 23:1–9). Observe how skillfully Paul breaks up the Pharisaic and Sadducean conspiracy against him by speaking about the issue on which they disagreed: the resurrection. Paul knew his facts. Good learning has an important part to play in the presentation of the gospel (24:10–21; 26:1–27).

d. PAUL THE EVANGELIST He is not only concerned about maintaining his rights as a Roman citizen (22:24–29); he has a passion for souls (26:18, 23, 27–29).

e. PAUL THE WITNESS He does not only present an objective evangelistic appeal, but he speaks out of his own experience of the transforming grace of God. He knows what Christ has done for him and longs that others might also experience his Lord's love and power (22:3–13; 26:3–19).

f. PAUL THE PRISONER As a Roman citizen he has the right of appeal to Caesar (26:31–32; 27:1; 28:19–20). He uses these uncomfortable circumstances for spiritual purposes (28:8–10).

g. PAUL THE TEACHER The closing portrait is of the apostle "in his own rented house" (28:30) engaged in a ministry of expounding, testifying, persuading (28:23), preaching and teaching (28:31), "without hindrance" for two full years.

That Greek word "unhindered" is a magnificent word with which to bring this book to a close, for this unhindered work still goes on: all over the world men and women continue to proclaim God's kingly rule and Christ's unique work and do so with boldness.

Romans

his epistle has shaped the course of Christian history more than once. Augustine, Luther and Wesley were transformed by its message. The great theme of the letter is "the gospel of God": God initiated the gospel. It is also called "the gospel of his Son" (1:9): God effected it. Paul describes it as *his* gospel (2:16): he experienced it. But the theme of *salvation* and *behavior* cannot be separated and *Romans* tells us as much about the one as the other. This good news of God's love, Christ's transforming power and the Spirit's indwelling presence is not only for those who will *believe it,* but for those who will prove the reality of their belief by the way they *manifest it.*

1. Chapters 1–4
HUMAN RUIN

After the opening salutation in which Paul describes himself as an apostle (1:1; see also 1:5), servant (1:9), debtor (1:14), and preacher (1:15), the main theme is announced: the wrath of God upon man's sin. Man's ruin has alarming characteristics:

a. MORAL CORRUPTION (1:18–32) Ingratitude (21), ignorance (22), idolatry (23) and immorality (24) go hand in hand. Note the repetitive, "God gave them over" (24, 26,

28); the same verb is found in 8:32: "gave him up . . . ." In the apostle's teaching God's justice and mercy are perfectly balanced.

b. RELIGIOUS PRIDE (2:1–29). The Jews would agree with Paul thus far in his description of Gentile impurity and godlessness. They imagined themselves better but they are just as bad (2:11, 17–24) and their rebellion is just as offensive to God. By their disobedience God's name is being blasphemed rather than glorified throughout the Mediterranean world.

c. SPIRITUAL APATHY There is no difference between Jews and Gentiles (3:9–23). Note the recurrent "no one" in 3:10–20. God's answer to man's sin is the miracle of redemption. Look at Paul's use of Old Testament and contemporary imagery to describe this mercy:

- the law court—legal, being "justified" (3:24)
- the marketplace—commercial, "redemption" (3:24)
- the Temple—religious, "a sacrifice of atonement through faith" in Christ's unique offering (3:25)

These aspects of Paul's doctrine of salvation are amplified in other places.

Chapter 4 is a vital link chapter; it introduces the main ideas of the next section. Abraham (4:1–5) and David (4:6–8) illustrate the truth that salvation is not by works. All man can do is *believe* the humanly impossible but divinely credible miracle of grace (see 4:16–25).

2. CHAPTERS 5–8
CHRIST'S REDEMPTION

We might summarize the leading ideas of this magnificent passage as follows:

a. HE OFFERS PARDON (chapter 5) We need to be pardoned, and it was accomplished for us not when men and women pleased God by good works but when they offended him by arrogant aggression (vv. 8, 10). We all sinned in Adam; he not only initiated the experience of sinning, he typified it. "Every man is the Adam of his own soul" (2 Baruch). But through Christ man is justified. As Adam's disobedience led to the condemnation of many, so Christ's obedience led to the justification of many (vv. 12–21).

b. HE IMPARTS NEWNESS (Chapters 6–7) Justification is not a heavenly transaction without earthly consequences. It makes a difference. The sanctification theme emerges here (for example, 6:4). In chapter 5 Christ is crucified *for us* (5:6–10); in chapter 6 we are crucified *with him* (6:6). The same power which raised Christ from the dead is at work in us to make our deliverance from sin possible (6:4). But this deliverance involves a believer in conflict. Paul shares his own experience of the struggle (7:14–25).

c. HE PROMISES COMPANIONSHIP (chapter 8) A. Skevington Wood describes this chapter as "Paul's Pentecost." The believer does not have to fight alone (8:13–14). Spiritually-minded believers:

- please God (vv. 8–9)
- obey God (v. 14)
- love God (v. 28)
- trust God (v. 31)

The chapter which began with "no condemnation" (v. 1) ends with no separation (v. 39). Paul was not theorizing when he wrote about tribulation (v. 35); he had personally experienced these hazards in his travels.

3. CHAPTERS 9–16
OUR RESPONSIBILITY

a. TO THE LOST (Chapters 9–11) Naturally the apostle was burdened about his own people, the Jews (9:1–5): "a pain that never leaves me" (v. 2, J. B. Phillips' paraphrase). Are we as concerned for the lost? These chapters move from the theme of evangelism to that of election. Paul naturally finds it important to discuss the immense issue of the Jew in the purpose of God, but never allows the missionary theme to go far away (10:1, 12–15, 20–21).

b. TO THE LORD (chapter 12) The theme of offering ourselves which has already been mentioned (6:13) is developed here (vv. 1–2). *Presentation* involves *separation* ("do not conform") and issues in *transformation* (v. 2). This sacrificial surrender to God will affect our relationship with the Church (vv. 3–13) and the hostile world (vv. 14–21).

c. TO THE STATE (chapter 13) This was a grave issue in the first century (see Titus 3:1; 1 Peter 2:13–14). Paul's doctrine of God's sovereignty obviously involves his control over magistrates and Roman officials, and his ability to make use of them as he wills (vv. 1–5). This means that the believer must pay his taxes (v. 6) and respect those in authority (v. 7). Two things motivate our actions: love (vv. 8–10) and hope (vv. 11–12); they issue in holiness (vv. 13–14).

d. TO THE CHURCH (Chapters 14–16) This closing section looks at some problems in connection with *weak believers,* some Christians have customs which do not commend themselves to others, while other believers have weaknesses that cause irritation. The apostle urges this local church:

- to pursue peaceful things (14:19)
- to pursue pleasing things (15:2)
- to pursue encouraging things (15:3–5)
- to pursue glorifying things (15:6)

Chapter 16 is a series of greetings to friends in the fellowship, and it closes with some great assertions about God: "the God of peace" (v. 20); "the eternal God" (v. 26), and "the only wise God" (v. 27). In the cruel days which lie ahead the believers at Rome will need this kind of confidence. God gives them *peace* in persecution. They do not fear the torture because they know that, as everlasting God, they can go to him who, in his wisdom will use even the fury of Nero to his praise.

1 Corinthians

orinth, a busy, Mediterranean seaport, was notorious for its low morals. "To Corinthianize" was a colloquialism in those days for "to degenerate." Many of its Christians had lived corrupt lives before they were converted (6:9–11). With this kind of background and a far from helpful environment, it is no wonder that this church had difficulties. Paul writes to correct a number of errors both of belief and behavior in a church which lacked love. He appeals for:

1. Chapters 1–4
HARMONY

Rival factions within the church (1:11–12; 3:3–4) are contradicting its essential nature as a *united* body (see 12:12–27). Paul brings these rivalries to the cross: "Was Paul crucified for you?"(1:13). "Christ crucified" has been his main theme, and God has been pleased to use weak, insignificant people to communicate it (1:26–31); all boasting, either of "party" or "group" is entirely out of place. We should glory in the Lord alone (1:31). Paul explains that when he came to preach at Corinth, he came not in pride or self-confidence, but in reliance upon God (2:1–5).

Note Paul's division of men into those who are *natural* (not knowing God), *spiritual* (having understanding), and *carnal* (fleshly), (see 3:1–4). God's truth is revealed to spiritual men (2:6–13); natural men cannot understand it (2:14–16).

Disharmony is clear evidence of carnality. The apostle emphasizes the importance of harmony and teamwork in Christian service (3:5–11) and presents us with vivid images and metaphors to emphasize the nature of his work:

- gardener (3:6)
- builder (3:10)
- slave (4:1. The word translated "servants" in the NIV and RSV, means literally "under-rowers," those who rowed in the lower bank of oars on a large ship)
- steward (4:2)
- apostle (4:9)
- fool (4:10)
- father (4:14–21) He has become their spiritual parent and as such has the responsibility of instructing and correcting them.

2. CHAPTERS 5–7
PURITY

This next section concerns more particular relationships. Chapter 5 deals with a serious moral offense (5:1) to which the church has been carelessly indifferent. The offender must be temporarily excommunicated (5:5) for this evil can infect the entire church (5:6–8). They must be prepared to take disciplinary action in such matters, and not resort to legal aid from the world (6:1–8). The church must maintain its purity (6:9–14) for the bodies of believers (and the church itself is viewed as a body, see 12:12–30) are the temples of the Spirit (6:15–20).

The Corinthians had sought Paul's advice about some marriage questions (chapter 7). His teaching here has been seriously misunderstood. It must be remembered that it is more a defense of celibacy than a disparagement of marriage. The Lord's return was "on the immediate horizon" of his thinking, the times were urgent (see 4:5; 5:5; 6:2–3; and especially 7:29–31).

3. CHAPTERS 8–10
LIBERTY

Another problem is now discussed: the eating of meat offered to idols. Paul stresses the importance of Christian liberty. Some believers eat such meat without an uneasy conscience because "an idol is nothing" (8:4) but Paul's own position is that if such a practice causes a brother to stumble it is best to refrain (8:9–13). He illustrates this principle of voluntary self-denial for the benefit of others from his own apostleship (chapter 9, especially 9:19). He does not please himself but seeks by every possible means to win others for Christ (9:20–27).

Chapter 10 discusses the seriousness of Christian life and service with an illustration from the Old Testament. In the days of the Exodus most of the people were disqualified from entering the Promised Land even though they were "baptized" and ate "spiritual food." Thus external rites are valueless if we are not right with God and obedient to him. These Old Testament events are warnings to believers of the disastrous effects such idolatrous practices will also have on them if not abandoned (10:11, 14–22). All our behavior must glorify God (10:31). Christian liberty does not ignore Christian example. We are free, but our freedom must commend Christ and encourage others.

4. CHAPTERS 11–12
UNITY

Some further problems are mentioned here: public prayers, conduct at the Lord's Supper, and spiritual gifts. Remember it is a young church and has many questions to ask, for example, *about prayer.* Jews prayed with heads covered, as did

Romans, but Greeks did not cover their heads when sacrificing. What are the members of this Greek church to do? Paul gives instructions in 11:1–16.

The Lord's Supper has become an occasion of grief because of their unchristian behavior (11:18–34). Such practices are contrary to its purpose and will provoke the judgment of God.

The exercise of *spiritual gifts* has also raised problems. Paul points out that there are various gifts (12:4), distributed by the sovereign action of the Holy Spirit (12:11) and for the edification of the church as a whole (for example, 12:14–27). The inference of 12:28–30 is surely that a negative reply is expected.

5. CHAPTERS 13–14
CHARITY

Love is the best gift (12:31) and chapter 13 presents us not only with majestic language but with a persistent challenge. It is love alone which *counts* (13:1–3), *costs* (13:4–6), and *endures* (13:7–13), says Karl Barth. Chapter 14 discusses its practical application (14:1) to speaking in tongues and the gift of prophecy, or proclamation for edification (14:3–5).

6. CHAPTER 15
CERTAINTY

What a confused and uncertain church this is. Its members are not loyal to the truths of the revealed Christian message (15:1–8): some appear to have doubted the doctrine of the resurrection of the dead (15:12). But Paul points out that you cannot abandon one aspect of Christian doctrine without losing others at the same time (see 15:13–19).

The chapter begins with Christ's resurrection (v. 12: *past*) and ends with our own (vv. 51–57: *future*) but as always Paul introduces a practical note about the *present* (58): stand firm and work hard.

7. CHAPTER 16
GENEROSITY

Just before concluding with a few final greetings (vv. 19–24), this epistle gives some instructions regarding a collection for the needs of the poor in the Jerusalem church (16:1–4, see Acts 11:29; Rom. 15:25). "Love" in Paul's teaching is something more than a beautiful word (13:1–13); it expresses itself in giving that is:

- compassionate (16:1)—for God's people
- systematic (16:2)—first day
- proportionate (16:2)—"in keeping with his income"
- generous (2 Cor. 8:2)
- eager (1 Cor. 9:2)

This letter has relevant things to say to late twentieth century Christians in these days of declining moral standards and doctrinal indifference.

2 Corinthians

emetrius, an old Greek literary critic, once said that everyone reveals his own soul in his letters. It is particularly true of 2 Corinthians. George Herbert, that outstanding seventeenth century pastor, said of it: "What an admirable epistle is the second of Corinthians. How full of affections! He joys and he is sorry, he grieves and he glories; never was there such care of a flock expressed, save in the great Shepherd of the fold who first shed tears over Jerusalem and afterward blood." In this letter Paul has to defend himself against those who do not recognize his leadership. The letter shows that the best of people often have to suffer at the hands of people who ought to know better.

1. Chapters 1–2
APOSTOLIC INTEGRITY

After an opening salutation, a great biblical theme: the consolations of God (1:3–7). He comforts us in adversity so that we may extend that comfort to others (or "strengthen," "encourage" others, Greek *parakalein*). Paul knows this; he has suffered great trials (1:8–11) but they have taught him *dependence* upon God (1:9), *hope* for the future (1:10), and the value of *prayer-partnership* (1:11). There are those at Corinth who insult and slander Paul, and he deals with some of their complaints later, but at this point he defends his own integrity, commenting on:

a. his sincerity (1:12–14)
b. his stability (1:15–22) Possibly some people have complained that he is always changing his mind and therefore is unreliable.
c. his compassion (1:23–2:4) It is out of love for them that he has not visited them lest his visit cause them pain.
d. his mercy (2:5–11) The "offender" in the congregation (perhaps the ringleader of the opposition?) must be forgiven and loved. Paul clearly implies that to refuse pardon is to help the devil (2:11).
e. his confidence (2:12–17) The work of God sometimes suffers setbacks caused by human weakness (2:12–13), but the triumphal procession of Christ's conquest moves steadily across the world (2:14–17).

2. CHAPTERS 3–6
APOSTOLIC TEACHING

Paul's message to the Corinthian church is:

a. EFFECTIVE TEACHING (3:1–3) It certainly works. The converts at Corinth are Paul's letter of commendation, his reference.
b. AUTHORITATIVE TEACHING (3:4–6) It is God who has qualified Paul and his companions to be ministers.
c. LIBERATING TEACHING (3:7–18) The old covenant—the Law—had its splendor, but, as Knox says, "its glory is now dimmed like the shine of lamps when dawn comes." The old covenant convicted; the new makes a transformation, even Christlikeness, possible (see 3:18).
d. FAITHFUL TEACHING (4:1–6) Some were tampering with God's word (see 2:17). The true message strikes at man's conscience and by this test men know it to be true (4:2). To distort it by our own interpretations or ideas is to

rob the loss of its benefits (4:3). The devil keeps them in the dark; we must not help him (4:4). The message is a *Person:* Christ proclaimed as *Lord* (4:5) and the unique illuminating manifestation of God's glory (4:6). Here is a clear echo of Paul's own conversion experience.

e. GLORIFYING TEACHING (4:7–18) It does not glorify the preacher or teacher (4:7) but the God who is proclaimed. He is thereby exalted (4:15). However difficult this work, its trials are nothing when viewed in the light of coming glory (4:16–18).

f. SERIOUS TEACHING (5:1–10) Paul does not deal with marginal trivialities. His message is a matter of life and death. It concerns the issues of *death* (5:1–2), *salvation* (5:5), *faith* (5:7), and *judgment* (5:10).

g. PERSUASIVE TEACHING (5:11–6:2). Notice the verbs of appeal: *persuade* (5:11), *appeal* (5:20), *urge* (6:1). Paul is not cold and detached. He feels the constraint of God's love and urges men to turn to the compassionate (5:14), transforming (5:17), reconciling (5:19), and sin-bearing (5:21) Christ for salvation, and to turn now, while there is opportunity, respond to this astonishing, undeserved grace (6:2; see Isa. 49:8).

h. COSTLY TEACHING (6:3–13) God uses all manner of experiences and agencies, and sometimes adverse circumstances, to communicate his word. The apostle describes how he faced nine hardships (6:4–7). He takes the seven scurrilous opinions of his enemies: imposter, unknown, dying, punished, sorrowful, poor, having nothing (8b–10) and turns them to positive affirmations of his faith and ministry.

i. DECISIVE TEACHING (6:14–18, or more accurately, 7:1) Paul's teaching states that we are the temple of God and therefore demands purity of life. Unmarried Christians do well to ponder this clear teaching, or they may enter into unrelieved grief.

3. CHAPTERS 7–9
APOSTOLIC COMPASSION

Paul's words, "Make room . . . in your hearts" (7:2) set the tone of the next section. The relationship between the apostle and this church has obviously been strained as a result of Paul's earlier letter (7:8). But Paul had only written in love that repentance might follow (7:8–13) and Titus' news of their response to Paul's message has given Paul immense joy (7:14–16), and confirmed his high opinion of their faith.

Paul's compassion is not only expressed in his concern for spiritual purity. Chapters 8–9 deal with the collection for Christians in Judea in dire need. In Paul's view true giving:

- begins with the offering of ourselves (8:5)
- is inspired by the self-giving of Christ (8:9–10)
- is continuous and not sporadic (8:10–11)
- is in proportion to our income (8:12)
- is worthy before God and men (8:20–21)

Paul believes that those who are mean will not receive God's gifts (9:6–15). How can we ever repay him for the indescribable gift of Christ (9:15)?

4. CHAPTERS 10–13
APOSTOLIC AUTHORITY

Here Paul addresses the disgruntled minority who had not been won over by his previous letter (10:8–11). They do not like the way he has acted ("in worldly fashion": 10:2, RSV). Paul explains that his work is not worldly; it concerns spiritual and eternal realities (10:3–6). He was the first to bring them the gospel (10:14) but he is not boasting of that (10:17–18).

His critics appear to have complained of his writings (10:10), physical appearance (10:10), preaching (10:10; 11:6) and lovelessness (11:11). His opponents may have been led away by Judaizers (11:2–4, 22). Do the false apostles (11:13) know what hardship and suffering are (11:24–33)? But Paul will not boast, unless it be of his weakness and his reliance upon Christ in physical need (12:1–10).

Paul will do anything for the Corinthians (12:15) but he does not want to find some of them impenitent and factious when he visits them (12:20). He urges his readers to examine themselves (13:5), mend their ways (13:11), and agree with one another, the three Persons of the Holy Trinity *are* their helpers (13:14).

Galatians

n *Galatians* Paul is not defending himself, he is defending the gospel. This dynamic letter played an important part in the spiritual experience of both Martin Luther and John Wesley. Both the sixteenth century continental Reformation and the eighteenth century Evangelical Revival owe an immense amount to *Galatians*.

1. Chapters 1–2
THE APOSTLE AND HIS AUTHORITY

The Galatian churches appear to have been troubled by Judaizers who insisted upon circumcision (observance of Jewish legal and cultic requirements) as a necessary part of salvation. The keynote of this letter is: "by faith *alone*."

Paul's opponents discredited Paul as an apostle, so the letter begins with a vindication of his apostleship (1:1). He calls this legalism "a different gospel" (1:6), a perversion of the truth (1:7). He declares that his authority as an apostle comes directly from Christ (1:11–12). He outlines his own experience of Christ; a story of *arrogant rejection* (1:13); *religious superiority* (1:14); and *undeserved grace* (1:15–16). Note that he was not only *called* and *converted* but *commissioned* (1:16). The Lord who saved also instructed him in the nature and content of the Christian gospel (1:16–17).

The desert experience in Arabia gave Paul a firm grounding in the message he had to proclaim. Only Peter (1:18) and James (1:19), the brother of the Lord Jesus, had doctrinal conversations with him when they must have told him much about Christ's earthly life and teaching. Years later he visited the church in Jerusalem, and was perfectly willing to check the revelation by what others believed and taught. He was no dogmatic isolationist or unthinking imitator. Paul points out that the Jerusalem church had not demanded the circumcision of Titus, a Gentile convert (2:3). Trouble had been caused by the appearance of "false brothers" (Judaizers) who had insisted on the necessity of legal observances (2:4); the true leaders of the Church (2:9), Peter, James and John, approved of Paul's mission and message to the Gentiles.

We next read of a clash between Paul and Peter (as in Acts 15:39 between Paul and Barnabas; even the early Christian leaders did not agree with each other in everything!) in the course of which Paul rebuked Peter for allowing himself to be persuaded to refuse table-fellowship to Gentiles (2:11–14). Paul knows that this is no marginal issue. If Gentiles have to be circumcised before they can be saved, the gospel is *of works* and not by grace through faith (2:15–21). The Judaizing message rendered the cross unnecessary.

2. CHAPTERS 3–4
THE LAW AND ITS FUNCTION

Paul's opponents are bound to raise the question: What is the present value, then, of the law? These two chapters present a brilliant, detailed argument asserting the primacy and superiority of faith. Paul invites his readers to think about:

a. THEIR OWN EXPERIENCE (3:1–5) They had not been converted by the works of the law, why now turn their backs on the message of grace and faith?

b. THE SCRIPTURES (3:6–29) Abraham was reckoned as righteous not on the basis of the law, but because of his faith. The law came 430 years after the Covenant (3:17). Abraham is cited and Habakkuk is also quoted (3:11). Note that it is not faith itself that saves (that would be a subtle form of salvation by works: by what *you* do in the act of believing). Faith is "the human attitude of receptivity which takes what God in his grace holds out" (Ralph Martin). Paul asserts elsewhere that even the desire to reach out is God-given (Eph. 2:8–9). Man *cannot* keep the law (3:10–11) and stands condemned, but Christ assumed the curse for us (3:13) and *all* (Jews *and* Gentiles) may believe through him (3:14).

Paul's argument is that the law would be enough if human beings could keep it, but that is utterly impossible (3:21–22). It has been likened to a railway ticket given to an imprisoned soldier during war; he would use it if he could, but he has to get out of the prisoner-of-war camp first! The law was our *paidagogos* (3:24), the disciplinarian slave who takes a boy to school. Similarly, the law rebukes and punishes us for our offenses but it cannot give us sonship. It is Christ who does that (3:26–29).

The theme of *sonship* is developed in chapter 4. Some are living as *slaves* in bondage to astrological speculation and fears: this is a word for our own highly superstitious times. Paul allegorizes the Hagar story from *Genesis.* The son born of Hagar was *of the flesh;* the child born of Sarah was *according to promise.* The women represent two covenants (4:24); those who are in Christ are the children of promise.

3. CHAPTERS 5–6
THE SPIRIT AND HIS WORK

These final chapters introduce us to some highly important aspects of the doctrine of the Holy Spirit in the life of the believer:

a. THE SPIRIT GUARANTEES ACCEPTANCE (5:5) We do not *work* to be accepted; we *wait.* In the coming Day of Judgment we shall be accepted as righteous, and the Spirit gives us the assurance of this. Paul makes it perfectly clear what he means by righteousness. It is not a glowing internal feeling of self-congratulation; it is the longing to give faith practical expression in loving deeds (5:6, 13–14).

b. THE SPIRIT PROVOKES CONFLICT (5:16–17) The Christian life involves a believer in warfare; there are things to be definitely and resolutely opposed in the power of the Holy Spirit. Some things are totally inconsistent with Christian life and faith.

c. THE SPIRIT OBTAINS FREEDOM (5:18–21) Being led by the Spirit gives liberty. The believer is not "under the law" as the Judaizers claimed.

d. THE SPIRIT CREATES HOLINESS (5:22–23) The "harvest of the Spirit" are the virtues of Christ. This is a superb portraiture of Christlikeness.

e. THE SPIRIT SANCTIFIES CONDUCT (5:25) Being led by the Spirit (5:18) is passive; walking is active (5:25), but in both verses the verb is in the present continuous tense. "Walk" in verse 25 means "to walk in line with."

f. THE SPIRIT ANTICIPATES ETERNITY (6:7–10) The worldly man ignores the future and lives as he wishes, sowing to the flesh (6.8). But the Spirit-filled man has a totally different set of values, and these are Spirit-inspired; he sows to the Spirit. This is not easy. The "family of believers" (6:10) may well be tested in coming days; as 6:12 hints, their profound faith in the cross of Christ may lead to persecution. But the believer knows that the cross is not only an historical event but a personal experience of profound importance (6:14, 17). Christ died for us and we die with him (see 2:20; 6:14).

Ephesians

ike *Romans,* the epistle to the *Ephesians* is a theological and literary masterpiece. It clearly expresses the inseparable nature of some immense themes, for example, Christ, the Christian and the Church; grace, faith and work. "Daily living" is a favorite theme and appears in several places (2:2, 10; 4:1, 17; 5:2, 8, 15). The letter, which may have been intended for a wider audience than the church in Ephesus, reminds the whole church of its unique privilege, unity, responsibility and destiny.

1. CHAPTERS 1–3
WHAT GOD ACCOMPLISHED

The main theme of this opening section is "our salvation." Notice the recurrence of the great words of the gospel:

- grace (1:2, 6, 7; 2:5, 7, 8; 3:2, 7)
- peace (1:2; 2:14, 15, 17)
- redemption (1:7, 14)
- blood (1:7; 2:13)
- salvation, saved (1:13; 2:5, 8)
- faith (1:15; 2:8; 3:12, 17)
- hope (1:12, 18; compare 2:12)
- love (1:4, 15; 2:4; 3:17, 19)

In these three chapters the apostle describes our salvation as:

a. A PREDESTINED SALVATION (chapter 1) The saving experience does not begin in the moment of man's response to the preaching of the gospel but "before the creation of the world" (1:4). Remember that the times in which Paul wrote were difficult for young Christians; there was much to oppose them. Ephesus itself was a city steeped in the traditions of heathenism and idolatry (see Acts 19:18–19, 23–41). This very letter was written from prison: it was costly to be a believer. Those young in the faith needed the reminder that their standing in Christ was God's gracious work in their hearts and lives. He had chosen them for his service (1:4) and his instruments must be holy. This choice was the act of his love (1:5). And because they *had been* chosen they *would be* kept.

Chapter 1 looks on eagerly and expectantly to a glorious future (1:14, 18). But this teaching on *predestination,* which could be interpreted in a highly individualistic way, is made a focus for Paul's rich teaching on the Christian community, the Church, the *body* of Christ (1:22–23), the *temple* (2:19–22). These believers are reminded that they belong to God and to one another.

b. A TRANSFORMING SALVATION (chapter 2) There was no shortage of "saviors" in the first century; the idea of salvation played some part in many of the contemporary religions and philosophical notions, for example, in Greek mystery religions. But the salvation which God offers is that which changes and transforms a man's life. It is not a series of speculative mystical ideas but a life-changing message of certainty and power. Many of the believers in this church knew their former life only too well (2:1–3). "But God" (2:4) had changed all that by his unlimited and undeserved mercy (his grace). Paul is eager to stress that it is not faith which saves a man, but grace (2:5–8). As we saw in our study of Galatians, if our salvation depended on faith, that would be a subtle form of salvation by works

("Look, I am saved by *my* believing!"). Faith is the term which describes the human response to what God has done and Paul asserts that even the desire to respond is God's gift to man (2:8–9). Grace has not only transformed man's relationship with God (inward) but man's relationship with man (outward). Christ has broken down the dividing wall between Jew and Gentile (2:11–18). It is through Christ that both Jew and Gentile have access to God, and by grace find themselves within the new community (2:19–22).

c. AN INCLUSIVE SALVATION (Chapter 3) This issue of Jew-Gentile relationships was a topic of immense importance in the first century Christian world. Paul had his problems in many churches because of the activities of the Judaizers who wanted to retain Jewish cultic practices (for example, circumcision).

We saw this in *Galatians* and we shall meet it again briefly in *Philippians*. In this chapter Paul explains that the mission to the Gentiles was God's clear revelation to him; "mystery" in New Testament thought is an "open secret" (3:3). Paul came to understand that the Gentiles are fellow heirs with the Jews (3:6) and members of the same body. Paul's understanding of this "mystery" is governed not only by the fact that Christ died for all (2:13–17) but that the Father cares for all (3:14–15).

2. CHAPTERS 4–6
WHAT GOD IMPARTS

"I therefore" (4:1, RSV) introduces one of Paul's superb *practical* sections. The various down-to-earth aspects are presented in the closing chapters with as much persuasive appeal as the "heavenlies" in the opening section. In Paul's teaching there is no sharp division between sacred and secular, doctrine and deeds, belief and behavior: the one conditions and regulates the other. The practical themes in these chapters are closely interrelated but three main issues stand out:

a. UNITY (4:1–32) Once again, we see here that although salvation is personal it is not individualistic but is corporate, for example, "bearing with one another" (4:2); "unity of the Spirit" (4:3); "one body" (4:4); "God's people," "the body of Christ" (4:12); "held together" (4:16); "members of one body" (4:25); "be kind . . . to one another" (4:32).

The sins which are mentioned in this chapter are those which mar good relationships (for example, 4:25–32). Believers in this church are urged to *put off* their former life of ignorance, hardness, callousness, immorality, greed (4:18–19) and *put on* (4:22–24) the new man of Christ-likeness and godliness.

b. LOVE (5:1–6:9) The key theme here is living a life of love. Note:

- Love's source: "as Christ . . ." (5:1–2)
- Love's standards (5:3–17) If love reigns then unhelpful things will be put away.
- Love's song (5:18–20) Love expresses itself in gratitude.
- Love's submission (5:21–6:4) Paul uses teaching about love in the *domestic* sphere to illustrate Christ's love for the Church ("as the church submits to Christ," 5:24). Children are urged to be obedient and the Old Testament is quoted as authority (6:1–4).
- Love's service (6:5–9) These lofty principles are now applied to *work*. Here again *submission* and *service* are key ideas. All work must be done out of love for Christ.

c. COURAGE (6:10–24) The closing verses of the epistle reflect the theme of warfare. There is need for strength as well as compassion. We are soldiers as well as servants. The various items in the armor have Isaianic verses behind them (see Isa. 11:5; 52:7; 59:17). The Bible and prayer are indispensable aids to victory (6:17–20).

The magnificent "little words" of the gospel—peace, love, faith, grace—bring this superb epistle to a close (6:23–24).

Philippians

lthough written in prison, this happy epistle abounds in references to joy (1:4, 18; 2:17, 28–29; 3:1; 4:1, 4, 10). During his imprisonment this one church sent Paul a monetary gift, and it was not the first time they had been generous to him. *Philippians* is Paul's "thank you" letter to them, expressing deep appreciation, and rejoicing in their genuine Christian lifestyle. Paul knows two things to be of supreme importance in the Christian life:

a. THE BELIEVER'S CONFIDENCE (1:12–14) God is sovereign and even an imprisonment can be used by him to the blessing of others.

b. THE BELIEVER'S CONTENTMENT (4:11–13) Christ is everything the Christian needs (see 4:19).

1. CHAPTER 1
THE CHRISTIAN'S TASK

Although imprisoned, Paul knows that there are important things he (and the Philippian believers) can still do. There are three essential tasks:

a. EARNEST PRAYER (1:3–11, compare v. 19). He prays for the Philippian Christians, and counts on their prayers for him. Notice the kind of praying it is:

- grateful (vv. 4–5)
- confident (v. 6)
- affectionate (vv. 7–8)
- definite (v. 9)
- lofty (vv. 9–11)

Paul is not content to pray for marginal things. He prays for the most important things in the Christian life—for their increased love, keen discernment and genuine holiness.

b. COURAGEOUS WITNESS (vv. 12–26) Paul knows that even his imprisonment has been used to bring the message to unbelievers (12–13) and to inspire courage in other Christians (v. 14). He knows that the devil sometimes uses other professing believers to hinder our witness (vv. 15–18). In great adversity, he rejoices in two facts: Christ's gospel is being preached (v. 18) and Christ's name is being exalted (vv. 19–20). Whether he lives *for Christ* here or goes to be *with Christ,* it does not matter. Eternity is gain.

c. EXEMPLARY BEHAVIOR (vv. 27–30) Our conduct must commend the gospel. It is not enough to witness *with words;* the committed Christian witnesses unconsciously *by works,* and regards suffering as a privilege (v. 29).

2. CHAPTER 2
THE CHRISTIAN'S CHARACTER

Some scholars believe the key passage here, 2:5–11, to be an early Christian hymn. It exalts Christ as the pre-existent, self-sacrificing Servant who subjected himself to the death on the cross for sinful men, later to be exalted as the victorious Lord of all. Believers need Christ's "attitude" (v. 5); this must be their outlook on life. Chapter 2 is therefore an exposition of three immense themes:

a. POSSESSING THE MIND OF CHRIST (2:1–11) In practical day-to-day living this means having a mind which is lov-

ing (vv. 1–2), humble (vv. 3–4), unselfish (vv. 5–6), surrendered (v. 7), obedient and courageous ("even death on
a cross," v. 8). Those who confess Christ's Lordship glorify the Father (vv. 9–11).

b. APPROPRIATING THE MIND OF CHRIST (2:12–13) This
"salvation" must not only be studied and possessed, it
must be appropriated and related to everyday life. God is
at work in us (v. 13) but we must work it out (v. 12). As
surely as Christ "worked" for God's good pleasure, so
must we (v. 13).

c. MANIFESTING THE MIND OF CHRIST (2:14–30) Here is a
delightful character study of three people who manifest
Christ's mind and character: Paul himself (14–18); Timothy (vv. 19–24); and Epaphroditus (vv. 25–30). The apostle points out that those who manifest Christ's mind
become:

- effective luminaries (v. 15)
- sacrificial offerings (v. 17)
- devoted servants (vv. 20–22)
- courageous soldiers (vv. 25–30)

3. CHAPTER 3
THE CHRISTIAN'S AMBITION

Philippians is a letter full of joy, but there are two problems
in the church to which the apostle addresses himself:

a. A DOCTRINAL PROBLEM—Judaistic legalism (3:2–3)
b. A PASTORAL PROBLEM (4:2)

The problem in 3:2–3 is the same as the problem faced in
Galatians. Paul describes these people as "dogs," a term of
reproach frequently used by Jews about Gentiles. Paul views
this as a desperately serious issue, a corruption of the gospel
of grace, making it a gospel of works.

Notice Paul's quest to "gain" Christ (v. 8), especially:

- its priority (v. 8)
- its cost (v. 10)
- its prospect (v. 11)
- its pursuit (v. 12)

These great spiritual ambitions are expounded under three divisions:

a. PAST (vv. 4–11) When contrasted with his experience in Christ, Paul regards all his previous moral, social and religious achievements as *skubala,* rubbish or refuse, the waste matter left on a dish and thrown to the dogs (3:8).

b. PRESENT (vv. 12–16) The past no longer interests him (v. 13), and in the present he presses on to higher spiritual and moral attainment (v. 14). Spiritual maturity is his only ambition.

c. FUTURE (vv. 17–21) The destiny both of Christ's opponents (vv. 18–19) and Christ's subjects (vv. 20–21), are mentioned, the one to destruction, the other to transforming resurrection (see 3:11) when the sincere Christian believer will be clothed in a body like Christ's resurrection body.

4. CHAPTER 4
THE CHRISTIAN'S CERTAINTY

This superb closing chapter begins with an entreaty to "stand firm" (v. 1) and continues with an appeal to two women to stand together in the work of the gospel. Disunity and disharmony hinder our effective witness (vv. 2–3). Paul's further appeal to "rejoice" (v. 4) is followed by a "handful of certainties." Although he does not know the way ahead, he knows the One above. Notice the repeated "will" (7, 9, 19). What are the Christian's certainties? They are in Christ's work for him:

a. HIS ETERNAL SALVATION—"whose names are in the book of life" (v. 3). See Exodus 32:32; Psalm 69:28;

Daniel 12:1; Luke 10:20; Revelation 3:5; 13:8; 20:12; 21:27 for examples of this vivid word picture of God's sovereign choice and note how the imagery was used particularly in times of crisis as a means of immense encouragement to believers.

b. HIS PROMISED APPEARING (v. 5) Conviction about the Lord's return should encourage tenderness and kindness. The Greek word translated "gentleness" (v. 5, NIV; translated as "moderation" in AV, and "forbearance" in RSV) also appears in 2 Corinthians 10:1 as the "gentleness" of Christ.

c. HIS PROTECTIVE PEACE (vv. 6–7) Prayerfulness dismisses anxiety, inspires gratitude, encourages dependence and dispels fear. "Guard" is military language; God's peace protects us like a sentry.

d. HIS SERENE COMPANIONSHIP (vv. 8–9) We must think about the right things (v. 8) if we are to be *assured* of God's presence with us (v. 9). *"Think"* about such things; "think" here means "reckon these things among your assets." It is a metaphor from accountancy.

e. HIS AVAILABLE STRENGTH (vv. 10–13) The apostle does not crave for material things because Christ's power within him makes him adequate for all situations.

f. HIS UNLIMITED WEALTH (vv. 14–23) God supplies our every need (v. 19). There is no lack for those who are "in Christ." As a prisoner, the writer has little; as a believer he has everything necessary for:

- a contented life (v. 11)
- an empowered life (v. 13)
- a useful life (v. 22, "Caesar's household": see 1:12–14)

Colossians

olossians, the third of Paul's four letters written during a period of imprisonment (the other three are Ephesians, Philippians and Philemon) was written to church members whom Paul had never met (2:1). The church at Colossae, a city set in the attractive Lycus Valley, had obviously been troubled by false teachers: either Judaizers or Gnostics, or a weird combination of both, that is, a form of Jewish teaching combined with Greek ideas. The Greeks (and many Gnostics) held that matter was essentially evil; the body was a prison in which the soul was compelled to dwell. The emphasis on Christ's assumption of human flesh is clearly directed against such teaching (1:19, 22; 2:9; and see 2:23). The Jews held on to their religious traditions, observance of ceremonial, circumcision, sabbaths, feast days, etc. (2:11–13, 16–17). The fear-ridden first century world had to realize that it was not under the control of hostile powers, stars or evil angels (for example, 2:18–23) but Christ (1:15–20).

Our division of the epistle is based on 1:4, suggesting two main sections, one doctrinal, the other practical. Colossians points to the centrality of Christ and tells Christians how they ought to behave as Christ's people in their homes, work, at church and in society at large.

1. CHAPTERS 1:1–3:11
FAITH IN CHRIST

The portraiture of Christ is fascinating and enriching. Paul knows that *Christ* is the answer to human need. He reminds his readers of:

a. THE REVOLUTIONARY CHRIST (1:1–14) He can change people, delivering them from Satan and the kingdom of darkness (1:13) by miraculously translating them to a kingdom of light (v. 12), freedom and pardon (vv. 13–14). This first passage is in the form of a superb prayer. Paul makes nine requests as he prays that the church will live: *sensitively* (v. 9, "knowledge of his will"); *worthily* (v. 10); *acceptably* (v. 10); *usefully* (v. 10); *dependently* (v. 11, "strengthened . . ."); *bravely* (v. 11, "great endurance"); *gratefully* (vv. 11–12, "joyfully giving thanks . . ."); *expectantly* (v. 12, "the inheritance of the saints," see 1 Pet. 1:4); *unitedly* (vv. 12–14, "saints," "kingdom." These words express corporate life; they are not individualistic terms).

b. THE PREEMINENT CHRIST (1:15–23) The key to this passage is 1:18. Paul believes Christ to be preeminent because of:

- His unique relationship. He is the "Son" God loves (v. 13). The phrase, "the firstborn" (v. 15) does *not* indicate that he is a created being, but that he is "prior to and supreme over" creation, the only-begotten Son.
- His creative achievement. He was not created; he shared in the work of creation (vv. 16–17, compare John 1:3). He not only created, but sustains the universe (v. 17, compare Heb. 1:3).
- His unrivaled leadership (v. 18). He controls the world and rules the Church. He is its only head.
- His divine nature (v. 15, "image of the invisible God," and especially v. 19). Christ is unique as the only Son of God. Here is Paul's undeniably clear statement about Christ's deity.

- His redemptive work. Redemption (v. 14) and reconciliation (vv. 20–22) are twin themes here. Christ's unique mission to mankind has obtained release from captivity (redemption) and the end of estrangement from God (reconciliation).
- His transforming power (v. 22). By his unique work, he is able to change men and women. The passage expounds what he has done, what he can now do, and what he will do ("present you holy . . .").

c. THE INDWELLING CHRIST (v. 1:24–2:7) Christ can only change our lives *from within;* that is where the revolution takes place (v. 27). Paul testifies of his experience of the indwelling Lord. He finds it:

- an exhilarating experience (v. 24, "*rejoice* in what was suffered")
- a costly experience (v. 24), that is, the suffering involved in the process of building up the body of Christ
- an enriching experience (v. 27) Paul rejoices in these "riches"
- a continuing experience (v. 28–29) Paul's pastoral ambitions are lofty; he longs to present every man "perfect" in Christ Jesus. Maturity takes a lifetime. It goes on and on until we see Christ face to face (see 2 Cor. 3:18; Phil. 3:12–14)
- a unifying experience (2:1–5) This consciousness of the indwelling Christ draws all believers together, united in love.

d. THE AUTHORITATIVE CHRIST (2:8–23) We have referred to the two problems of *gnostic asceticism* (2:8, 18, 21–23) and/or *Jewish legalism* (2:11–14, 16–17) which probably lie behind *Colossians*. Paul shows that all that matters is surrender to Christ not to philosophical systems and religious regulations (2:9–10). He alone is the dependable, unchanging reality (v. 17); other things are

but passing shadows. These believers are urged to hold
fast to the head, Christ Jesus (v. 19); no other powers
have any control (v. 20). Christ defeated them at the
cross (v. 15).

e. THE VICTORIOUS CHRIST (3:1–11) The Ascension is in-
disputable proof of his triumphant conquest (3:1–2). Believers must not have a limited, earthly vision; they must
set their minds (v. 2) on lasting heavenly, eternal things.
Unworthy things must be slain (v. 5) and abandoned (v. 8).
Christians have a *new* nature (v. 10) which has the divine
impress upon it (v. 10). They are not interested in worldly
divisions and classifications (v. 11). Christ is absolutely
everything.

2. CHAPTERS 3:12–4:6
LOVER FOR OTHERS

Faith, hope and love emerged at the beginning of this letter
as a divine triad (1:4–5, compare 1 Thess. 1:3). *Faith in
Christ* has been the main theme of chapters 1:1–3:11. *Hope
in Christ* has been clearly reiterated (1:23; 3:4). Paul now
turns to the theme of *Christian love* in its various practical
aspects. For the apostle it is:

a. FORGIVING LOVE (3:12–13)

b. HARMONIOUS LOVE (3:14–15) "Put on love," which
binds everything together—a salutary word for a church
torn and divided by false teaching (compare 2:2–4).

c. CORRECTIVE LOVE (3:16–17) Believers are expected to
"teach and admonish one another," but this must, like
everything else in life, be done "in the name of the Lord
Jesus" (v. 17).

d. PRACTICAL LOVE (3:18–4:1) "Love" in the New Testament is not a vague, emotional effusion; it is a grace
which turns immediately to action, affecting ordinary,
everyday affairs at home and work. Paul expounds it to
wives (v. 18), *husbands* (v. 19), *children* (v. 20), *fathers*

(v. 21), *employees* (vv. 22–25, a magnificent example of Paul's doctrine of work), and *employers* (4:1).

e. PRAYERFUL LOVE (4:2–4) This church's love would surely turn to intercession for the apostle and his work.

f. EXEMPLARY LOVE (4:5–6) Both works and words (vv. 5, 6) are to commend Christ.

The closing section (4:5–5) contains a series of salutations in which *ten workers* are mentioned; they are a superb study in the rich and varied qualities of Christ's servants.

1 Thessalonians

his is possibly the first of Paul's epistles (though some scholars think *Galatians* came first). It certainly reflects Paul's missionary and pastoral responsibilities at a very early stage. Paul is writing to encourage those who have been recently converted, to defend his apostolic methods against some critics, and to explain the importance of a consistent Christian lifestyle. He also corrects some misunderstandings about what happens when Christians die and what will happen at the second coming of the Lord Jesus.

We use 1:3 to summarize its three main themes. Paul's Christianity is:

1. CHAPTERS 1:1–2:16
A WORK OF FAITH

Paul is grateful for the "work of faith" of the Thessalonian church; this passage also offers some suggestive insights into Paul's own work of faith.

a. PAUL'S CONVERTS (1:1–10) These verses tell us five important things about the young Christians at Thessalonica:

- they are chosen (v. 4) Salvation does not begin with our response but in God's choice.

- they are encouraged (v. 5) It was not mere words which led to their conversion, but the work of God's Holy Spirit; this gives strength of purpose and assurance to them.
- they are tested (v. 6) This word brings affliction with it. There is always opposition when God's word is being used to change lives.
- they are used (v. 7–8) The believers have become an example (v. 7) and exposition (v. 8) of the gospel's power.
- they are changed (v. 9) They are different people; they have turned *from* dead idols *to* the living God.

b. PAUL'S AMBITIONS (2:1–16) Paul treasures three great ambitions, which are priorities throughout his whole missionary career.

- to please God (2:1–4) This is uppermost (v. 4). He has faced physical hazards of various kinds (v. 2, "opposition" is a term common in athletics and indicates strenuous exertion), and verbal insinuations about his sincerity (v. 3). He is only able to continue because he has a dominating passion to please God (v. 4).
- to help men (vv. 5–12) His accusers (possibly Jewish opponents, see Acts 17:5–9, 13) have suggested that in Thessalonica he was leading men astray and making money out of them (v. 5). But Paul and his colleagues helped the Thessalonians as mothers (v. 7), with loving care, and as fathers (vv. 11–12) earnestly training them.
- to proclaim truth (vv. 13–16) Some men and women have accepted the truth of God's word, but the apostle returns to the suffering theme. He knows that throughout Hebrew history those who have believed and proclaimed the word have been persecuted (v. 15). Similarly, he is constantly being hindered by hostile opponents (v. 16).

2. CHAPTERS 2:17–4:12
LABOR OF LOVE

The apostle expounds four great aspects of love at work. He
has proved that it is:

a. ENDURING LOVE (2:17–3:10) He longs to see these
Thessalonian believers again (2:17) but the devil has
caused hindrances to block his way (2:18). The devil still
does this when we want to help others; it is but one of his
devices (see 2 Cor. 2:11). But although Paul and his readers are separated, their love has not diminished. Not only
has Paul's love for them endured separation and accusation (from Jews probably), but their love for him is of an
enduring quality as well (3:1–10). Paul has been able to
withstand intense persecution knowing that these young
Christians are standing firm (3:7–8) in times of testing.
Our reaction to adversity can affect others.

b. UNBOUNDED LOVE (3:11–13) Paul's observations are soon
turned to prayer. He longs that their love will extend toward
one another *and* to everyone (v. 12). Love cannot tolerate
boundaries and barriers; it has to transcend them. Overflow-
ing, unlimited love is a sure sign of holiness of life (v. 13).

c. REFINING LOVE (4:1–8) Paul's teaching to this church is
not merely concerned with intellectual belief, but with
practical behavior, "how to live" (4:1). Sanctification (v. 3),
being set apart for God's use in the world, is *God's will*
and the *believer's responsibility*. We are to be holy because he is holy (5:23; 1 Pet. 1:15). How can a Christian
profess to believe in a holy God and be content with impurity of life? Paul, intensely practical, here as elsewhere,
then discusses the implications of holiness in the realm of
sexual behavior (4–8). The indwelling presence of the
Holy Spirit is ever a check against uncleanness (4:7–8).

d. COHESIVE LOVE (v. 9–12) This love not only keeps
them away from evil; it keeps them close together. God has
taught them how much they need each other (vv. 9–10).

Note that however rich love is, it can always be improved (v. 10, "to do so more and more").

Paul is also concerned about the "outsider"; for Paul pastoral responsibilities (love for the brethren) and evangelistic opportunities ("win the respect of outsiders," v. 12) go hand in hand. This will demand honest work (v. 11) as well as faithful words. The Greeks despised manual work; Paul does not. He regards it as a God-sent opportunity for sacrificial service (see Col. 3:22–25).

3. CHAPTERS 4:13–5:28
ENDURANCE THROUGH HOPE

Earlier in the letter Paul made several references to the Lord's return (1:10; 2:19; 3:13). He now turns to this great doctrine in greater detail. This teaching is strangely neglected in our own day. We should not be surprised at this (2 Pet. 3:3–4). The apostle makes three assertions about the return of Christ:

a. THE COMING OF THE LORD DISPELS GRIEF (4:13–18) We do not sorrow as hopeless unbelievers (4:13). The truth of Christ's return brings comfort (4:18) as we remember that we will be reunited with all those in Christ who have gone before (4:14). It will be the day of the Lord's triumphant victory (4:16). Those who die in Christ are not "finished," as the unbelieving world asserts, but are asleep (4:14).
b. THE COMING OF THE LORD DEFIES SPECULATION (5:1–7) It seems that there have always been those who have spent valuable time in the profitless pursuit of hidden information about the precise moment of Christ's return (see Matt. 24:3; Acts 1:7). The date is not to be revealed to us (Mark 13:32–33), but what we do know, however, is that he will return when he is least expected (5:3–4). We must be alert (5:5–7) and not live as those who are indifferent to his promised return.

c. THE COMING OF THE LORD DEMANDS HOLINESS
(5:18–28) This final passage is concerned with living in
the light, in the day (v. 8). Faith, hope and love return again
(v. 8, see 1:3). It has been suggested that these terse commands or exhortations may be cast in this form as instructions for converts to memorize (catechetical instruction).
Similar lists are found in other epistles (for example, Rom.
12; 1 Pet. 3). They emphasize once more the *practical* nature of the Christian life. Holiness is not some ethereal, im-
practical ideal; it is concerned with *real life,* for example,
with:

- mutual encouragement (v. 11)
- affectionate respect (vv. 12–13)
- gracious admonition (v. 14)
- unselfish goodness (v. 15)
- constant gratitude (vv. 16–18)
- sensitive discernment (vv. 19–21)
- moral purity (v. 22)

How is all this possible? Only because the One who demands it (4:3) is the One who effects it (5:23–24). Some
final salutations (5:25–28) bring Paul's earliest letter to a
close.

2 Thessalonians

he two Thessalonian letters are quite similar, and the second one cannot have been written long after the first. Paul writes again in order to encourage suffering Christians. He tells them to continue steadfastly in their faith, knowing that evil will certainly be punished. Paul's teaching about Christ's return is:

a. SCRIPTURAL He quotes frequently from the Old Testament.
b. URGENT He is concerned that erroneous teaching regarding the Second Coming (2:2) should be quickly corrected.
c. PRACTICAL False teaching soon produces bad living; some had become lazy and idle believing that they had nothing to do but sit and wait for the Lord's return.

The epistle clearly expounds four themes:

1. CHAPTER 1:1–12
THE BELIEVER'S AFFLICTION

Paul's first word is encouraging. He is delighted that their faith is growing and their love is increasing (v. 3). There is bound to be opposition (v. 4), but they should be encouraged by it. Paul points out the positive things to be gained from persecution:

a. IT ENRICHES TESTIMONY "we boast about . . ." (v. 4) Paul can tell other Christian communities about their fortitude, bringing encouragement to them (see Phil. 1:14).

b. IT STRENGTHENS CHARACTER (v. 4) It is trouble which has made them steadfast; constant case would eventually result in weakness.

c. IT PROVES SINCERITY (v. 5) The devil would not harass them like this if they were not true Christians. These trials are a guarantee of their sonship.

d. IT ENCOURAGES PRAYER (v. 11) Paul and his colleagues had been driven to prayer for them.

e. IT GLORIFIES CHRIST (v. 12) As they go through these fires of affliction, Christ is being glorified in their lives. Others can see what a gracious God they have.

Verses 7–10 focus attention on the fate of unbelievers who:

- ignore God (v. 8) that is, they do not want to know about him (see Rom. 1:28)
- disobey God, that is, they do not obey the gospel, which is not only an invitation, but a summons (Acts 17:30).

"Everlasting destruction" (v. 9) means being excluded from God's presence, his majestic power (v. 9), and glory (v. 10; see Isa. 2:10, 19, 21).

2. CHAPTER 2:1–12
THE BELIEVER'S ENEMY

a. THE LAWLESS ONE Paul's missionary work was frequently opposed, maligned and hindered. Apparently one letter at least had been written purporting to be from him saying that the "day of the Lord" had already come (2:2). Paul explains that although the precise moment is not known, certain events will precede his advent. A time of serious apostasy will be led by the anti-Christ, "the man of lawlessness" (or "of sin," v. 3) who will take titles of deity to himself (2:3–4). These warnings were not hypothetical impossibilities; in AD 40 the Emperor Gaius tried to set up his statue in the Jerusalem Temple (see 2:4; Mark 13:14).

b. THE RESTRAINING ONE (2:6–7) God is sovereign. The destiny of men and nations is not in the hands of the devil. Who is "the one who now holds it back" (2:7)? Some suggest the Roman Empire or the Emperor; even though at times the state opposed the gospel, in other ways, though without realizing it, the state furthered God's work (see Rom. 13:1–7; 1 Tim. 2:1–4; 1 Pet. 2:13–17; Rev. 13 for evidence that the state was seen in *both* a protective and persecuting role). Other commentators think "the restraining one" is the Spirit of God, and yet others prefer to think in terms of a promised leader of some special kind.

c. THE VICTORIOUS ONE (2:8–12) More important than the identity of the "restraining one" is the conquest of the evil one, the devil. Of this there is no uncertainty. He is to be destroyed by Christ (v. 8). Note that the Lord Jesus slays him with his word (see Isa. 11:4; Rev. 19:15). The one who is to be vanquished:

- opposes God
- deceives men
- perverts truth (v. 10; see Rom. 1:18–32)

3. CHAPTERS 2:13–3:5
THE BELIEVER'S CONFIDENCE

The apostle says that although many are being led astray, he has confidence in the Thessalonian believers (3:4). This is because he has confidence in the God who will protect them (3:3). Four things produce true Christian confidence:

a. GOD'S CHOICE OF US (2:13–15) He chose them from the beginning (2:13) and called them (2:14). Note the clear trinitarian reference here. Father, Son and Holy Spirit share in the miracle of man's eternal salvation.

b. GOD'S LOVE FOR US (2:16–17) Paul has earlier described the Christians in Thessalonica as "brothers loved by the Lord" (v. 13), but he now makes this immense truth more explicit (v. 16). The fact that Christ is mentioned first (v. 16) shows that "there is complete equality in the apostle's mind between the Father and the Son" (W. Neil). The Lord's love imparts comfort (v. 16), inspires hope (v. 16) and encourages witness (v. 17).

c. GOD'S WORD TO US (3:1–2) This church has gratefully received God's word (1 Thess. 1:5–6) and eagerly shared it with others (1 Thess. 1:8). They know that it is God's truth, not just men's advice (1 Thess. 2:12). Now Paul asks that they will pray for him. He longs that God's word may "speed on and triumph" (3:1, RSV), in the place of his present missionary work (Corinth?), just as it did in Thessalonica (see Ps. 147:15). Paul knows that there are many without faith.

d. GOD'S POWER IN US (3:3–5) Though some men are faithless, the Lord is faithful (3:3); he has promised to strengthen and protect his people from "the evil one" (compare Matt. 6:13). In view of what Paul has just said about Satan's activities (2:2–12), this is an immensely encouraging promise. Christ was *steadfast* in times of testing (for example Matt. 4:1–11), and in God's power his people can be the same.

4. CHAPTER 3:6–18
THE BELIEVER'S RESPONSIBILITY

This church is troubled by "adventist idlers" who maintain that as the Lord is about to return there is no point in getting down to any hard work! Paul exposes this erroneous thinking (v. 6). The church members are to engage in:

a. HARD WORK—like Paul, who "worked night and day" (v. 8)

b. EXEMPLARY WORK (v. 9) Paul might have expected to

be supported as a full-time Christian worker but he obtained local employment as "a model" for them to copy.

c. HELPFUL WORK (v. 13) The believers at Thessalonica are to give themselves unstintingly to good work (compare Gal. 6:9), that is, "stop fussing, stop idling, and stop sponging" (W. Neil).

Paul expects his readers to accept his teaching (vv. 14–15). However tumultuous life may be, they are reminded that "the Lord of peace" imparts his peace in all circumstances and in various ways (v. 16).

The closing salutation (vv. 17–18) is interesting in view of 2:2. The apostle dictated his letters but always added these gracious postscripts in his own handwriting.

Whatever their difficulties, the totally sufficient grace of Christ would not fail these Thessalonian Christians. Paul's own experience confirmed that truth (2 Cor. 12:9–10).

1 Timothy

his letter is the first of three "Pastoral Epistles" (1 and 2 Timothy and Titus). When Paul sailed for Greece, he left Timothy in charge of the church at Ephesus. It proved a difficult task for a young (4:12), timid (2 Tim. 1:4, 7), devoted (Phil. 2:19–21) colleague who was frequently unwell (5:23). Once Paul's strong leadership was removed from the scene, false teachers began to intensify their activities; they were probably Gnostics ("Gnostic" comes from the Greek word for "knowledge"), who taught that moral conduct was not important to believers. After his opening greeting to a "true son" we have:

1. CHAPTER 1:3–11
PAUL'S WARNING

This erroneous teaching is intellectually suspect (v. 4), spiritually profitless (vv. 5–6) and morally damaging (vv. 5–11: the teachers were probably "antinomians" who spoke "against the law"), and theologically indefensible. Its message is utterly contrary to "the gospel which tells of the glory of God" (v. 11, NEB). It occasions controversy, deflects from faith-inspired service (v. 4), desensitizes the human conscience, damages Christian love, promotes useless talk (v. 5) and encourages ignorance (v. 7).

Paul insists on the importance of God-given law. The law exposes sin (vv. 8–10), which is always likely to be minimized, excused or ignored. These teachers may have reduced the intentionally forceful moral impact of, say, the Ten Commandments, by allegorizing them, or by suggesting that a Christian is "under grace" and not subject to the law. But the law is not dismissed by the gospel. The law illustrates God's holiness and compassionate concern (note the sins against others); precisely identifies our rebellion; exposes our inability to live for God without the gospel and provides a basic code of behavior essential for the well-being of a clean, secure, caring community. Those who ignore law soon despise grace.

2. CHAPTER 1:12–17
PAUL'S GRATITUDE

As a convinced Pharisee, Paul knew and valued the moral law, but was in desperate need of the gospel. It was the gospel which changed him: from a Christ-rejecting blasphemer to a Christ-honoring worshipper; from a cruel persecutor to a loving preacher (vv. 12–14). This transforming miracle of grace took place not only so that Paul might be saved but also that others might be reached: since the "worst of sinners" has been converted (v. 16), nobody else could possibly claim to be too bad to be changed, or too far away to be reached by God. No wonder Paul becomes lyrical about the privilege of service (v. 12) and about God's generous mercy (v. 13), abundant grace (v. 14), dependable truth (v. 15), limitless patience (v. 16) and eternal reign (v. 17).

3. CHAPTERS 1:17–6:10
PAUL'S TEACHING

Once he has shared his deep and practical convictions about law and gospel, the apostle provides his son in the faith with essential "instruction" (1:18; 3:14; 5:21; 6:3) to pass on to

others. Sound teaching is of the greatest possible importance
in the Pastoral Epistles. Essential truths (entrusted by Christ
through Paul to Timothy) must be passed on faithfully to
others (2 Tim. 2:2). Paul here presents vital teaching on five
main themes concerning the church's:

a. WORSHIP (2:1–15). Prayer for *everyone* (including first
century godless emperors) is a "first of all" priority (2:1).
This injunction may well have been prompted by the
Gnostic heresy which made salvation an exclusive blessing strictly reserved for a favored few who had been personally initiated into secret truths. But God wants *all* to be
saved (4:10). Christ's death was a ransom for *all*. The only
mediation is through him, not by private Gnostic privileges (2:3–5). Praying worshippers must also offer the
sacrifice of holy, peace-loving lives, and women must be
tastefully adorned with appropriate conduct. Paul's concern about the congregation's teachers has the Gnostic
heresy as its context: it is possible that some women may
have been offenders in this respect (4:7), some had certainly been captivated by the false teaching (2 Tim. 3:6).
b. LEADERS (3:1–16) Paul's concern here is about:

- consistent living—the leader's personal qualities, financial affairs, domestic circumstances, spiritual maturity and social behavior must be "above reproach"
- loyal teaching—verse 16 is possibly an early Christian hymn concerning the living God, ascended Lord
  and authenticated Spirit.

c. OPPONENTS (4:1–16) The same Spirit who vindicated
Christ also warns believers about deceptive and demonic
heresy (vv. 1–2). Some Gnostic teachers insisted that all
physical matter was evil, so marriage and certain foods
were alike forbidden. But God has created all good things
and they are to be thankfully received and prayerfully
consecrated to God's glory (vv. 3–4). False doctrine must
be counteracted by good teaching (4:6, 11, 13–14, 16),

disciplined godliness (vv. 7–8), confident hope (v. 9), exemplary speech (v. 12), as well as the public reading and exposition of Scripture (v. 13).

d. MEMBERS (5:1–6:2) Here Paul gives Timothy pastoral advice about both elderly and young members (5:1–2), and the widows, leaders and slaves as well as offering a few words about self-care, easily neglected by busy workers (5:21–25).

e. MONEY (6:3–10) Some false teachers were making money out of their dangerous doctrines (vv. 3–5). Paul recalls the quality of Christian contentment (vv. 6–8), a blessing which eludes the avaricious rich who ruin others (v. 9), spawn evil, destroy faith and inflict severe wounds on themselves (v. 10).

4. CHAPTER 6:11–21
PAUL'S COUNSEL

The concluding paragraphs remind young Timothy that there is a quest to pursue (v. 11), a battle to fight (v. 12), a commandment to keep (vv. 13–16, remembering Christ's courageous testimony and promised return), a warning to share (vv. 17–19, once more to the rich), and a deposit to guard (vv. 20–21), the saving gospel of which he is a trusted steward.

2 Timothy

his message, the last of Paul's letters, was written during imprisonment (1:8; 2:9) and under the shadow of impending execution (4:6). It is the apostle's final opportunity to counsel his young colleague, and is primarily about the Christian leader's personal values and the inevitable suffering his work will entail. After the customary salutation (vv. 1–2) the prisoner writes about:

1. CHAPTER 1:3–7
MEMORIES

With his earthly life almost at an end, Paul naturally looks back and he gratefully recalls his forefathers' spiritual example (v. 3), Timothy's deep affection (v. 4), genuine faith, godly upbringing (v. 5) and divinely imparted gift (v. 6) as well as, above all, God's generosity (v. 7).

2. CHAPTER 1:8–18
PRIVILEGES

There are times when Paul feels lonely (v. 15; 4:16), but his hold on spiritual realities is more firm than ever. In God's power he endures suffering (v. 8), through God's Son he proclaims grace (vv. 9–11) and by God's Spirit he treasures truth (vv. 12–18).

Paul's saying about guarding the good deposit (v. 12) may refer to the commitment of his life to Christ or, more likely, to Paul's confidence that the Holy Spirit protects the gospel which Christ has entrusted to him. We guard (v. 14) what he preserves (v. 12). Paul recalls that in tough times, when many deserted him, one family was specially and sacrificially kind (vv. 15–18) in two different and distant pagan cities.

3. CHAPTER 2:1–26
IDEALS

Chapter 2 gives seven fascinating metaphors to illustrate the ideal in Christian life and service and Paul longs that people of this caliber should take up the work he is soon to lay down (vv. 1–2). In times of adversity, hostility and persecution, service for Christ demands:

- the devoted soldier (vv. 1–4), who is determined to please his superior;
- the obedient athlete (v. 5), who conforms to the rules;
- the energetic farmer (vv. 6–7), whose industry is rewarded;
- the submissive sufferer (vv. 8–13), who remembers Christ's victorious conquests, God's unfettered word and dependable promises;
- the faithful interpreter (vv. 14–19), who "correctly handles [literally, plows a straight furrow. The Greek version of the Old Testament uses the same word in Prov. 3:6; 11:5] the word of truth" (v. 15). He does not traffic in quarrelsome, profitless, ruinous (v. 14), godless (v. 16), damaging (v. 17), destructive (v. 18) chatter;
- the useful vessel (vv. 20–22), varied in function (v. 20), but clean, dedicated and utterly at the Master's disposal (v. 21);
- the kind slave (vv. 22–26), who will be gentle, even toward fractious ensnared opponents.

4. CHAPTER 3:1–9
DANGERS

For Paul, and ourselves, "the last days" have already arrived. His description of self-loving (3:2), rather than God-loving (v. 4) humanity is tragically illustrated in the columns of our daily newspapers. Note the highly relevant exposure of perverted love. Love is not meant to flow inward to selfish, avaricious pleasures (vv. 2, 4), but outward to the good (v. 3) and to God (v. 4). The apostle knows that there are insincere and inconsistent (v. 5) people around who not only adopt such corrupt standards for themselves but make strenuous attempts to win converts (vv. 6–9). Jannes and Jambres (v. 8) were Egyptian magicians whose names are not mentioned in the Old Testament but who appear in Jewish, pagan and early Christian literature. Their opposition to Moses was totally and evidently ineffective as will be the work of the false teachers (v. 9).

5. CHAPTERS 3:10–4:8
PRIORITIES

Paul's concluding commission to Timothy is the instruction to engage in faithful teaching. He is to recognize:

a. ITS COST (3:10–13) Paul mentions present endurance (3:10), past suffering (3:11, during the first missionary journey) and predicted difficulties (vv. 12–13).

b. ITS NATURE (3:14–17) The message Timothy received from his mother, grandmother (1:5) and the apostle (2:1) is contained in authoritative, uniquely inspired Scripture which imparts wisdom, presents salvation, exalts Christ, offers instruction, provides correction, inspires discipline and describes resources.

c. ITS IMPORTANCE (4:1–8) This word must be earnestly preached at all times (4:2), through hard times (4:3–4) and to the end of time. Paul's closing "charge" to Timothy be-

gins and ends with a reference to Christ's promised return
(4:1, 8). The apostle contrasts the doctrinal loyalty of
Timothy (4:5, "But you . . .") with the doctrinal instability
(4:3–4) of some contemporaries. Paul, a model of dedicated ministry, has been the soldier, athlete and interpreter
who has guarded the deposit (4:7).

6. CHAPTER 4:9–22
HELPERS

Paul knows that all this could not have been achieved on his
own. Some friends have certainly been disappointing. Demas
defected (v. 10) and Alexander was damaging (vv. 14–15),
but others were wonderfully supportive, especially the dependable friend and greatly loved Doctor Luke (v. 11; Col.
4:14), loyal colleagues like Crescens, Titus (v. 10), Tychicus
(v. 12), the thoroughly helpful and no longer useless Mark
(v. 11; Acts 13:13; 15:36–40), the hospitable host, Carpus
(v. 13) and a cluster of other believers (vv. 19–22) whose
precise service is not known.

The apostle closes the letter by mentioning—including
Timothy himself (v. 21)—seventeen people who have been
his helpers and supporters and will carry on the work after
Paul's fight has ended and his race been successfully won
(v. 7). The Lord who accompanied and fortified the apostle
(v. 17) is alongside all his servants (v. 22) and brings them
safely home (v. 18).

Titus

aul wrote this short letter to Titus, one of his Gentile converts (1:4; Gal. 2:3) and his valued colleague (2 Cor. 2:12–13; 8:23; Gal. 2:1–4; 2 Tim. 4:10) in order to offer him affectionate encouragement, pastoral counsel and sound teaching. After Titus had worked hard in the difficult church at Corinth (2 Cor. 7:6–7, 13–15; 8:6, 16–18; 12:18), the apostle entrusted this young minister with another demanding assignment, this time the care of the churches on Crete (1:5). It was a far from easy task; there were highly divisive doctrinal (1:10–11) and moral (1:12, 15–16) problems on the island.

In his *opening greeting* (1:1–4), Paul begins by describing himself as God's *slave* and Christ's *apostle*. His confidence is in the God he serves and the Christ who sends. Christians are *chosen* ("God's elect"), *changed* ("leads to godliness") and *used* ("the preaching entrusted to me by the command of God.") Paul then expounds three main themes:

1. Chapter 1:5–9
LEADERS

Good leadership is essential if these young churches are to be firmly established, morally protected and spiritually quickened. Titus must look out for suitable elders. Low moral standards were typical of Cretan social life; "to cretize" was a popular first century synonym for lying (v. 12). That kind of behavior must not be found in the homes of Crete's spiritual leaders. The elder must have an exemplary lifestyle, totally different from his pagan contemporaries. His children need to be converted (v. 6), not "wild and disobedient" like so many fellow Cretans, and his home must be a welcoming haven (v. 8) offering good hospitality in an alien environment. His life must be characterized not only by love for what is good but also by self-control, and a grasp of sound truth (vv. 8–9).

2. CHAPTER 1:10–16
PROBLEMS

The Cretans' wild and immoral behavior was no recent phenomenon. Paul quotes the words of a famous sixth century BC Cretan, Epimenides, to prove it (v. 12). There are false teachers around as well as people with virtually no moral standards. Judaizers (v. 10) are pressing the claims of the ceremonial law but that will do little to transform the lives of the corrupt islanders. Several are even making money out of their heretical teaching. Knowing God must be a moral as well as a spiritual experience (v. 16). Unworthy behavior is a denial of the gospel.

3. CHAPTERS 2:1–3:11
TEACHING

The Cretans need good teaching (2:1). This section first discusses the doctrine of consistent behavior, then goes on to expound the doctrine of the Savior who alone makes it possible.

a. TEACHING ABOUT CONDUCT (2:2–10) Some Cretan heretics are only out to make money (1:11), but the life of the Christian on the island must draw people to the gospel

(2:10). Christian doctrine is to be taught (2:1), exemplified (2:7) and made undeniably attractive by appropriate living (2:10). Different groups of people must be helped to apply the message to their own lives: older men must be loving and steadfast (2:2); older women reverent and kind; younger men need to be self-controlled; and slaves submissive and honest. Above all, the teacher must make sure that his own life preaches a thoroughly consistent message (2:7). Some unbelievers may well be looking out for something "bad to say about us" (2:8), so that God's word can be maligned (2:5). The morally upright lives of Cretan believers must be so clearly evident that teaching about their saving God is visibly adorned in each local community.

b. TEACHING ABOUT CHRIST (2:11–3:11) A further appeal for consistent behavior (3:1–2) is set between two passages about the Savior. Paul tells Titus to remind the believers of what they once were (3:3), and then of who Christ is (3:4). The transformed lives, evident in the island's Christian community, have only been made possible by Christ's unique work. Without that, every exhortation to good conduct would be utterly ineffective. Paul reminds young Titus of the comings of Christ: the unique fact of his first appearance at Bethlehem (2:11; 3:4) and the "blessed hope" of his promised return (2:13). The incarnation and the consummation are twin truths which not only *encourage* holiness of life but *effect* a transformation of lifestyle.

The incarnate Christ is God's generous gift to *all* mankind, slaves (2.9) as well as freemen; it is for *all* who believe in his saving work (3:5), and is not reserved for those who rely on legalistic ceremonial (1:10) or good works. Notice how effectively Paul links together as saving truth, the birth (12:11; 3:4), the atonement (2:14; 3:5), the achievements (3:6–7), demands (2:12) and return (2:13) of Christ. Jesus came into this world to redeem us and he will return to complete that unique redemptive work. The truth of Christ's return is not a theme for profitless speculation, but an incentive for radical transformation. Believers want to be at their best, morally and spiritually, when the Savior returns (1 John 3:3).

The apostle knows that neither on Crete nor anywhere else will everyone be devoted to doing good (3:8, 14). Though the message is profitable for everyone, it will not be heeded by everyone. Some prefer to argue about profitless things rather than believe unshakable truths (3:9). Such people will not only debate useless topics, but will also divide unsuspecting churches (3:10). Heretics of that kind must be seen for what they are and not be allowed to damage the lives of others.

In Paul's *final greetings* (3:12–15) he turns with relief from quarrelsome cranks to reliable colleagues. Do we do everything we can to help the Lord's servants? We should "see that they have everything they need" (3:13).

The believers on Crete must work hard so that they can give generously (3:14). Unproductive lives dishonor the Lord "who gave himself for us" (2:14). Loving and "doing what is good" (1:8; 2:14; 3:8, 14; compare 1:16) are the outward evidence of the renewing work of God's indwelling Spirit (3:5).

Philemon

nesimus, formerly a "useless" slave (v. 11) in the household of the Christian leader Philemon, appears to have run away from home and work, possibly having stolen some of his master's money (v. 18). God's sovereignty is such that, thinking he was getting away from Christians, he was actually getting closer to them! He ran into the company of the apostle Paul during the apostle's imprisonment (v. 9). Onesimus was converted through Paul's testimony to the power of the gospel (v. 10). Perhaps Paul told the young man of his own earlier opposition to the good news of Christ and the people who were of "the way" (Acts 7:58; 8:1; 9:1–2). Paul, too, knew what it was to be an enemy of the gospel, but had been forgiven, reconciled and changed (1 Tim. 1:12–16).

Now that Onesimus is a Christian he must be reconciled to his master as well as to his Savior. It is essential for him to return home, no longer "useless" but now true to his name: the Greek word "onesimus" means "useful" (v. 11). Paul had benefited from the young slave's devoted service, but it would not be right to keep him. In order to make the difficult task of returning home a little easier, the apostle gives him a letter to take to his Christian master appealing for a loving welcome to this new Christian. After an opening salutation (1:1–3), this delightful personal letter introduces us to three themes:

1. VERSES 4–7
THANKSGIVING

Although he is confined as a prisoner, the apostle is grateful
for so many good things. His joy is not dependent upon his
circumstances. It is as he comes to God in daily thanksgiving (v. 4) that he is reminded of his blessings and benefits.
We ought to set aside at least a few minutes in every day to
reflect on the many good things that God has done for us.
Notice how important a place "unceasing thanksgiving" has
in Paul's life and how particularly evident it is in the letters
he wrote from prison (Eph. 1:3, 16; 5:20; Phil. 1:3; 4:6; Col.
1:3, 12; 2:7; 3:15, 17). He might well have been frustrated
that he could not continue his vigorous missionary activity.
Instead he counted his blessings and gratefully acknowledged that God knew best (Phil. 1:12–14).

  a. THANKSGIVING IS EXPRESSED IN PRAYER Even in a
Roman dungeon Paul can still pray. This short letter has
several references to prayer (vv. 4, 6). It is a mutually supportive exercise (v. 22) which accomplishes more than we
can ever imagine.
  b. THANKSGIVING IS DEEPENED BY FELLOWSHIP Paul is
deeply grateful for other believers (v. 7). He is not able to
travel and do what he would like to further the çause of
Christ, but he rejoices that, while his activities are re-
stricted, other Christians are constantly at work confessing their faith, expressing their love, increasing their
knowledge and deepening their fellowship (vv. 5–7).
  c. THANKSGIVING IS GLORIFYING TO CHRIST Paul's greatest
encouragement lies not in what other Christians have done
for Christ, but what the Lord has done for them. He rejoices
in "every good thing" we have in Jesus. Those resources are
endless and unlimited. Some of them are mentioned in this
opening section of the letter: grace, peace (v. 2), assurance
and security ("my God," v. 4), faith, love (v. 5), spiritual insight ("full understanding," v. 6), the privilege of sharing

(*koinonia,* v. 6) that knowledge within the Christian community and beyond it in evangelism, joy (v. 7).

2. VERSES 8–22
CONFIDENCE

The heart of the letter contains Paul's request that Onesimus be reinstated in Philemon's household so that the reconciling gospel can be seen in practice as well as heard in preaching. Paul's spiritual confidence is vividly reflected in these verses. He knows that:

a. GOD IS SOVEREIGN Three times in this brief letter Paul describes himself as the prisoner of Jesus Christ (vv. 1, 9, 23). He is not Caesar's convict. Even his enforced removal from strategic missionary work is within the sovereign control of an Almighty God (Rom. 8:28; Phil. 1:12–14). And the same sovereign God who was at work within the lives of Paul and Epaphras in the Roman jail, was also pursuing the runaway Onesimus as he hurriedly escaped from Philemon's Christian influence but not from God's pardoning mercy.

b. PEOPLE CAN CHANGE Paul really believes in the power of the gospel he preaches so persuasively. He has seen it at work during his missionary journeys and here is yet another example of its transforming work within human life. The young man who was "formerly useless" is now thoroughly useful (v. 11). When Martin Luther gave his lectures on this letter in the late 1520s he said: "Thus no one ought to despair about anyone else . . . see how brethren are to be handled if they fall."

c. CHRIST WILL CONQUER Christ's conquest had earlier taken place in *Paul's* life to make him the passionate Christian evangelist he has become. Here is this formerly insular, exclusive, self-confident, persecuting Pharisee (Phil. 3:4–6) now writing about a Gentile slave, and a delinquent at that, as "my son" (v. 10), "my very heart" (v. 12), "very dear to me" (v. 16). Paul would have given anything to have kept Onesimus alongside him as a supportive helper (v. 13). Here some of the great gulfs of the first century world have been crossed by the power of Christ's reconciling gospel: Jew and Gentile, free citizen and slave, cultured, well-educated intellectual and social outcast. This same reconciling message has clearly worked in the life of Onesimus as he has turned from his sins and found new life and a better freedom in Christ. It will surely work too in the life of Philemon, the recipient of the letter. In those days runaway slaves were either branded on their return with an "F" (*fugitivus*), or were executed, but Paul has confidence in Philemon's grasp of the gospel and is sure he will welcome the runaway back (v. 21).

3. VERSES 1–4, 23–25
PARTNERSHIP

Within this short letter (only 300 words in the original text) Paul refers to his greatly valued colleagues: *ten* of them. Timothy offers his friendship (v. 1), Philemon his home (v. 2). Archippus probably has pastoral oversight as he is mentioned at the beginning of the letter (v. 2; see Col. 4:17); Epaphras gives his physical and prayer support as a fellow-prisoner (v. 23; Col. 4:12). Mark and Luke (v. 24) are to devote their literary gifts to the service of this reconciling gospel. Paul knows that the spread of such momentous news is only possible through teamwork. In such an enterprise he is deeply grateful for his "fellow-workers" (v. 24).

Hebrews

his "letter" reads more like a sermon (13:22) addressed to Jewish Christians who were either in danger of abandoning the distinctively Christian aspects of their faith or were tempted in time of threatened or impending persecution to minimize those aspects and live solely in the more socially acceptable Jewish part of their Christianity. Possibly some of their Jewish neighbors had become offended by their claims concerning Christ's deity and the uniqueness of his sacrificial work. The writer, or preacher, a highly gifted church leader, who does not identify himself in this letter, urges his readers not to slip back into reliance on outward religious observances, pleading with them to recognize that the ceremonial provisions of the Law were temporary (7:11), partial (9:13–14), imperfect (7:18; 8:7) and now obsolete (8:13). The readers are exhorted not to abandon their confidence in Christ (10:35), but to accept the fact that some element of suffering has been (11:1–40) and always will be (12:1–12) part of authentic godliness and true faith. The letter can be divided into three parts.

1. CHAPTERS 1:1–6:20
GOD'S UNIQUE WORD

In Old Testament times God used a variety of different means to communicate his message, but he now addresses us uniquely in Christ (1:1–3). The "word" is very important in *Hebrews* (2:2; 4:2, 12; 6:5; 11:3; 12:19, 27; 13:7, 22); these first century readers were reminded of the completeness and finality of God's perfect revelation in Christ. God speaks to us more eloquently in Christ's person, life, teaching, sacrifice and saving achievement than anywhere else. Christ is far more than a divinely appointed messenger (angel, 1:4–14). To minimize, ignore or reject him as the unique Word has the most serious consequences (2:1–4). Notice how Christ's deity (1:1–14) and perfect humanity (2:5–10) are deliberately set alongside one another. In a series of six portraits the Lord Jesus is presented as:

- brother (2:11–13)
- liberator—from death, the devil and sin (2:14–18)
- apostle—sent by God to establish a new "house" or believing community (3:1–6)
- partner (3:14)
- priest who was appointed by God, tested like us and victorious over sin (4:14–5:10)
- forerunner—see 6:20, where Christ is described as the *prodromos,* a military term used by the Greeks to describe an advance guard sent to explore and prepare the way for those who will follow (see also 2:10; 10:19–21; John 14:2–3).

These opening chapters contain four increasingly serious warning passages; they expose the dangers of carelessness (2:1–4), unbelief (3:7–4:13), immaturity (5:11–14) and apostasy (6:1–8). In our understanding of these verses, it is essential to remember their first century context. The words about apostates do not describe the occasional drifter, or spiritually weak or insecure backslider; the terms used indicate people who wish to be included among those who now fiercely oppose Christ and would crucify him again (6:6); such unhappy people do not wish to be numbered among his followers. Those who deliberately choose to reject Christ in this hostile manner do not believe he is the world's Savior.

But people will not be saved when they forcefully spurn the only means of salvation. A later passage (10:26–31) takes up the same theme.

2. CHAPTERS 7:1–10:18
CHRIST'S PERFECT WORK

The central section of the letter uses three vivid word pictures to expound and interpret the eternal achievement of Christ through his saving death. He is the *eternal priest* (7:1–8:5) who inaugurates a *better covenant* (8:6–9:5) through a *unique sacrifice* (9:6–10:18).

Christ's redemptive work perfectly accomplished that which was never possible under the old covenant. The Old Testament itself constantly looks beyond its own provisions to something which will be far "better," a key concept in this letter (1:4, 6; 7:19, 22; 8:6; 9:23; 10:34; 11:16, 35, 40; 12:24).

However godly they may have been, the old Jewish priests eventually died, but Jesus lives forever (7:23–24).

Their ministry was limited by time; his is eternal (7:25).

They were sinners, but he is perfect (7:26).

They offered sacrificial animals, but he offered himself (7:27).

They had to keep on presenting their offerings, but his eternally effective sacrifice was offered once for all (9:12).

They made the worshipper ceremonially clean; he purges our sin-stricken consciences (9:6–14).

They stood in God's presence on earth; he sat down in God's presence in heaven, his priestly sacrifice complete and the unique work finished (10:11–12).

3. CHAPTERS 10:19–13:25
OUR OBEDIENT RESPONSE

Believers are here called to a life of:

a. STEADFAST HOPE (10:19–39) They must *draw near* to the place of prayer, cleansing and faith (10:19–22) and help others to do so (10:23–25); *keep close* (some will want to lure them away, 10:26–34) and *press on* (10:35–39).

b. COURAGEOUS FAITH (11:12–29)—constantly encouraged by the inspiring lives of heroic men and women who have entered into their reward (11:1–40), by the unique example of Jesus (12:1–4), by God's present fatherly love (12:5–17), and our eternally secure future prospects (12:18–29).

c. MUTUAL LOVE—expressed in practical help (13:1–3), moral example (13:4–8), doctrinal integrity (13:9–12), courageous witness (13:13–14), grateful worship (13:15–16), loving obedience (13:17) and supportive prayer (13:18–19), knowing that the risen Shepherd has promised every necessary provision (13:20–21).

James

hen the seventeenth century Puritan, Thomas Manton, was expounding this very practical letter in a time of persecution, he said *James* is "fraught with excellent instructions, how to bear afflictions, to hear the word, to mortify vile affections, to bridle the tongue, to conceive rightly of the nature of God, to adorn our profession with a good conversation, with meekness and peace and charity." It is a good summary of the letter's main message, which reminds us of the necessity of consistent, daily, godly behavior. The letter is among the earlier New Testament writings, and may well have been written by our Lord's brother (Matt. 13:55; Acts 12:17; 15:13; 1 Cor. 15:7; Gal. 1:19; 2:9). That could explain the frequent references or allusions to Christ's teaching, for example 1:4 (Matt. 5:48); 1:5, 17 (Matt. 7:11); 1:5; 4:2 (Matt. 7:7–8); 1:6 (Matt. 21:22); 1:22–25; 4:17 (Matt. 7:21–27); 2:5 (Luke 6:20–23); 2:8 (Mark 12:31); 2:10 (Matt. 5:19); 2:13 (Matt. 5:7; 18:32–35), as well as further echoes in James 3:12; 4:4, 6, 10–12, 13–17; 5:2–3, 7–9, 12.

The letter offers Christian insights into *ten* practical themes:

1. Chapter 1:1–18
TROUBLES

Believers are not to grumble when adversities come. These times of "testing" can produce fine spiritual qualities which could not develop if life were always smooth and unruffled. They help to make us mature people (v. 4), dependent upon God for wisdom to react to trials in the most fitting and creative way (v. 5), grateful for the unchanging values and blessings of the spiritual life (vv. 9–11), all the more appreciative of those promised treasures in store for us (v. 13), and assured of the gifts of an unchanging Father (vv. 13–18).

2. Chapter 1:19–27
OBEDIENCE

Man's words are sometimes destructive (1:19–21), but God's word is thoroughly and uniquely beneficial. Like a mirror, it exposes our need (vv. 23–24) and in addition it demands our response (v. 22). It must not simply be heard (vv. 22–23), but practiced; its teaching, if obeyed, will control our speech (v. 26), touch our hearts and sanctify our character (v. 27).

3. Chapter 2:1–13
LOVE

Like Jesus, James is concerned about the poor. There is no room for class-conscious favoritism in the church (2:1–4). The economically deprived Christian may be rich in faith and we may need his or her spiritual wealth if we are to mature in Christ. In today's global village we need to hear, through these verses, the agonizing cry of the world's hungry; they are our desperately needy neighbors (v. 8).

4. CHAPTER 2:14–26
DEEDS

The command to love can fall on deaf ears, or be senti-
mentalized into compassionate thoughts which are not
matched by sacrificial deeds. Words alone are not what
God requires of us (v. 15). True faith is always expressed
in consistent good works. Paul is opposed to ceremonial
works (like circumcision, Gal. 5:2–6) or moral works as a
means of *achieving* salvation, but both Paul and James believe in the necessity of works for *expressing* our new life.
Both Abraham the righteous (v. 21) and Rahab the sinner
acted on what God had said (v. 25, Josh. 2:8–11, 18, 21;
6:17; Heb. 11:31).

5. CHAPTER 3:1–12
TALK

James has a great deal to say about both appropriate and un-
fitting speech (1:26; 2:3, 16; 3:1–12; 4:13, 15; 5:9, 12). The
tongue has astonishing potential for good or evil. It is like the
bit in the horse's mouth, the rudder on a ship, the few sparks
which can lead to a forest fire. With the tongue we can glorify God (3:9), or create havoc in relationships—which is our
writer's next theme.

6. CHAPTERS 3:13–4:12
RELATIONSHIPS

Christians need the wisdom promised by God (1:5–8); this
is the knowledge of the best way to act in given circumstances (1:13–17). That is much more important in life than
gathering huge quantities of academic information. God's
wisdom will not make us proud but pure, not superior but
submissive. It is clear that numerous problems are damaging
relationships in the church (or churches) to which James
writes: evil (1:21); disobedience (1:22–25); favoritism

(2:1–13); insensitivity to other people's needs (2:14–17); damaging conversation (3:2–12); envy (3:14); and now, here, a quarrelsome spirit (4:1–2); prayerlessness (4:2–3); worldliness (4:4); pride (4:5–10); slander (4:11–12). It is a grim catalogue of human failure; all these things destroy any sense of harmonious community.

7. CHAPTER 4:13–17
HUMILITY

Some of James' readers were acting as though their human lives were within their own firm control. They failed to recognize that life is like a vanishing mist (4:14), or, as earlier in *James* (1:10–11), and in the following New Testament letter, like a fading flower (1 Pet. 1:24); or the quick flash of a weaver's shuttle (Job 7:6), a fast runner (Job 9:25), a mere handbreadth, or smoke passing from a fire (Ps. 39:5; 102:3). With a true sense of humility and meekness the believer ought to subject all his life to God's sovereign will, and not boast and brag about either his achievements or ambitions. It is better to use the opportunity of each day not simply to think about good things but do them (4:17).

8. CHAPTER 5:1–6
MONEY

Here James returns again to the "rich and poor" theme. Some rich people had amassed wealth (5:1–3), but at the expense of their poor employees (5:4). The passage is reminiscent of the eighth century prophets like Isaiah (1:21–23; 3:13–26); Amos (2:6–7; 3:15; 4:1; 5:12; 6:4–6); and Micah (6:8–15); where oppression by the greedy citizens and landowners is exposed and condemned with righteous anger. Note that while the rich rob them, the poor can only pray; their cries are heard by God, but they must be answered by us also. In our time millions of our neighbors in the Third World (2:8) "cry out" for help; we must live more simply, avoid wasteful practices, pray, work, plead, campaign, make sacrifices and give generously for the hungry.

9. CHAPTER 5:7–13
ENDURANCE

Whatever life's circumstances, God's servants need to develop qualities of endurance like a patient farmer (v. 7), a steadfast prophet (v. 10), or a patriarch severely tested and found true to God (v. 11). Such people remember the Lord's past faithfulness (helping Job and the prophets), present compassion (v. 11) and promised return (vv. 7–9). If God is true to his word, we must certainly be true to ours (v. 13).

10. CHAPTER 5:14–20
PRAYER

Perhaps the reference to Job forms a natural link with the problem of suffering (v. 13) and mention of the prophets recalls Elijah (vv. 17–18). But prayer is not simply an exercise for moments of trouble. It is equally important when life seems specially kind to us (v. 13). Here prayer is corporate (v. 14), dependent (v. 15), powerful (v. 16), exemplary (v. 17, Elijah was remembered for the power of his prayer, will we be?), costly ("fervently," v. 17, RSV). Those who are spiritually sick (vv. 19–20) also need our help (see 1 Pet. 4:8; Prov. 10:12).

1 Peter

eenly aware of impending persecution, Peter here uses a variety of word pictures to remind his readers of what it means to be a Christian. Like the author of *Hebrews* Peter tells his readers that Christians who suffer are privileged people because they follow in the steps of their Lord. He emerged victorious, and so will they.

1. CHAPTER 1:1–21
STRANGERS

Peter's readers are greeted as "strangers in the world" (1:1; 2:11). Just as devout Jews had been dispersed throughout the known world, so Christians were the new Israel, purposely scattered as God's witnesses who travel throughout many nations. This present world is not their ultimate home. Although, as God's chosen people (v. 2), Christians now enjoy new life in Christ (v. 3), their salvation is also portrayed here in its future aspect (vv. 5, 11) as a reserved inheritance (v. 4), rich prospect (v. 7), necessary goal (v. 9) and promised grace (v. 13). It is a salvation anticipated by prophets, predicted by the Spirit, proclaimed by the apostles and admired by angels (vv. 10–12). Christians are like those Jewish exiles who left Egypt, with its moral and spiritual ignorance (v. 14), because they had been called to holiness (vv. 15–16; Lev.

11:44–45). They have been redeemed by Christ, the uniquely perfect Passover Lamb (vv. 17–21) whose resurrection inspires faith and encourages hope.

2. CHAPTERS 1:22–2:3
CHILDREN

Christians have been "born again" (1:3, 23), and their new life is expressed in love for God's people (1:22) and God's word (1:23–2:3). A constant appetite for his life-imparting, imperishable word ensures that Christians "grow up" spiritually.

3. CHAPTER 2:4–10
STONES

Peter goes on to emphasize the corporate aspects of the Christian life. Believers are both "living stones" in God's church, and the priests who offer its spiritual sacrifices. Christ, their cornerstone, has been chosen by God, rejected by opponents (2:4) and treasured by believers (2:7). For those "builders" who despise and disobey him, the coping stone becomes the stumbling stone (2:8–9). Christians rejoice that the privileged titles which described the old Israel now apply to them (v. 9), God's new, called, vocal, enlightened people, to whom he has been generously merciful (v. 10).

4. CHAPTER 2:11–25
SLAVES

Christians are:

    a. RELEASED SLAVES (2:11–12) Conspicuously delivered from bondage to sin's tyranny, they are irrefutable proof of the gospel's transforming power.
    b. OBEDIENT SLAVES Christians witness by their good citizenship. They submit to magistrates (vv. 14–15), respect

their contemporaries (vv. 15–17), honor the Emperor (v. 17) and serve their employers, even those who are inconsiderate (vv. 18–20).

c. CHRIST'S SLAVES (vv. 21–25) The cruelly treated slaves find inspiration and strength by recalling Christ's sufferings. He is their "example" (v. 21, the word describes letters of the alphabet copied by the child during a writing lesson at school). Jesus suffered unjustly (v. 22), silently, confidently (v. 23), purposefully (v. 24) and effectively (v. 25).

5. CHAPTER 3:1–7
PARTNERS

Peter's exposition of Christian responsibility in church (2:4–10), neighborhood (2:11–12), nation (2:13–17) and work (2:18–25) is followed by witness at home, especially where a Christian woman has an unbelieving husband. Wives are to be submissive "in the same way" as Jesus (3:1). The life must preach. Peter reminds wives of their moral responsibility (3:2), and spiritual priorities (3:3–4), and cites biblical examples (3:5–6). Husbands are to be considerate, respectful and sincere. Inconsistent behavior seriously hinders prayer (3.7).

6. CHAPTERS 3:8–4:19
SUFFERERS

Peter now develops his main theme, the Christian attitude to suffering (3:14, 17; 4:1, 12–13, 16, 19). The apostle began his letter by warning of coming trials which test faith's reality (1:6–7). As peacemakers, believers must certainly not inflict pain on one another or anyone else (3:8–13). When trouble comes, they must be fearless before men (3:14), surrendered to Christ's Lordship, always prepared for well-informed, gentle, consistent testimony (3:15–16). Christ suffered unjustly and uniquely (3:17–18) on the cross, and, as the victorious Lord, he announced the benefits of his saving conquest to those who had died before he came (3:19; 4:6). Salvation for the remnant in Noah's time is used as a symbol of baptism. The water does not wash away sin; we are saved by Christ's risen, ascended, authoritative life (3:20–22).

The believers' new lifestyle illustrates that they forsake sin (4:1–2), expect reproach (4:3–4), remember eternity (4:5–7), love others (4:8–9), offer service (4:10), proclaim truth, receive strength and glorify God (4:11). Suffering as a Christian is to be expected (4:12), and regarded as a unique privilege. By such adversity we are identified with Christ (4:13), blessed by the Spirit (4:14) and preserved by the Creator (4:19).

7. CHAPTER 5:1–14
SHEPHERDS

Peter closes by commissioning Christian leaders to care for the flock as willing (5:1–2), humble (5:3–6), unworried (5:7), alert (5:8–9), confident (5:9–11) shepherds.

The concluding greeting salutes a faithful brother (5:12, possibly the amanuensis and postman), a chosen sister (probably a local church in adverse circumstances, perhaps Rome, Rev. 18:2, 10), and a transformed son (v. 13, Acts 15:37–39).

2 Peter

eter's second letter has many features in common with the letter of Jude. False teachers are creating serious problems within the life of the first century church. Members need to be warned of their destructive message.

1. Chapter 1:1–21
THE CALLING OF SAINTS

Believers are "called" by a righteous (v. 1), gracious (v. 2) and powerful (v. 3) God and they are to be like the God who called them (v. 4, "participate in the divine nature"). Some corrupt teachers were putting around the notion that once we have trusted in Christ we can behave entirely as we wish. But Peter here says that a true believer does not merely hear God's call but obeys it and confirms (v. 19) its reality by consistent conduct. Peter's message is a necessarily strong corrective against effortless (v. 5), unproductive (v. 8) and ethically forgetful (v. 9) forms of Christianity. True Christian living is marked by moral consistency, a quality of life made possible by God's unfailing promises (v. 4), Christ's unique testimony (vv. 16–19) and the Spirit's inspired word (v. 20–21).

Because Peter knows that he does not have long to live (v. 14), he wants to remind his contemporaries that they should listen to God's word, not to the fanciful interpretations of dangerous heretics. During Christ's earthly ministry Peter was privileged to hear the confirming word of God at the Mount of Transfiguration: "This is my Son . . . Listen to him" (v. 17; Matt. 17:5). The Old Testament writers did not suddenly appear on the national scene with their own religious ideas; they only shared what God had given to them. They were "carried along" by the Holy Spirit (vv. 20–21, the nautical imagery is of a ship with the strong wind in its sails). The deluded false teachers are not inspired by God and their message must be recognized as the morally damaging nonsense it is.

2. CHAPTER 2:1–22
THE ENEMIES OF TRUTH

There were false, as well as genuine, prophets in Old Testament times (2:1) and the same could be said of the first century scene. Verses 1–3 portray such prophets. They act secretly, disloyally (even denying the Lord who redeemed them), rebelliously (ignoring God's sovereignty), destructively (bringing ruin to themselves as well as others), successfully ("many will follow," v. 2), immorally ("shameful ways"), greedily (only thinking of gain) and inauthentically (with stories they have made up). These condemned enemies of the gospel are moving steadily to their own destruction (v. 3).

Three examples of divine judgment are used as warnings: the rebellious angels (v. 4), Noah's (v. 5) and Lot's (vv. 6–7) godless contemporaries. But the reader is reminded that God is able to deliver the genuine believer even when he is surrounded by spiritual rebels, ungodly teachers and moral offenders (2:8–9).

Another Old Testament illustration, the story of Balaam (Num. 22–24), is pressed into effective service to remind these early Christians that there have always been people who will do anything for money ("experts in greed," v. 14), but God can stop them in their tracks (vv. 15–16). As well as referring to the avarice of such people, Peter exposes their arrogance (2:10), blasphemy and ignorance (v. 12), impurity (vv. 13–14), insincerity and instability (v. 17).

They are enticing charlatans who promise what they have no power to bestow, depraved prisoners enslaved by their passions (vv. 18–19); people entangled in lust when they might have enjoyed liberation (vv. 20–22).

3. CHAPTER 3:1–18
THE RETURN OF CHRIST

Jesus is coming back. Christians must be given to "wholesome thinking" (3:1), not to the corrupt living described in the previous chapter. The concluding section of the letter draws attention to:

a. THE WORLD'S ATTITUDE: people deliberately despise Christ's return (vv. 3–7). Like Noah's contemporaries, they greet his message with blatant unbelief.
b. THE LORD'S ATTITUDE: he deliberately postpones his return (vv. 8–10). The narrow confines of time mean nothing to him. He waits patiently, determined that some Christ rejecters should become committed believers. Men and women are not divinely operated robots; they must have the freedom to make their own response or their love will not be genuine. The privileged freedom to turn to him must allow for the abused freedom to turn from him. "Anyone ... everyone" (v. 9), expresses the divine appeal, but rebels are determined not to hear it. When the day comes, it will be endless night for some (v. 10).
c. THE CHRISTIAN'S ATTITUDE: we deliberately anticipate his return (vv. 11–18). Believers prepare for their glorious future and "speed its coming" (v. 12) by holiness (vv. 11, 14), expectancy (v. 13), watchfulness (v. 17) and increasing maturity (v. 18).

1 John

subtle and dangerous error appears to have harassed several of the New Testament churches. Sometimes described as Gnosticism, it was a counterfeit gospel, fervently preached at a time when first century society was littered with religious notions of various kinds. Some pagan teachers presumed to offer a way of salvation through knowledge (from the Greek, *gnosis*); they claimed that certain spiritual mysteries, which they secretly imparted to a favored few, had the power to save. Ideas of this kind gradually gained a footing in the churches.

Several gnostics held that physical matter was essentially evil, and therefore Christ could not possibly have come "in the flesh"; for them the Incarnation was a serious stumbling block. Others said that Jesus only appeared to be human—these were called Docetists (from the Greek *dokein*, "to seem"). Some said he did not actually die on the cross, but at the last minute someone else took his place.

It is for this reason that John insists on the unique deity and essential humanity of Christ (4:1–3, 7–10, 14–15). He stresses the uniqueness and sufficiency of God's revelation in Christ, God's only Son (2:23) who came "in the flesh" (4:2): our Savior from sin (1:7; 2:2; 4:10, 14); our Advocate in heaven (2:1); perfect example (2:6); invincible conqueror (3:6); and returning Lord (3:2–3).

The phrases "if we claim" (1:6, 8, 10), and "the man who says" (2:4) may actually introduce us to the views of some gnostic teachers whose message John is refuting, for example, their superior claim to unique communion with God (1:6; 2:6); to entire sinlessness (1:8, 10); to exclusive knowledge (2:4), and privileged spiritual illumination (2:9).

John's theme is "Fellowship with the Father." He deals with:

1. CHAPTER 1:1–10
ITS CONVICTIONS

The Christian message about our fellowship with the Father is:

a. factual—rooted in firm historical events (1:1–4). It is not a series of highly speculative notions as the gnostics believed. It is anchored in verifiable events in history which have been seen, touched and heard. Christ came physically to this world.
b. radical—It demands a change of life. Professing Christians cannot make spiritual claims (1:6) which are not attested by a transformed and consistent lifestyle. It is not simply a case of confessing religious belief and then living as we like. We must *keep on* walking in the light (1:7) and he will *keep on* cleansing us (1:9): both verbs are imperfect tense, denoting a continuous action.
c. reliable—God will never let us down. He keeps his promises. However close we try to live to him we cannot possibly be perfect in this life (1:8, 10), but if we are genuinely penitent and confess our sins, he will forgive us. The pardon does not depend on the eloquence of our confession or the depth of our grief; it is based on the constancy of God's nature. He is faithful and just (1:9).

2. CHAPTER 2:1–17
ITS DEMANDS

John now goes on to explain the high standards of the Christian life, but before doing so he reminds his readers of the uniqueness of Christ. Without his unique work for us, all our lofty ideals would be unattainable dreams. Life at our best (not life without mistakes) is possible because:

- Christ is our righteous advocate (2:1)
- Christ is our atoning sacrifice (2:2)
- Christ is our perfect teacher (2:3–5; see John 15:15)
- Christ is our loving example (2:6)

Jesus lived a life of compassionate service and so must we. This is not a new command (2:7; 4:21; Lev. 19:18; Deut. 10:19), but there is an element of "newness" about it in the supreme importance (Matt. 22:37–40), depth (John 13:34) and range (Luke 10:29–37) Christ gave to it.

Fellowship with the Father demands love for the needy world (2:9–11, see 4:14), not love of the hostile world. The word "world" is used in two different senses in the letter: it describes the *people* who live within it and it also describes the spirit or outlook of people without God, those who are "mobilized in defiance of the divine purpose" (W. F. Howard). Worldliness is living by the spirit of this spiritually alien world. Christians receive pardon (2:12), assurance and deliverance (2:13), and power (2:14) while those who are committed to a world-controlled life are lured away from God (2:15). They are attracted by merely external things (2:15), greedy for additional possessions, fascinated by their own petty achievements (2:16), failing to recognize that all those things which occasionally give them immediate satisfaction will ultimately disappear (2:17).

3. Chapter 2:18–29
ITS OPPONENTS

John knows that heretical teachers have lured some away from the church (2:18–19) by damaging and dishonoring teaching about Christ (2:22–23). The enemies of true Christian teaching say that their highly exclusive message is for the favored few who will be "saved" by special knowledge, but John emphasizes that true believers are *all* taught by the Holy One (2:20, 27).

4. Chapter 3:1–24
ITS CHARACTERISTICS

These are presented first negatively (3:1–10), then positively (vv. 11–24). The true child of God does not willfully and deliberately go on sinning. The tense in verses 6 and 9 is important: the present tense means "keeps on sinning." This refers to habitual and impenitent sinning committed by someone who is utterly indifferent to the moral demands of the gospel. Some gnostics said that the "spirit" or "soul" was all that mattered and the "flesh" could do whatever it liked. This is what John is striving to combat here.

But we must accept the challenge of these verses and remind ourselves that while John does not teach that it is *impossible to sin* he does suggest that it is *possible not to sin* in any given situation. In other words, our sinning in particular circumstances is not inevitable; if it were otherwise a statement like 2:1 ("so that you will not sin") is meaningless. But John also makes it plain that, vulnerable as we are, there will be times when we are likely to fail (see 2:1 again, "But if anybody does sin").

Positively, the Christian is not only holy (3:1–11), but loving (3:11–24). The compassion he has in mind *distinguishes* believers from unbelievers (3:11–15):

- it is sacrificial (3:16)
- it is practical (3:17)
- it is genuine (3:18)

Love is an act of basic Christian obedience; there is nothing remotely optional about it (3:21–24).

5. CHAPTER 4:1–21
ITS TESTS

There are different ways of testing whether a profession of Christian faith is genuine. Here John mentions a *doctrinal* test: is Christ accepted as fully human (vv. 1–3)? Elsewhere in his epistle John refers to a second doctrinal test: is Christ accepted as fully divine (1:3; 2:22–23; 4:15; 5:1, 10, 13)?

There is also a *fellowship* test (4:4–6). True Christians enjoy the partnership and confidence of those who love this message of truth, imparted and verified by the Holy Spirit (4:6; see John 16:13).

The *practical* test is love (4:7–21). God's love (vv. 8, 19), Christ's incarnation (v. 9), his saving mission (v. 14) and sacrificial death (v. 10) are models for our loving. Genuine Christian love is God's gift, and *evidence* of new birth (v. 7), personal knowledge of God (v. 8), his indwelling life (v. 16) and likeness (v. 17). Like God's love, ours must also be visible (v. 9, "God showed his love") and eager to take costly initiatives (vv. 10, 19). Merely verbal "loving" is one of John's greatest fears (v. 20, see 3:18).

6. CHAPTER 5
ITS CERTAINTIES

John closes the letter by returning to familiar themes: love (v. 1); obedience (vv. 2–3); faith (vv. 4–12); prayer (vv. 13–17); holiness (v. 18); assurance (vv. 19–21).

2 John

John takes up some of the themes of *1 John,* dealing with them more briefly, stressing their relevance to the "Elect Lady."

1.
TEACHING

Aspects of the apostle's message which emerge again here are:

- the truth (vv. 1, 2, 3, 4, see 1 John 2:21; 3:19)
- the new yet old commandment of love (v. 5, see 1 John 2:7; 3:11, 23; 4:21)
- the importance of our daily "walk" ("that we walk in obedience . . . that you walk in love," v. 6; see 1 John 1:7; 2:6)
- the sinister activities of the antichrist (v. 7; see 1 John 2:22; 4:1–3)
- doctrinal loyalty to the truths of the deity and humanity of the Lord Jesus Christ (vv. 7–11; see 1 John 2:22–23; 4:2–3, 15; 5:1, 9–10)

2.
READERS

Who is "the chosen lady" (v. 1)? The expression has puzzled many readers over the centuries. It may be a person known to the apostle but, in view of the fact that women teachers were hardly encouraged in the early Church, this is unlikely (1 Tim. 2:12, but see Acts 21:9). What is more probable is that "the chosen lady" is a personification of a particular local church, and "her children" are the members of this local fellowship of Christian people. The apostle's use of the term *may* have been dictated by the uneasy circumstances of the time, for example, danger of persecution if precise details of the church's location were made known in a letter which could fall into the hands of unbelievers.

3.
PURPOSE

The occasion of the letter is quite straightforward. The first letter made it clear that a number of false teachers were moving around the early church (4:1–2) and the apostle is warning this little church that such teachers may well visit their meeting. However, they are not even to offer overnight hospitality to these "deceivers" (vv. 7, 10).

The inns of the first century world were notoriously immoral, dirty, and flea-infested, and hospitality was an important issue in the early Christian church (Rom. 12:13; Heb. 13:2; 1 Pet. 4:9). Some people traded on this generous and gracious Christian custom, even though they were imposters. Lucian (in his *Peregrinus*) writes about the itinerant charlatan who lived on the generosity of Christians; as soon as he was found out, he moved on to another company of equally benevolent, guileless believers!

The Didache (an early Christian document) lays down regulations about hospitality to traveling preachers: "If he that comes is a passerby, succour him as far as you can; but

he shall not stay with you longer than two or three days, unless there be necessity. But if he is minded to settle among
you, and be a craftsman, let him work and eat. But if he has
no trade, according to your understanding, provide that he
shall not live idle among you, being a Christian. But if he
will not do this he is a Christmonger (*Christemporos,* a traf-
ficker in Christ); of such men beware."

4.
MESSAGE

Truth is the unifying theme of this second epistle. The apostle says that believers must:

    a. KNOW THE TRUTH (v. 1) The members of this church
("her children") are greatly loved. The "I love" is em-
phatic; possibly John is contrasting his own deep sincerity
and genuine affection with those who are endeavoring to
destroy the church: they hate rather than love (see 1 John
3:11–15). True believers are those who *have come to
know* the truth. The verb is in the perfect tense, which
speaks of a decisive event in the past.
    b. WELCOME THE TRUTH (vv. 2–3) The truth is not some
statement of doctrine which we merely accepted once, in
the past. It is saving truth and we constantly receive it and
live by it. It should live in us and stay with us (v. 2). Notice how the apostle relates closely to the whole Christian
fellowship; it is the truth which "lives in *us*": not "in me."
Westcott observes that "the truth" is "that which is identical with Christ's message (John 1:17) and with Christ's
Person (John 14:6)."
    c. OBEY THE TRUTH (vv. 4–6) Truth is not something
merely to store away in our minds; it has to be *applied* to
every part of our daily lives. It must be acted upon: we
must *walk* in his commandments. This means that mutual
love must be earnestly pursued. If we have really grasped
the truth (v. 4), it should make us more loving (vv. 5–6) to

all those who love the truth. Barclay says: "The only proof
of our love of God is our love for the brethren."

d. GUARD THE TRUTH (vv. 7–11) John warns his readers
against those who oppose Christ by denying his deity and
humanity. Subversive teachers must not be entertained in
Christian homes; this only helps to prosper their mission
(v. 10). John would lead the modern Jehovah's Witness
straight to the garden gate!

Note that John is not only concerned for the spiritual welfare of those who entertain the false teachers, but the well-
being of the whole church; in some manuscripts verse 8
reads: "that you may not lose what *we* have worked for."
This second epistle closes with joy (vv. 12–13), as the first
epistle opened with it (1 John 1:4). New Testament faith is
both jubilant (v. 12) and jealous (vv. 10–11).

3 John

John was written to encourage a loyal Christian worker who was coping with some difficult problems. *2 John* deals with *principles, 3 John* is concerned with *personalities.* These two epistles are the shortest letters in the New Testament, and they deal with a similar practical issue: *hospitality.* In *2 John* this is discussed in relation to those who, in the course of their extensive travels, are seeking to corrupt and destroy the life of the Church. In *3 John* it is discussed in relation to genuine Christian teachers.

3 John is a warm and honest pastoral letter. Its realism is both striking and appealing. Where encouragement and commendation is deserved, it is generously given. Where unspirituality is evident, it is clearly exposed and firmly handled. Has this little letter something to say to us all about mutual love and discipline? Our fear of losing people sometimes results in a form of toleration which is both unbiblical and unloving. We allow some folk to grow up in the church with irritating, uncorrected failings which cause great hurt and even serious damage to God's people over the years. If only these people had been quietly told years ago of their serious failings and had been lovingly corrected they might well have been wonderful saints today.

The apostle mentions three people, and what is said about them forms the natural divisions of the epistle:

1. VERSES 1–8
GAIUS SERVES OTHERS

John knows that Gaius is spiritually healthy and so do those
who visit the apostle. Other Christians speak well of him; that
is a lovely tribute. He is not only *saved* (v. 2), he is *used*
(vv. 5–8), his part in the work being *generous hospitality*. In his
second letter John warned the church about receiving false
teachers into their homes (2 John 10–11). Here he commends
one who eagerly receives genuine Christians into his home.
Are our *homes* really at the disposal of Christ? An open home
is a magnificent means of grace to saved and unsaved alike. An
immense amount is being done all over the country just now
by Christians who are willing to invite their neighbors into
their homes for a film, a talk, a discussion. Coffee evenings
and coffee mornings of this kind are being widely used.

Verses 6–8 suggest that Gaius is *generous* as well as hospitable. It looks as though local Christians made themselves
financially responsible for the next stage of a traveling
preacher's journey. Are we doing our utmost for our missionary friends? For the sake of Christ's Name "they went
out." Therefore, says John, "we ought . . ." (vv. 7–8). If we
do not give them maximum support we are not "allies of the
truth" (Moffatt). We prove our loyalty to the truth of God by
our concern for the servants of God.

2. VERSES 9–10
DIOTREPHES HINDERS OTHERS

What a wonderful local church it would have been if everyone had been like Gaius! But John is realistic and we come
now to a sharp contrast: Diotrephes, who was not disciplined in former years. Note:

a. HIS ARROGANCE (v. 9) Diotrephes likes to put himself
first. He appears to be a leader of a local congregation.
Leadership is a very solemn and serious responsibility and

pride is one of its occupational diseases. This aggressive elder or leader is doing a great deal of harm to the local fellowship of Christ's people by lording it over them. He is unhappy if they do not exalt him at every possible opportunity. If you had to propose a vote of thanks in that church, his name would have to go down first. Woe betide the member who forgets to acknowledge the part played by Diotrephes! How sad this is, especially when we think of the humility of the Lord Jesus and his apostles (Mark 10:45, and note the context: Mark 10:35–44; John 13:1–5, 12–17; Acts 20:19; Rom. 12:16; 1 Cor. 15:9; 2 Cor. 10:1; Phil. 2:3–11; 1 Pet. 5:5).

b. ACCUSATIONS (v. 10a) John says that Diotrephes has been slandering him. Most of those who set themselves up love to run others down. They can only exalt themselves by decrying others.

c. ACRIMONY (v. 10b) What an unattractive character he is. He is not only against John; he seems to be opposed to everyone. Gaius welcomes the brethren, but Diotrephes casts people out (v. 10). Bitterness toward any one Christian can soon rob us of love for all. Not content to turn good teachers away himself, Diotrephes is annoyed when others minister to them.

3. VERSES 11–25
DEMETRIUS ATTRACTS OTHERS

Demetrius lives a consistent Christian life: he is the kind of man we should copy (v. 11). The apostle says that there is a threefold witness to the sincerity and holiness of Demetrius (v. 12). The witnesses are:

a. EVERYONE: there is widespread recognition of his many attractive spiritual qualities.

b. THE TRUTH ITSELF: his life conforms to all we read in God's word: he embodies the principles of the Christian life in his own personality.

c. THE APOSTLE HIMSELF: and they know they can trust what John says.

This short letter leaves two final thoughts with its readers:

a. PEACE—with a man like Diotrephes making war against God's children, how much this church needed the peace that Christ can give.
b. LOVE—"Greet the friends," everyone, "by name," that is, not just the ones we like. Everyone comes within the circle of sincere Christian love.

Jude

he writer of this short letter may have been either a younger brother of the Lord Jesus (Mark 6:3), or "Judas, not Iscariot" of the original twelve disciples (Luke 6:16). The words "brother of James" may point to the former (Matt. 13:55). The letter's main theme is identical to that of 2 Peter, with which it has many structural, illustrative and verbal similarities. Some Christians are in danger of going astray by imagining that, as long as they are believers, moral conduct does not matter, and Jude warns them against this false teaching. He also assures his readers that whatever our difficulties we are not left to live the Christian life on our own: God keeps us from falling (1, 24).

After the opening salutation (vv. 1–2), which has two examples of the author's familiar triads (called—loved—kept; mercy—peace—love), there are two main sections:

1. VERSES 3–16
CONTEND FOR THE FAITH

Jude would prefer to have written a doctrinal exposition about the salvation they all share, but it is important to respond to more immediate needs by warning his readers about the message entrusted to faithful stewards in the past but corrupted by godless charlatans in the present. Jude emphasizes the errors:

a. THE SERIOUS NATURE OF THE HERESY The false teachers appear to distort the biblical concept of grace and deny the uniqueness of Christ.

b. HISTORICAL EXAMPLES (verses 5–7) He illustrates the seriousness of this moral and theological error by using three striking Old Testament examples of rebellion:

- the unbelieving Israelites (1 Cor. 10:5)
- the unsubmissive angels (2 Pet. 2:4)
- the ungodly citizens (Gen. 18–19)

Those who despise God's warnings deserve God's judgment.

c. THE DESTRUCTIVE CHARACTERISTICS OF THE HERESY (vv. 8–13) Another of Jude's triads describes their impurity, arrogance and irreverence (v. 8). These people are so intent on evil that they blasphemously slander angels.

In this short letter Jude twice quotes from Jewish literature. First (vv. 9–10), a story from *The Assumption of Moses,* which depicted a verbal contest between the archangel and the devil, who brought the charge of murder against Moses. Michael did not use contemptuous language, but left it to the Lord to rebuke the slanderer. Lacking the archangel's restraint, the false teachers are not only ignorant and immoral, but are more like animals than men.

Another triad, about Cain, Balaam and Korah, offers further illustrations of loveless, mercenary and insolent rebellion (Gen. 4:8–9; Num. 22:1–25:3; 16:1–3, 31–35). Vivid word pictures drive the warning home; these dangerous teachers are greedy shepherds, useless clouds, fruitless trees, uncontrolled waves and wandering stars (vv. 12–13).

d. CERTAIN JUDGMENT (vv. 14–16) Jude's second use of Jewish literature, from the *Book of Enoch* (first or second century BC) asserts that the returning Lord will come in judgment to convict these dangerous offenders who grieve God by their sins of speech, sensuality and pride.

2. VERSES 17–25
CONTINUE IN THE FAITH

In face of such strenuous opposition, sincere believers must remember:

    a. PAST WARNINGS They must recall the warnings they received from the Apostles (vv. 17–18) about such selfish, unspiritual men with divisive ambitions (v. 19).

    b. PRESENT RESPONSIBILITY (vv. 20–23) They are to build up their faith (contrast the destructive aims of their opponents), keep themselves (compare vv. 1 and 24) in God's love, pray in the Spirit (contrast v. 19) and, as they themselves wait for Christ's promised mercy, show practical mercy to others (vv. 22–23).

    c. FUTURE HOPE (vv. 24–25) Although they have been urged to keep themselves in God's love (v. 21), the letter opens (v. 1) and closes with the assurance that God will keep them "from falling" (v. 24, literally, "surefooted"). God enables us to stand firmly in this life so that we will stand finally in the judgment. Those who are dependently surefooted now will be gratefully surefooted then.

Revelation

ritten by John while he was a prisoner on the Aegean island of Patmos, this is not an easy book to understand. Its central message, however, is crystal clear: the Almighty reigns (19:6). *Revelation* reminds every reader of God's eternal sovereignty (4:2, 9–10); Christ's eternal victory (1:5, 17–18), and the Spirit's eternal presence (1:10; 2:7; 22:17).

Occasional confusion over interpretation may be due to the fact that its key truths had to be presented in code so that if the book fell into the hands of some first century Roman official, he would not immediately regard it as dangerously subversive. It depicted the triumph of the church and collapse of the Roman empire, as well as the ultimate defeat of all evil, but its teaching, brilliantly conveyed by means of language and symbolism drawn from the Jewish Scriptures, would be unintelligible to someone without a knowledge of the Old Testament. It would, however, be immediately clear to someone with that rich literary background. There are five main sections:

1. CHAPTER 1:1–20
THE LIVING LORD

John is an exile because of his loyal proclamation of Christ's truth (1:9). The ever present, eternally sympathetic, victorious Christ (vv. 12–16) comes to his suffering companion with the assurance of peace and hope and with new work for John to do (vv. 17–20).

The portraiture of Christ in this opening vision (vv. 12–18) is a good example of the book's dependence on Old Testament imagery; note that it mostly belongs to periods of adversity in Hebrew history, reminding John afresh that God sees his people through dark and bewildering times (Isa. 41:4; 49:2; Ezek. 1:26–28; Dan. 7:9–14; 10:5–6).

2. CHAPTERS 2:1–3:22
THE REDEEMED CHURCH

God's people are not perfect; that blessing is part of the rich delight which awaits them in the future he has prepared. There is no attempt here to hide or minimize the early Church's failures. Five out of the seven Asia Minor congregations (each at the heart of a known postal district, so that the letter could be more widely available) are rebuked for serious spiritual and moral offenses.

Each letter opens with an inspiring reminder of Christ's uniqueness (2:1, 8, 12, etc.) and closes with a dependable promise (2:7, 11, 17, etc.). The two churches which are specially commended (2:8–11; 3:7–13) both exercise their difficult ministry in persecution contexts. They are reminded of their spiritual wealth (2:9), promised life (2:10), immediate access (3:7), evangelistic opportunity (3:8), assured love (3:9), divine protection (3:10), and eternal security (3:11–12). The open door of witness at Philadelphia is sharply contrasted with the closed door of communion at Laodicea (3:8, 20). Material possessions can minimize spiritual values (3:17–18), but God's exposure of these mistakes and sins (3:19) is a token of his enduring love.

3. CHAPTERS 4:1–5:14
THE SECURE THRONE

A closed door on earth (3:19) is followed by an open door in heaven (4:1). These two chapters provide the Church with a necessary dimension of stability and security. In times of spiritual failure (2:4), religious opposition (2:9), doctrinal disloyalty (2:14), moral corruption (2:20), ecclesiastical pretense (3:1), numerical weakness (3:8), and materialistic preoccupation (3:17), the Church needs to know beyond doubt that God is sovereign (4:2), merciful (4:3; Gen. 9:12–16), holy, everlasting (4:8) alive (4:10) and omnipotent (4:11). They are assured that Christ is the conquering Lion (5:5), the sacrificial and victorious Lamb (5:6–14). Only the enthroned Father and saving Lamb are worthy of eternal and universal praise (4:11; 5:13).

4. CHAPTERS 6:1–20:15
THE INEVITABLE CONFLICT

These central chapters depict the warfare which is bound to follow when God's Son and Christ's people are active in the world. The dramatic story makes use of unforgettable imagery: seals are broken, trumpets blown, bowls of wrath poured out. The famous four horsemen of the Apocalypse depicting aggression (6:1–2), violence (6:3–4), famine (6:5–6) and bloodshed (6:7–8) are a sad reminder that such realities were not confined to the world of antiquity; they are a disturbing feature in every news bulletin throughout the contemporary world.

But within the immediate context of unfolding doom the story is also disclosed of God's secure people, emphasizing that however grim their adversities, the hand of the Lord is upon them for good. They are marked by the seal of God's protective ownership (7:3; 9:4; 14:1; 22:4), and numbered with his saved people (7:4–10), the believing multitude (7:14), for whom Jesus is not only the Lamb (7:9), but Redeemer (7:14), Shepherd (7:17) and King (7:17).

In the developing story, "eternal Rome," as she conceitedly described herself, is overthrown (chapters 17–18). Every evil influence is brought to the feet of the conquering King of kings (chapter 19) and the archenemy, the devil, is destroyed forever (chapter 20).

5. CHAPTERS 21–22:21
THE ETERNAL CITY

The victory and presence of God among his people guarantees the end of loneliness (21:3), sorrow, death (21:4), need (21:6), sin (21:8, 27; 22:3, 15) and darkness (21:23–25).

The book closes with the confident words of the dependable God (21:5; 22:6), the returning Lord (22:7, 12, 20), and the persuasive Spirit (22:17).